J. Henry Shorthouse

Kipling T. O

Woolner

Anthony Shorthouse

Oscar Wilde

Charles Kingsley

H. G. Wells

Charles Kingsley

Thomas Hardy.

WB Yeats

Edward A Freeman

LETTERS TO MACMILLAN

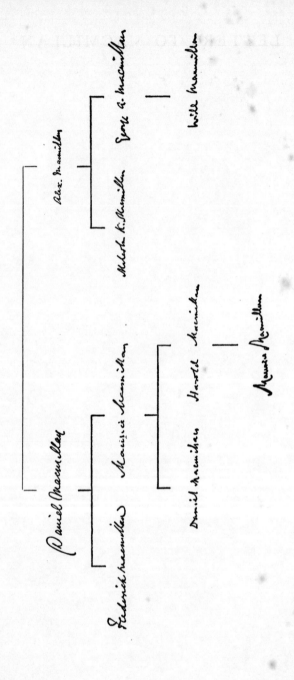

LETTERS TO
MACMILLAN

SELECTED AND EDITED BY

SIMON NOWELL-SMITH

Our guiding principle . . . is that publishers
exist to satisfy their authors.

HAROLD MACMILLAN

MACMILLAN

LONDON · MELBOURNE · TORONTO

ST MARTIN'S PRESS

NEW YORK

1967

MACMILLAN AND COMPANY LIMITED
Little Essex Street London WC2
also Bombay Calcutta Madras Melbourne

THE MACMILLAN COMPANY OF CANADA LIMITED
70 Bond Street Toronto 2

ST MARTIN'S PRESS INC
175 Fifth Avenue New York NY 10010

Library of Congress catalog card no. 67–24488

PRINTED IN GREAT BRITAIN

CONTENTS

LIST OF ILLUSTRATIONS

ALPHABETICAL LIST OF CORRESPONDENTS

INTRODUCTION

The history of Macmillans in their first hundred years was written in the centenary year by Charles Morgan.* The present volume is not a history, though it contains a number of footnotes to history. It is in the nature of a scrapbook drawn from the firm's correspondence files which began to be preserved, at first somewhat haphazardly, in the eighteen-fifties. By 1965 the Macmillan archives up to the beginning of the second world war contained something like half a million letters — incoming letters from authors, illustrators, editors, travellers, printers, binders, agents, solicitors and the public at large; copies of outgoing letters to the same categories; correspondence with branches oversea; and letters, a few only, which had passed between the partners or directors, usually when one or another was abroad on business, or combining business with holiday — Frederick Macmillan, for instance, writing about a new author from Paris on Christmas Day.

This notable accumulation, apart from the space it filled in Macmillans' substantial Victorian building in St. Martin's Street, Leicester Square, proved a source of embarrassment as well as of pride to its owners. A busy publishing house, concentrating upon the present and the future, is ill equipped to satisfy the demands of scholars whose concern is with the past, scholars who wish to pursue one author, or one aspect of literary or publishing history, through perhaps several scores of box-files, copyletter volumes and ledgers. In 1964–5 Macmillans opened an up-to-date warehouse at Basingstoke and moved their offices to a smaller and more convenient modern building in Little Essex Street, Strand. It was then decided to retain the correspondence files only from 1939 and to make the rest accessible to scholars and students in public collections. The autograph letters of some hundreds of Macmillan authors, together with some 130,000 copyletters in 400 bound volumes, covering three-quarters of a century, passed into the keeping of the department of manuscripts in the

* Charles Morgan, *The House of Macmillan 1843–1943* (1943).

British Museum, and a valuable residue of miscellaneous correspondence, running into tens of thousands of letters, was presented to the library of the University of Reading.

Out of this mountain, a mouse. The sorting of the archives revived a project long cherished in St. Martin's Street — a scrapbook of letters. This at best could contain only a minute fraction of the whole, and it seemed best to confine the selection for the most part to letters from authors. (No living authors are included.) Within that general limitation it is designed to illustrate the variety of types of letter which in the course of his day-to-day business a publisher receives and to which he must make appropriate response. His responses are quoted when they assist a narrative or illumine his character, or his correspondent's: but primarily this book is concerned with the author, his aspirations and achievements, his troubles and vanities, rather than with the publisher, whose interest was to encourage talent and soothe discontent.

Selection has inevitably been limited by the nature of the surviving material, and indeed also by the absence of material. The most interesting or brilliant or durable of authors do not necessarily write the most interesting or brilliant or durable of letters, at least to their publishers. Some whose books are soon forgotten regard their publishers as, so to speak, emotional wastepaper-baskets, filling folios with cries of anguish more poignant than the preoccupation of celebrities with misprints, rights of reproduction or the fancied malice of their critics. Authors' problems, set out at length in their letters, may be solved in personal interviews or by telephone — the files all too often leave a pregnant narrative half told — or the publisher from tact or exasperation endorses a complaining letter 'Not answered'.

Some letters — Tennyson's for example, of which there must have been many spread over three decades — long ago disappeared from the files; Kipling, associated with Macmillans for the greater part of his writing life, communicated with them almost entirely through his literary agent; because *Gone with the Wind* was first published by the Macmillan Company, New York, the author seldom had occasion to write to St. Martin's Street. At the other extreme were copious correspondents abundantly represented in the archives. Whole books could be based on individuals' letters in this class: indeed whole books have already been made of the Rossettis' letters to Macmillans and of Matthew Arnold's correspondence with Macmillans and with Smith, Elder. But abundance is not all. Some authors of great significance in the history of Macmillans find no place here: the scientists, doctors and musicians; Bryce and Bury among the historians; the New Testament scholars Bishop Westcott and Dr. Hort; 'Hall and Knight' of algebra fame, and many more. Either their letters are of no interest or the stories they have to tell do not fall into the pattern of a scrapbook. Among memorable Macmillan figures of the nineteenth century are the editors of *Macmillan's Magazine*, *Nature*, the *English Illustrated Magazine* and the *Statesman's Year-Book*. The correspondence relating to periodicals seems only to have found its way into the general files by chance, when for instance a partner in the firm had become personally involved with a contributor. Stray letters from David Masson and George Grove, both editors of *Macmillan's*, are quoted as occasion serves, and something of their quality as editors emerges.

It is in the nature of the author–publisher relationship that certain themes should be recurrent. Certain attitudes of mind have coloured that relationship since long before Macmillans entered the trade. In the eighteenth century there were roughly speaking two principal types of author: on one side the nobleman, gentleman or well-found scholar who cared little for the financial rewards of writing, and on the other the poor scholar and the Grub Street hack to whom reward was anything but immaterial. The nineteenth century, in the middle of which the firm of Macmillan was founded, witnessed a levelling process — and not only in authorship — in which the scholar and creative writer became of necessity, if he was to succeed, his own man of business. Advertisement was a subject rather ungentlemanly to Matthew Arnold and Coventry Patmore. Towards the end of the century Alfred Austin tentatively asks, 'Do you think it wise to desist from advertising *Savonarola* altogether? You know best.' In the new century the advertising of their books is of passionate importance to Kipling and Maurice Hewlett, Hugh Walpole and Edith Sitwell. The author as business-man is well exemplified in Charles Morgan, who at one period himself booked and paid for advertising space in *The Times* for his own novels and plays. Few modern publishers, however, share, though they may indulge, their authors' faith in the paramountcy of press advertisement; and few authors understand the business of publishing as well as their publishers do. Economists like Neville Keynes and Alfred Marshall are entitled to be heard on half-profits, royalties and net prices. But when the novelists or historians, the Kiplings and the Fortescues, presumed to tell Frederick Macmillan how to run his business they touched his pride and earned their rebukes. If there are few allusions to literary agents, a profession evolved in the late nineteenth century as a cushion between the rapacious publisher and the defenceless author, that is because the uses of the profession are little canvassed in the correspondence. From time to time one Macmillan writing to another might call some agent a parasite or a shark, but seldom if ever when writing to an author.

Another recurrent theme is the author–publisher conflict over Grundyism. No author relishes censorship, whether the dispute is over four-letter words like 'damn' and 'Hell' (as it was with the Reverend T. E. Brown); or over *lèse-majesté* (as with the Honourable Caroline Norton); or the attributes of an Oread (Tennyson) or the appetites of an English maiden (H. G. Wells). No publisher, at the same time, sees himself as Mrs. Grundy. In 1856 the first Daniel, most devout of Macmillans, disarmingly confessed to a pusillanimous 'fear of Mrs. Grundy' if atheists should figure in *Tom Brown's Schooldays*; in 1866 the editor of *Macmillan's Magazine* disclaimed opposition 'to outspokenness, or to strength of opinion or language, as such', but objected to Mrs. Norton's indulgence in them all the same; in 1908 Frederick Macmillan, of the second generation, finds *Ann Veronica* unedifying and 'exceedingly distasteful to the public which buys books published by our firm', though a few years later he admits that if the firm is 'to deal in literature at all' it must, short of actual indecency, move with the times. (The Macmillans were perhaps less strict with books for their American public: in 1897 Maurice Macmillan had negotiated the sale to the New York branch of Vizetelly's translations of Zola.) In 1954 an editor removed from Sean O'Casey's autobiography expressions which, permissible perhaps on the stage, are not such as are wont to appear in Macmillan books. It is the public, it seems, not the publishers, who are prudes. It was the wife of a west-country vicar who

protested on behalf of herself and other mothers that *The Woodlanders*
was unfit reading for pure-minded English girls.

Moving with the times Macmillans had rejected a rather shocking
novel by Marion Crawford, one of their regular authors, in the eighties,
only to recover it several years later. The rejections of great publishing
houses are often as instructive as their acceptances. This volume is not,
like many publishing histories, a *Festschrift — ad majorem Macmillan-
orum gloriam*: it can afford to record failures of judgment as well as
successes. Macmillans lost *Lorna Doone* through squeamishness over
Blackmore's earlier novels; they refused Hardy and Bernard Shaw
while recognizing that there was promise in their prentice work, and
A Shropshire Lad and *Dubliners* with apparently no such recognition.
In each instance, as in many more — Baroness Orczy and Ethel M.
Dell, Arnold Bennett and Norman Mailer might have been added —
they erred in good company: several other publishers rejected the
same books.

Few authors have the arrogance of Marie Corelli, who expected her
books to be taken on trust without benefit of publisher's reader. (More
than once Macmillans' habit of sending established writers' books
unread to their printer landed them in trouble.) But once a writer is
established he has no need to expound to his publisher in advance the
scope and intention of his work. The letters of tyros tend to hold more
interest than those of celebrities — Kingsley plotting *Westward Ho!*
(his first real success as a novelist, and the first novel to be published by
the theological and educational firm of Macmillan); J. R. Green
outlining his *Short History* and James Frazer *The Golden Bough*;
Hardy on the motive behind his first, abortive novel; Wells with a
long-term blue-print for consolidating with serious fiction 'a large
confused reputation'. The young, or younger, writer also figures in
another congenial aspect when his claims are pressed by a contemporary, as Henley's by Stevenson, or more often by a discerning senior
— Christopher Hassall's by Eddie Marsh, Sydney Goodsir Smith's by
Edith Sitwell, or James Stephens's by 'A.E.' and Lennox Robinson's
by Yeats. It will be seen how greatly the loyalties of writers of the
Irish literary renaissance strengthened Macmillans' list.

Readers' reports, which have survived only patchily, are drawn upon

scarcely at all. They open up altogether too wide a field. But the
differing attitudes of reviewers and publishers' readers appear in some
of their letters. Jebb is proud that he should have refused to review a
book by a rival Hellenist with whom he had been involved in public
controversy: he could not trust himself to read it 'with that detachment from prejudice which I desired'. Maynard Keynes likewise
returned unopened the manuscript of a social economist to which,
though its authorship assured it of a respectable circulation, he knew he
would be hostile. Sir Lewis Namier on the other hand, in a letter too
intemperate for present reproduction, was confident that strong
personal antipathy would not affect his judgment of another Jewish
historian's work. A masterly and judgmatic report by the scholar
Walter Raleigh on a book about Shakespeare by the unscholarly Frank
Harris is admitted because it was couched in the form of a letter.

Public controversy is yet another theme. Merely to rake over the
embers of old quarrels — Maurice and Jelf, Kingsley and Newman,
Jebb and Mahaffy — would be gratuitous were it not for the part
played and the advice given by the publisher as a kind of extra-
publishing activity. Successive generations of Macmillans are sometimes seen at their best in extra-publishing activities, which may vary
from pacifying the controversialists to raising money for poor Johnny
Green and attending his foreign deathbed, or testifying in the witness-
box to the artistic integrity of the three Sitwells. For the distinctive
attributes of the Macmillans of the earlier generations the reader may
go to Charles Morgan's book, and to some of his sources.* But a brief
note is appended to this introduction on those partners and directors of
the firm to whom letters are addressed. It is often, of course, uncertain
to which 'Mr. Macmillan' a letter is addressed.

A scrapbook is by definition scrappy. A different book could have
treated the material thematically, with chapters devoted to the various
themes adumbrated above: this would have involved dismembering
many letters, extracting a sentence or two here and there for dis-

* Thomas Hughes, *Memoir of Daniel Macmillan* (1882); *Selected Letters of
Malcolm Kingsley Macmillan* (privately printed 1893); *Letters of Alexander
Macmillan*, edited by George A. Macmillan (privately printed 1908); Charles L.
Graves, *Life and Letters of Alexander Macmillan* (1910).

tribution among the chapters, and thus losing the impact and intimacy of whole letters in the context in which they were written. As it is, the sections devoted to individual correspondents do not pretend to cover the whole of their relations with their publishers but merely to tell stories interesting in themselves or illustrative of some particular aspect of publishing practice. Moreover the sifting of half a million letters, or of such of them as time and energy have allowed, must reflect the taste, even the prejudices, and perhaps also the serendipity (if he can lay claim to it), of the sifter. He is not concerned to rebut charges of partiality. Others would have chosen other letters, detected other themes, ranged more widely into theology or the education of the backward races, or into infringements of copyright or suits for libel; or they might have approached some authors or topics with greater sympathy, or with less. Henry James's *Partial Portraits* (Macmillan, 1888) — a brilliantly amphibolous title — was originally to have been called 'Half-Length Portraits'. If the portraits here are partial in both of James's senses, and if many of them fall far short of half-length, the blame must be shared between the sitters themselves who wrote the letters, the publishers who preserved not all the letters, and the editor of the selection. In the last resort responsibility rests with the editor, to whom the publishers gave not only unstinting help but a free hand.

The correspondents have been arranged in the order which seems to give the book most shape rather than according to any strict system of chronology. I have taken some liberties with my texts, fewer than Victorian editors were wont to take but more than is now fashionable among scholarly editors of texts for student reading. Abbreviations have been spelled out, authors' second thoughts preferred to their first, and obvious slips of the pen silently corrected. To print '& I sh.d' or 'my receipt ⟨appended⟩ enclosed', as one editor of letters to the Macmillans has lately done, or to spatter the page with '[*sic*]', would be, in a scrapbook, to obtrude pedantry between the dead author and the living reader. Dates and addresses are given in a standard form at the head of the letters and, where lacking in the originals, have been supplied from such evidence as is available: in most cases where no address is printed the letter or extract may be presumed to have been written from the writer's last printed address. Similarly the beginnings and endings of many letters have been omitted if there has been no change in the personal author–publisher relationship, as from 'Dear Mr. Macmillan' to 'My dear Mac', or from 'Ever yours truly' to 'Affectionately yours'. Spelling, pointing and the use of capitals have been standardized except where a writer's idiosyncrasy adds flavour to his style. The aim throughout has been to make for readability within the limits of what a recent writer in *The Times Literary Supplement* has called 'judicious, if minimal, alteration'.

SIMON NOWELL-SMITH

MACMILLAN PARTNERS AND DIRECTORS

A MACMILLAN family tree appears as frontispiece to this book. In 1843 the brothers DANIEL (1813–57) and ALEXANDER (1818–96), Scots of humble origin and little formal education, set up as publishers in London and Cambridge. (From 1844 to 1857 the publishing business was carried on only in Cambridge, after 1863 only in London.)

DANIEL had earlier worked in a bookshop in Cambridge, where the brothers formed friendships with many scholars, philosophers and theologians. A victim of tuberculosis from his twentieth year, he was sustained by a strong Christian piety, grounded in Calvinism but enlarged by sympathy with the Christian Socialists of the school of Frederick Maurice. In spite of recurrent absences owing to illness, Daniel dominated the business, but he seems to have retained a somewhat puritanical belief that profit was inimical to the vocation of publisher.

ALEXANDER, though of marked sincerity and generosity, and something of an idealist, did not altogether share this belief. His was a more dynamic character and he had a keener eye for business. Under his rule the firm expanded from the issue of fewer than forty titles in 1857 to more than 150 (excluding American and colonial books) in 1889 when, at over seventy, he retired from active publishing. He founded, and took much pride in, *Macmillan's Magazine* (1859) and *Nature* (1869). He visited America in 1867 and set up what was to prove a flourishing branch in New York two years afterwards; and he developed the London house into one of the foremost publishers not only of educational and theological books, but of fiction, poetry and general literature. He believed in personal contact with his authors, and for many years weekly entertained the more congenial of them at evening 'tobacco parliaments' in the firm's premises in Henrietta Street (later in Bedford Street), Covent Garden.

In 1865 Alexander took into partnership GEORGE LILLIE CRAIK (1837–1905), an energetic administrator and the husband of the author of *John Halifax, Gentleman*. Craik was comparatively little concerned with authors, or with the literary and editorial sides of the business. His demeanour on encountering Dr. Stone on the staircase, as recorded on page 148, is no proof that he was incapable of courtesy and tact when these were called for. Morgan prints an excellent short letter of his to Mrs. Humphry Ward on the occasion of her being seduced from Macmillans by another firm.

After Daniel's death in 1857, at the age of forty-three, Alexander brought up his brother's sons FREDERICK ORRIDGE (1851–1936) and MAURICE CRAWFORD (1853–1936) with his own sons MALCOLM KINGSLEY (1853–89) and GEORGE AUGUSTIN (1855–1936). A note on MALCOLM appears on page 201. The other three Macmillans of the second generation were active in the family firm until all three died, in their eighties, in the same year. They have been described as 'Galsworthy characters to a man'. Certainly Frederick's letter to his brother Maurice, intended also for the eye of his cousin George (page 305), might have been written by a Forsyte to Forsytes.

FREDERICK went straight into publishing from his public school. He had had practical experience in Macmillans' various departments, as well as in printing and retail bookselling, and had spent five years in the firm's New York office, before he was admitted into partnership in 1876. He became deeply interested in trade practices outside the firm, was the chief architect of the 'net book system', played a leading role in the book war with *The Times*,[*] and served two terms, in 1900–2 and 1911–13, as president of the Publishers' Association. He was knighted in 1909. There was no aspect of Macmillans' business on which Sir Frederick did not keep, or seek to keep, a controlling hand to the end.

MAURICE alone of the trio, went to a university. With a first class in classics from Christ's College, Cambridge, he taught at St. Paul's School for five years before joining the partnership in 1883. His initial

---

[*] See *The Net Book Agreement, 1899, and the Book War, 1906–1908*, by Frederick Macmillan, privately printed 1924.

sphere was education. His tour of schools and universities throughout Australasia and India in 1884–5 resulted in a large expansion of Macmillans' business oversea. Besides scholarship at large, his main preoccupation in the years before the first world war was publishing in the empire and the far east. He was socially the most reserved member of the family.

GEORGE, the youngest, entered the firm when he left Eton in 1874 and became a partner five years later. His principal interests were music (fostered by George Grove, of *Grove's Dictionary*) and Greek literature and archaeology. He was at different times honorary secretary of the Hellenic Society (for forty years), the British School at Athens and the Royal College of Music, as well as chairman of the music publishers Stainer & Bell. George inherited his father's good head for business and taste for good company, both assets in a publisher.

On the death of Alexander in 1896 Macmillans were incorporated as a limited company, with Frederick as chairman, and next year they moved into newly built premises in St. Martin's Street, Leicester Square, their home until 1965.

The members of the third generation of the family who appear in this book are George's son WILLIAM EDWARD FRANK (1880–1954) and Maurice's sons DANIEL DE MENDI (1886–1965) and MAURICE HAROLD (born 1894).

WILLIAM ('WILL') was a good classical scholar and a keen musician and natural historian. He joined the board of Macmillans in 1911 and was also a director of Stainer & Bell.

DANIEL ('DAN') was also a classical scholar and, like his father, was keenly concerned with maintaining the continuity of the firm's publications and in developing its educational list. He joined the board when he was twenty-five and was chairman from the death of Sir Frederick in 1936 until his own death in 1965.

HAROLD, whose university career was interrupted by the 1914–18 war, entered the firm in 1920. He has held a directorship, except when a Government minister, since then. He was deputy chairman 1936–40 and 1945–51, and again, after his resignation as prime minister, in 1963, succeeding his brother Daniel as chairman in 1965.

THOMAS MARK (1890–1963) joined Macmillans in 1913 and, after some years as secretary to the board, was appointed a director in 1944. He retired in 1959, but continued as literary adviser to the firm — and as guide, mentor and friend to many of its authors — until his death.

HORATIO ('RACHE') LOVAT DICKSON (born 1902), who had previously edited literary periodicals and conducted his own publishing house, entered Macmillans in 1938. He joined the board in 1941, and retired from it in 1964. His second volume of autobiography, *The House of Words* (Macmillan, 1963), describes his early years with the firm.

MAURICE VICTOR MACMILLAN (born 1921), the son of Harold Macmillan, entered the firm in 1946 and has been a director, except when he was a Government minister in 1963–4, since 1949. He became deputy chairman in 1966 and chairman in 1967.

ACKNOWLEDGMENTS

Besides present members of the staff of Macmillans, the editor has cause to be grateful to the genius of the late Thomas Mark, whose notes for Charles Morgan's *House of Macmillan* laid the foundation for that book and for this; to Colin Cooke for help in the choice and annotation of the letters; to Kay Soper for her skill in deciphering difficult hands; to Derek Hudson for the loan of typescripts of Lewis Carroll's letters; to Rache Lovat Dickson and William Plomer for judicious advice; and, for assistance in matters of detail, to Leon Edel, Henry Maas, Hilda Morgan, Christopher Ricks, and Geoffrey and Kathleen Tillotson.

The editor and publishers wish to thank the following copyright-holders for permission to reprint the letters from those named in parentheses: Mrs. Rossetti Angeli (Christina Rossetti, D. G. Rossetti, W. M. Rossetti); Simon Asquith (J. M. Barrie); Bedford College, University of London (A. C. Bradley); Professor Bradford A. Booth, for the letter from *Letters of Trollope*, Oxford University Press; George P. Brett (G. E. Brett); the Rt. Hon. the Lord Brooke (Stopford A. Brooke); Jonathan Cape Ltd. (Laurence Housman); Capt. J. M. Carew (Sir J. W. Fortescue); the Hon. Randolph Churchill (Sir Winston Churchill); Dame Isobel Cripps (R. Stafford Cripps); John Farquharson Ltd. (James Hilton and Henry James); Charles A. Gladstone (W. E. Gladstone); Miss Jennifer Gosse (Sir Edmund Gosse); Sir Rupert Hart-Davis (Hugh Walpole); Nigel William Henley (W. E. Henley); David Higham Associates Ltd. (Sir Edward Marsh and Dame Edith Sitwell); Michael Hillary (Richard Hillary); Vyvyan Holland (Oscar Wilde); Sir Julian Huxley (T. H. Huxley); Philip Dodgson Jacques ('Lewis Carroll'); Lord Kahn (J. M. Keynes); Sir Geoffrey Keynes (J. N. Keynes); Henry Maas (A. E. Housman); J. Maurice (F. D. Maurice); J. C. Medley (Charles Morgan); Mrs. G. A. Morley (John Morley); Mrs. Eileen O'Casey

(Sean O'Casey); A. D. Peters & Co. (Maurice Henry Hewlett); Presses Universitaires de France (Henri Bergson); the Public Trustee and the Society of Authors (G. Bernard Shaw); Mrs. Eva Reichmann (Sir Max Beerbohm); Royds, Rawstorne & Co. (Matthew Arnold); Diarmuid Russell ('A.E.'); the Rt. Hon. Earl Russell and Continuum 1 Ltd. (Countess von Arnim); the Society of Authors as the literary representative of the Estate of the late Laurence Binyon; the Society of Authors as the literary representative of the Estate of the late James Joyce; the Society of Authors as the literary representative of the Estate of the late R. L. Stevenson; Robert J. Stopford (J. R. Green); Lord Tennyson (Alfred and Hallam Tennyson); Thorold, Brodie, Bonham-Carter & Mason (A. V. Dicey); Mrs. Mary T. Trevelyan (G. O. Trevelyan); Trinity College, Cambridge (Sir J. G. Frazer); Deputy Treasurer, University of Cambridge Financial Board (Alfred Marshall); Miss Gabrielle F. Lilian M. Vallings (Charles and Henry Kingsley); Vandercom, Stanton & Co.; Professor G. P. Wells (H. G. Wells); Miss Irene Cooper Willis (Thomas Hardy); Mrs. Iris Wise (James Stephens); and Mr. M. B. Yeats and A. P. Watt & Son (W. B. Yeats).

The publishers have made every effort, but have failed, to trace the other copyright-holders concerned and they would be happy to make the necessary arrangements at the first opportunity.

The illustration of 'Psyché et l'Amour' facing page 56 was photographed by D. E. Flowerdew in the Victoria and Albert Museum. The copies of *The Children of the Castle* and *Cranford* illustrated facing pages 225 and 224 were kindly lent by Roger Lancelyn Green and Ruth Harris respectively. The letters reproduced are from the Macmillan archives, with the exception of that from Tennyson on page 113 (W. S. G. Macmillan). The other illustrations are from the editor's copies.

THE LETTERS

THE DRIFTERS

FREDERICK DENISON MAURICE

1805–1872

Maurice, a close friend of Daniel and Alexander Macmillan, was in
1853 professor of ecclesiastical history at King's College, London. He
had already once been cleared by the council of the college of a charge
of heterodoxy arising out of his opinions as a Christian Socialist. In
June 1853 Macmillans published his *Theological Essays*, whereupon
the principal of the college, Dr. Richard William Jelf (1798–1871),
quarrelling with his interpretation of eternal punishment, called upon
him to resign his professorship. Arguing, as he wrote to Daniel
Macmillan, that 'a Principle which is more than a Principal is at stake',
Maurice refused to resign. On 28 October Daniel wrote to Alexander:

My dear Brother,

I have just seen Mr. Maurice. I spent about an hour with
him. He is dismissed — and at once. He is not even allowed
to lecture today. As he expected this from the first he is not
greatly surprised. I think he does feel the mode in which it
has been done — that is, the suddenly being forbidden by
the Principal to lecture even to the historical students. Never
mind ! God rules over all !

I asked him about the future and half repent having done
so. His answer was, *'sufficient unto the day is the evil thereof'*.
Mrs. Maurice is rather a 'cheeping body'. I wish he had a
more lively and braver wife. But pray don't whisper this to
any one. I may be mistaken. He is a grand man ! — and
must endure like other Prophets. The good people of the
next age will build his tomb.

He has lent me the correspondence and given me his own
defence. He has asked leave to print and publish the whole,
most likely with such additions and prefaces as may seem

needful. I wish we could do it, and should like to write offering to do so at latest on Sunday night. It is sure to pay — most likely it would have a very large sale. I should be glad if it sold so well that we could give him £20. . . .

Your loving brother,   DANIEL

The 'defence' which Maurice had left with Macmillan was a pamphlet which he had had printed for private circulation. Macmillans published this as *The Word 'Eternal' and the Punishment of the Wicked, a letter to the Rev. Dr. Jelf*, after Jelf had issued his own pamphlet, *Grounds for laying before the Council of King's College, London, Statements in 'Theological Essays' by F. D. Maurice*.

21 Queen Square, Bloomsbury, 31 October 1853

My dear Macmillan,

In a letter to the secretary of King's College in which I acknowledged the receipt of the minutes of the council I said that I did not perceive any reference in the resolutions to the publication of the correspondence, that I supposed the Principal would wish to superintend the publication of that part of it which he had asked to be printed, that *I* would publish my final letter, but that, if there was any considerable delay, I should feel myself authorized to publish the whole. In his answer the secretary said that he communicated my letter to the Principal and that he undertook to publish the correspondence, with some footnotes, by Thursday next at the latest. I should therefore be glad to publish about Friday.

I have just ascertained from Wilson & Ogilvy, who printed 100 copies for me, that the greater part of the types are not dispersed (2s 6d they say would set them to rights), so I will ask as many to be printed as you think desirable. I will add a short account of the proceedings at King's College and perhaps one or two notes. . . . As to terms, I can

settle with Wilson, and pay advertisements such as you think
fit, and you can publish *for me*. . . .

I do not like to speak of it ; but the considerable reduction
of income which my expulsion will cause me must oblige me
I fear to trust the matter in your hands, as I shall not be able
to meet the expenses of the press. I owe £130 at least for my
house, besides some other unusual demands. . . .

Kind regards to you both. Ever yours affectionately,

F. D. MAURICE

2 December 1853

Dr. Jelf has just published a third edition of the correspondence with a rather impertinent preface.

2 January 1854

All New Year blessings to you. . . . Is the third edition of my
letter published yet? I have compunctions about the preface
as I hear that Dr. Jelf is ill.

THOMAS HUGHES

1822–1896

Tom Hughes, later Q.C. and M.P., wished his novel of public-school life to appear anonymously because, he said, his vocation was the law, not the pen, and 'I don't want credit with an adulterous and corrupt Mrs. Grundy'. *Tom Brown's Schooldays*, 'by an Old Boy', was published in 1857, and *Tom Brown at Oxford* in 1861; the proposed London sequel was never written. Messrs. Routledge had been advertising new novels in cheap yellowback form; Holywell Street, Covent Garden, was the home of pornographic publishing and bookselling.

3 Old Square, Lincoln's Inn, 11 October 1856

Dear Mac,

Thanks for your note. I shall now go right ahead. I don't, however, hold you pledged, of course, if you find anything you think outrageous in the remainder. I don't think you will in this volume, but if folk read it, and I ever get to a second and third, I mean to raise their hair a bit, I tell you ; only you needn't father the Oxford and London volumes ; I can go to Routledge, or some cove in Holywell street. . . .

Yours ever,   THOS. HUGHES

Daniel Macmillan was delighted with the book as it progressed, but with reservations. Tom Brown's protégé Geordie, in a fever, dreams of some great work being accomplished not only by good men, but by others 'whom they called atheist and infidel'. To include atheists, Macmillan urged, would injure Hughes's influence. 'If it were changed for Methodists or Dissenters or something of that kind it would answer the purpose and save you from giving offence to many good people.' Hughes replied that he would consult Frederick Maurice.

Cambridge, 22 October 1856

Dear Hughes,

... My objection to 'men called atheists' is mere cowardice — a fear of Mrs. Grundy! — and you are going to ask
Mr. Maurice who has not had the least notion of what
cowardice means! This is keen irony. I deserve it. ...

Ever yours faithfully,   D. MACMILLAN

The atheists were allowed to stand. But Mrs. Grundy had not
finished.

18 February 1857

Dear Macmillan,

... As to the 'dammes' I give you *carte blanche.* I can't
remember above two altogether. Only mind, boys then swore
abominably ; I did myself until I was in the Fifth. I dare say
they do still. Besides, if mamas won't buy for young hopefuls,
young hopefuls will for themselves. ...

Ever yours,   THOS. HUGHES

2 March 1857

Now as to your corrections and prudery in my affair. Of
course you may do as you please, because in any case you
will. I can't remember any words myself necessary to be
erased or changed, but when you tell me that you have altered
'beastly' into 'inhumanly' drunk — I suppose etc. — I
really think that it is time for me to give up in despair. However my name's Easy ; please yourselves, gentlemen, and
you'll please me.

5 March 1857

As to 'inhumanly', *vice* 'beastly' cashiered, I don't care a
straw. ... The 'damns' I was prepared for ; I suppose you've

put this sort of thing for them '——'. (I prefer 'damn' myself, but no matter.) But what have the poor 'infernals' done? and what have you substituted? — 'gracious'? 'heavenly'?

Tom Brown's Schooldays appeared in April. Hughes had sold the copyright for £150, but unexpected success led to the immediate preparation of a new edition and to revision of the contract: by November 11,000 copies were sold, and the author received £1,250 in these seven months.

John Malcolm Ludlow (1821–1911), barrister and social reformer, collaborated with Hughes in a history of the United States (Macmillan, 1862).

3 Old Square, 29 May 1857

Dear Mac,

I suppose I must have been drunk when I wrote to you last, though I sincerely thought I wasn't; I say this judging from your last answer. Why, man alive, am I not a man and a brother, go to! and a lawyer, go to! and a man who has the only common room in England in his house, go to! Who am I that I should sweat even my publishers, who are (generically speaking) as hard to sweat as flints, by the witness of all writing coves in all ages? To speak the language of soberness, I never had the slightest idea, wish, notion, or intention to upset our written contract about Tom Brown. As it stands at present, no doubt there is some small ambiguity, because it was never stated whether our agreement affected only the first edition or the editions for ever and ever, amen; but this no doubt the custom of the trade will decide, to determine which I shall leave to you. Now, if you like the old agreement, stick to it, for second edition as well as first; but if you like better to give the £150, why, give it, and take the two editions as your own. I don't want to get a penny out of the book or anything else which ought by the strictest laws of honour and equity to have gone into the pockets of any other son of man — even Louis Napoleon — which is going as far as I can, short of the Devil, whom I own I should like to cheat. So, as I said above, construe the contract as you like ; I shan't grumble. I only wrote about the copy I have corrected because your brother seemed to talk as if you wanted it directly. However, here it is, and can stop till you send for it.

I mean to go on writing, unless trade improves here, which I fear it won't for some years, until these changes have time to work themselves straight and suitors recover courage. What I wanted to know was whether I should go on to Oxford, etc., with some of my old characters, or start a new line at once, e.g. law students' life or some life in London. You haven't solved my difficulty ; but there's no hurry, and before writing a line I must get the prophetic sanction.

Kindest regards to everybody. I am deeply sorry to hear of your throat.

Ever yours, THOS. HUGHES

Saturday

The enclosed was written yesterday, when Ludlow came in, read your letter, said of course I ought to accept your very liberal offer of £150, that at any rate I must submit the whole to my wife, which I did accordingly last night at home, and she is with him. However, my impression from your letter is still that you think I wanted to alter our contract, which is a chimaera dire, so shall leave the whole in your own power either to stick to the half-profits plan or to buy the two editions.

B

CHARLES KINGSLEY

1819–1875

Kingsley was rector of Eversley in Hampshire. His first novel, *Alton Locke* (1850), was published by Chapman & Hall, to whom he was committed for another, and his next two novels, *Yeast* (1851) and *Hypatia* (1853), by John W. Parker. His *Phaethon, or Loose Thoughts for Loose Thinkers*, and F. D. Maurice's sermons, *The Prophets and Kings of the Old Testament*, were published by Macmillans at the end of 1852. George Brimley (1819–57), librarian of Trinity College, Cambridge, was brother to Alexander Macmillan's wife.

These letters deal with *Westward Ho!* (Macmillan, 1855), a novel of Elizabethan adventure written during the Crimean war. Kingsley's mother came of a family long settled in the West Indies. James Anthony Froude (1818–94), the historian, was Kingsley's wife's brother-in-law.

Eversley, 17 February 1853

My dear Friends,

For in answering one I answer both, never being able to tell either your writing or your thoughts apart. I ought to have written to you long ago. But I have been ill, and Mrs. Kingsley very ill; item, I have been busy, which is, I hope, an excuse.

I have thought much upon your novel, and you shall have it if I can fairly get off Chapman without damage to my pocket, which I am bound, having debts to pay, to consider in justice to my tradesmen. But I will tell you (*in the most strict confidence, of course,* for Chapman's sake) what it will be.

The autobiography of a knight of Queen Elizabeth's time, a pet of Grenville and Raleigh, who goes out with Drake to the West Indies, has to do with Caribs, the Inquisition, the

Spaniards, and all the rest of it, and finishes by helping to fight the Armada. Froude, who knows that period better than any man, is giving me good counsel thereanent continually, and I go, *Deo volente*, to him in May to talk it over. The West Indian part of it I have known from a child. The English I am reading up; and I think that, considering these times of the Pope and the French Invasion, it may make a hit and do good. I am, you mentioned, a worshipper of Queen Bess, and as ready as Raleigh would have been to do battle *à l'outrance* for the Honour of her Stainless Virginity. We want her and her old heroes up from the dead again; and I'll try and conjure them.

Hypatia is near ended — thank Heaven! It, too, is something done, but I fear will be caviare to the many.

Give my kindest remembrances to Brimley, and tell him from me that his review of Maurice was perfect; and that while he thinks thus of my master's book, I will forgive him any hard thoughts which he chooses to have about *mine*. It *was* a righteous review; and if Mrs. Kingsley had not been so poorly, and I in bed for two days ! ! ! — oh wonder! for the first time in ten years — I would have written him a long letter of praise.

I am delighted to hear of your success in the important matter of bairns.* I must ask to be godfather to one apiece of the futures — for, arguing by analogy, there are more 'looming'. I wish I knew your two goodwives: but when I shall happen at Cambridge I see not: and if it was not for you and Brimley, I would never enter it again.

I am very well, and busy as a bee. But this is a sickly season among my poor folk. The frost, however, will set all right, and stop fever and rheumatism.

Phaethon I like better than anything which I have yet

---

* Daniel Macmillan at this date had one son, Frederick: the second, Maurice, whose godfathers were Frederick Maurice and Charles Kingsley, was born in the following April. Kingsley also stood godfather to Alexander Macmillan's first son, Malcolm Kingsley, the baby referred to in Mrs. Kingsley's postscript.

done. It will live. But as for making a noise at once, that no one could expect. I have no brother for it yet born — one or two conceived, though. The next on the difference between Aristotle and Plato.

Yours sleepy and tired,   C. KINGSLEY

P.S. Please to accept my warm congratulations on the dear new Baby. I should love to see them both and their parents.

FANNY E. K.

Babbacombe, 1 June 1854

My dear Macmillan,

Many thanks for your letter. A *sine qua non* for a curate is that he shall either be married, or have a mother and sisters living with him who will interest themselves in the parish. If you can find me such a one, a tolerable *High* Churchman, but no Puseyite, pray do. . .

My book thrives apace. I have got now nearly all my materials, much of them quite new and unknown. I have written, up and down, several chapters, whereof Froude approves much. It only now remains to me, after having picked up a little more material round here, to go and settle down (as please God I shall soon do) for twelve months on the very site of my story, Bideford, on the north coast, and write straight away from eyesight. But unfortunately I cannot settle about moving till I hear from you about money matters. So without hurrying you I should like very much to know *when* you think you could make me any advance on the book, as I shall then see my way.

The book is so far complete in my head that I can promise it you certainly by Xmas, and even before, if you wanted it.

I have taken the autobiographical form, and intend to call it *The Tracey Papers* or some such name, and coolly and impudently to assume the reality of the whole story, making him comment on known documents, and if he chooses correct them in details. I have lots of good stories, both English and Spanish, as episodes ; and I think, what with Drake, Hawkins Oxenham, Gilbert, Raleigh, Grenville, Sidney, Burleigh, Elizabeth, Grey of Wilton, the Jesuits, the Inquisition, Ballard's conspiracy, and the Spanish West Indies, the discovery of Virginia, and the North West Passage, and, for a finale, the defeat of the Armada, we may make a book which people will read in these war-times and learn what glorious fellows their forbears were.

Kindest regards to your brother, and blessings to my god-child.

Daniel Macmillan replied with a cheque for £100 by way of advance. Thackeray's *Henry Esmond* (1852) is said to have owed something of its archaic diction to *The Maiden and Married Life of Mary Powell* (1849) by the prolific historical novelist Anne Manning (1807–79).

Cromer, June 1854

My dear Kingsley,

. . . We are greatly taken with all you tell us about the plan and character of your novel. Of course you will not adopt the pseudo-antique manner in which *Esmond*, *Mary Powell* etc., are written. The style is now getting a bore. The free march of your own style will be much more Elizabethan in manner and tone than any you can assume. We feel sure it will be a right brave and noble book, and do good to England. . . .

Yours ever faithfully,   DANIEL MACMILLAN

Chelsea, 18 June 1854

My dear Macmillan,

You have behaved very generously and trustfully to me, and you need not fear that I shall ever forget the obligation

under which you have laid me. As for the book, I have just
been talking to Thackeray about it; and he thinks that the
archaic form, slight as it was, injured *Esmond*'s sale, and
that it must be avoided. . . .

Nicholas Trübner (1817–84), an export-import bookseller, was
arranging to sell Kingsley's novel in the United States. The title as here
given differs in several small particulars from the form as published in
February 1855: the spelling 'Burrow' was altered to 'Burrough' before
publication, though not in Macmillans' early advertisements. The next
extracts were addressed to Alexander Macmillan:

Bideford, 29 September 1854

Your brother asked me to send Trübner through you the
name of my book. It is

Westward-Ho.
being the Voyages and Adventures
of Sir Amyas Leigh, of Burrow,
Co. Devon,
in the Reign of Queen Elizabeth
of Glorious Memory.

. . . I shall expunge all preachments — your criticism was
quite right.

Eversley, 30 August 1855

I hope you approve of the review in *The Times*. I think it,
though wrong in point of fact about the Jesuits, yet very kind
and good, and certain to help the book very much. I hope
you are of the same opinion. As for extravagant praise, the
book don't deserve it, and my wonder is that he has not fallen
foul of the clumsy way in which it was put together. As for my
not having Walter Scott's genius, well, it is quite true in the

first place, and in the second no one expects me to have, and in the third, if I had it I should use it in another direction, and shock the world still *more*, not less, than now.

I want to caution you on one thing. Our country postman is proved a rogue, having, no doubt, purloined various money letters : but being a government officer, that is not the least reason for his being turned out, as the government system in small employés, just as in great, makes (on a complaint) the defendant himself witness, jury and all but judge, while his superior (i.e., the man whose work he does for him) is both attorney and counsel. Hence it is nearly as difficult to convict a government employé in England as it is in Prussia — though not quite, owing to a free press.

But as we are liable to have monies stolen with impunity, *don't* send your cheque here, but in a registered letter to my account at Messrs. Stephens, Blandy & Co., Market Place, Reading.

Mrs. Kingsley is anxious about Mrs. Macmillan, and says she must be ill, or you would have told us how she went on. Pray let us know thereanent, and also how Daniel is.

HENRY KINGSLEY

1830–1876

Charles Kingsley's younger brother, after five unproductive years in
the Australian gold-fields, returned to England in 1858 to live by his
pen. Macmillans published his first six novels — *The Recollections of
Geoffry Hamlyn* (1859); *Ravenshoe* (1862); *Austin Elliot* (1863);
The Hillyars and the Burtons (1865); *Leighton Court* (1866); and
Silcote of Silcotes (1867). The first of these letters was written early in
1863, when *The Hillyars and the Burtons* was on the stocks, and the
second later in the same year, when that novel was appearing in
Macmillan's Magazine. In the interval the Alexander Macmillans had
moved from Cambridge to Upper Tooting, outside London.

David Masson (1822–1907) edited *Macmillan's Magazine* from its
start in 1859 until 1868. Clay was the printer. Charles Kingsley never
wrote his novel about Babylon.

Eversley

Dear Macmillan,

Would it be too much if I were to ask you to send me a
cheque for the first number of the new story, for I am very
low at my bankers, and if you could kindly do an unbusiness-
like action in my favour, you would save me from calling in
any money, a proceeding I have the greatest horror of? If
business stands in the way, never mind.

I long to see my first proofs. I suppose I shall have them as
soon as you get this. Masson sent the first number to Clay on
Monday. He seems taken with it. I hope the public will be
the same. Nearly four numbers of it are written, and it is
progressing in a rapid ratio. I dare say you would like to hear
something of it, but the plot is very intricate and so overborne
by incident that it would be difficult to give a précis of it.

I will talk with you about it when I come to town, and tell you the general bearings of it.

Today's news from America was, to me, utterly unexpected. The wave has turned again, this time long before I expected it. If the Southern luck keeps good for a little longer, this is the most important crisis of the war. For there are slight symptoms of weariness in the North, which would, after a few disasters, grow serious. Again, there is very little doubt that the French are intriguing at Richmond, and may be driven to recognize the South, for cotton or for some other reason. I don't believe the story about Texas being the price paid for recognition because I don't believe that the French want Texas, or any other extension of territory. But they are a restless and immoral nation, and may do anything. I don't care much what happens so long as the American Union goes to smash ; and after that the Negroes are slowly and carefully emancipated. I like the Northerners better than the Southerners on the whole, but I hate both, and the Union worst of all three.

How does the little dog suit you? I have not heard of it. If it won't do I will get you another. Pray remember me to Mrs. Macmillan and Mrs. Daniel, and believe me, yours ever sincerely,

HENRY KINGSLEY

Dear Macmillan,

The Nemesis of all general invitations has swooped down on your unhappy head. Can you take me in on Wednesday next? I bring my mother up to stay a week with Lord and Lady Chelsea, and if I may accept your invitation at the same time, I should have your company, that of Mrs. Macmillan and Mrs. Daniel, not to mention the 'kids', instead of being boxed up at 19 Henrietta Street, with nothing to think of. If it is the least inconvenient you will let me know of course, and I will sleep in London and come and see you occasionally in the day time. . . .

Charles expressed to me a wild intention of going into the high-fellooting historic novel line of business again. Scene Babylon, Time Nebuchadnezzar. He will make a fine thing of it you may depend. It is his *especial* line. The works of his which will live best are *Saint's Tragedy*, *Hypatia*, and *Westward Ho!* I am glad he has got out of the absurd idea that it was *infra dig.* to write novels. As I pointed out to him on Sunday night, Cabinet Ministers did. A man who has forced his way to the front rank *by* literature, must not throw literature overboard. It won't do. Besides, with his literary reputation, it is actually wicked not to make use of that reputation to increase his fortune. I told him so some time ago, and now the leaven has worked. I need not tell you how sacred this little confidence of mine is. Don't let him know that I have discussed the matter with you ; but I think that he ought to come before the public again with some carefully finished work. It won't do him to be forgotten. He has not made his great hit, yet.

I should be glad if he wrote his book from end to end and published it all at once, for these reasons. 1st, it will rather take the wind out of my sails if he starts at once in your *Magazine*. 2nd, that two brothers, writing two novels at one and the same time in one magazine, is a new and astounding spectacle to gods and men. And 3rd, that his book will be far too good to be parcelled out into monthly doles. I should almost wish now that we had kept my book back, sooner than that we should clash. I shall see you next week.

Yours affectionately,   HENRY KINGSLEY

Kingsley married in 1864. In the following summer he was having difficulty with a novel to be called *Aunt Mary*. What story Mrs. Carlyle told is beyond conjecture.

Upper Tooting, 12 June 1865

My dear Henry,

I am so sorry to hear of your wife's relapse. I wish very much that you could have stayed with us for a few weeks. The Craiks come on 1 July, but if you could come for a fortnight before that we should be so glad to see you, and perhaps the change might do her good. I do so hope she will soon get over this weakness.

As to the novel, here is my idea : a plain simple story with quiet but interesting plot, neither squalor nor vice nor crime. Mrs. Carlyle told me one such charming story that would work beautifully into a story. I give it very roughly within. I was meaning to send it to you. Tell me if you can do it. If you don't, I will send it to Tennyson for a poem. But it would make the charmingest little one-volume affair in the world, and you would do it like an angelic artist. Play not a bit of the fool. Quiet pathos and humour. Kindest regards to the wife. I do so hope you can tell me better of her soon.

Ever affectionately,   A. MACMILLAN

Wargrave, Henley-on-Thames, June 1865

Dear Mac,

I will let you know all about my goings on in the 'litery' line as you wish. I have been very busy, as heaven knows I need be.

I put *Aunt Mary* on one side at once, and started an entirely new thing. Pathetic, instructive and genteel, in which Mrs. Carlyle's story is interwoven. (I like Tennyson's impudence in offering to bone it.) I have entirely absorbed myself in this, and it will be done in two months, the time which Mudie especially recommended, which is what I have been driving at. You can see some of it in the rough form as soon as you like.

I am sorry to hear of your going to America, though if it does you good and sets you up again I should be glad were it

even Australia. There is not much chance I fear of communi-
cating to you by the Atlantic telegraph, I am afraid it is all
over with that. You will be in time to see Jefferson Davis
executed. I think they are going to make an example of him,
and prevent any future secessions. They are in a sad mess
over there, they had better, far better, have let the South go to
the devil their own way. The North seems to me to have paid
too terrible a price for what they have got. They hardly
realize yet the price they have paid. Meantime Johnson is
disappointing his enemies, and showing himself a statesman.

I was in hopes that you were going to have a new edition of
Austin Elliot by now, for the fearful expenses of pulling a sick
wife about the country, literally to save her life, and setting
up a new house, have superinduced an alarming financial
crisis, and left me without any money at all. I suppose that
one's first year is always a squeezer, but to be forced into
extravagance by the doctors is too hard. However I can see
my way quite clear if I can tide over Xmas.

My dearest wife is quite recovered. If she goes on like this
I shall actually begin to believe in the possibility of a Cherub,
though I see nothing of his appearance yet. I hope Mrs.
Macmillan and Mrs. Daniel are very well. Will *you* come and
see *me* before you cross the briny. Meet we must, in London
or somewhere ; I wish you had time to read my new story.

Ever yours affectionately, HENRY KINGSLEY

Caroline Norton's *Old Sir Douglas* (page 78, below) was being
serialized in *Macmillan's Magazine*, where *Silcote of Silcotes* was due
to appear from July 1866 to September 1867.

1866

Dear Mac,
My new story for you is called *Silcote of Silcotes*, and I am
patching and puzzling to make the first number brilliant and

interesting and bowl over Old Mother Norton (how dreadfully old she must be, it is exactly thirty years since she was talked of with Lord Melbourne).

I shall utilize the best part of the defunct *Aunt Mary* in *Silcotes*. I shall not altogether eliminate humour, as I have in *Leighton Court*, but what little there is of it will be very dry. There will be no *fun* ; but it would be an utter mistake to be dull, as I have left very much inclined to be since the handling *The Hillyars and the Burtons* got from the *Saturday* and *Spectator*. . . .

Love to all, H. K.

JOHN HENRY NEWMAN

1801–1890

The exchange of letters between Newman and Charles Kingsley that
led to Newman's *Apologia pro vita sua* is well known, but Alexander
Macmillan's intervention, sincere if naïve, may pertinently be re-
hearsed here. Kingsley's provocative article appeared, over the signature 'C.K.', in *Macmillan's Magazine* for January 1864. The text
of Newman's two letters (the second* in extract — the original runs to
some two thousand words) is taken from *Mr. Kingsley and Dr. Newman, a correspondence on the question whether Dr. Newman teaches that
Truth is a Virtue* (1864).

The Oratory, 30 December 1863

Gentlemen,
    I do not write to you with any controversial purpose,
which would be preposterous; but I address you simply
because of your special interest in a *Magazine* which bears
your name.
    That highly respected name you have associated with a
Magazine, of which the January number has been sent to me
by this morning's post, with a pencil mark calling my attention to page 217.
    There, apropos of Queen Elizabeth, I read as follows:
'Truth, for its own sake, had never been a virtue with the
Roman clergy. Father Newman informs us that it need not,
and on the whole ought not to be; that cunning is the weapon
which Heaven has given to the saints wherewith to withstand
the brute male force of the wicked world which marries and
is given in marriage. Whether his notion be doctrinally

---

* Newman printed his second letter, without mentioning Macmillan's name, as
addressed to 'a gentleman who interposed between Mr. Kingsley and Dr. Newman'.

correct or not, it is at least historically so.' There is no reference at the foot of the page to any words of mine, much less
any quotation from my writings, in justification of this
statement.

I should not dream of expostulating with the writer of such
a passage, nor with the editor who could insert it without
appending evidence in proof of its allegations. Nor do I want
any reparation from either of them. I neither complain of
them for their act, nor should I thank them if they reversed
it. Nor do I even write to you with any desire of troubling
you to send me an answer. I do but wish to draw the attention of yourselves, as gentlemen, to a grave and gratuitous
slander, with which I feel confident you will be sorry to find
associated a name so eminent as yours.

I am, Gentlemen, your obedient servant,

JOHN H. NEWMAN

Bedford Street, Covent Garden, 5 January 1864

Reverend Sir,

Your letter concerning a paper of Professor Kingsley's in
the January number of our *Magazine* reached me last
Monday. I delayed answering you till I had seen and talked
with him on the subject.

Precious memories of more than twenty years since, when
your sermons were a delight and blessing shared (and thereby
increased) with a dear brother no longer living, but for whom
the mists and misunderstandings have, as we believe, been
dispelled by the Light Himself, would add strong weight to
my desire to answer such a letter from you with peculiar care
and reverence.

I cannot separate myself in this case from whatever injustice, and your letter convinces me that there was injustice,
there may have been in Mr. Kingsley's charge against you
personally. I had read the passage and I will confess to you
plainly that I did not even think at the time that you or any of

your communion would think it unjust. Nothing has given
me more pleasure for long than to learn as I do from your
letter that I am mistaken at least in one instance. It is many
years since I have had intercourse with members of the
Church that holds us heretics. My intercourse then was
mainly with young men — some of them as noble and good
men as I have ever known. On the point alluded to in Mr.
Kingsley's article as well as another point — namely the duty
of enforcing penally conformity to one form of thought concerning the Revelation of God to man in Christ Jesus — I
received an impression that it was generally true that the
Roman Catholic way of looking at these matters was what
Mr. Kingsley says it is. I cannot now recall particulars, and
it is quite possible I may have done them injustice. I never
identified them personally with their theory — that truth is a
matter of *enactment*. I believed and still believe of those I
knew best that they loved truth in their souls perhaps better
than I did. I can conceive now that I may have allowed heat
of controversy to blind myself. While they were talking of
English Christian gentlemen as wolves towards whom the
combination of serpentine wisdom with the innocence of the
dove was the proper line of conduct, those who felt that they
were not wolves but sought to live and think as Christian
men ought, may have seen only the former quality without
the redeeming one. A man who like myself is brought into
near contact with very various phases of human thought in
men equally noble has often occasion to mourn over harsh
unjust words spoken by men who would not consciously
wrong any. I really ought in no way to aid — even by carelessness — increase of wrong like this.

I am sure that Mr. Kingsley and Mr. Masson both will do
all in their power to repair any wrong and print a full retrac-
tion of what you feel unjust. Mr. Kingsley wished to write
you himself, and I hope that before you have had this letter
his will have reached you. I spoke also to Mr. Masson, who
is equally anxious that you should have every, the fullest,

means of being set right in our pages. I am perfectly sure that both these gentlemen are incapable of wilfully slandering any man, and surely not more one whom all thoughtful Englishmen must owe so much to.

I am, Reverend Sir, with deep respect, your very obedient servant,   A. MACMILLAN

8 January 1864

Dear Sir,

I thank you for the friendly tone of your letter of the 5th just received, and I wish to reply to it with the frankness which it invites. I have heard from Mr. Kingsley, avowing himself, to my extreme astonishment, the author of the passage about which I wrote to Messrs. Macmillan. No one, whose name I had ever heard, crossed my mind as the writer in their *Magazine* : and, had anyone said it was Mr. Kingsley, I should have laughed in his face. Certainly, I saw the initials at the end ; but, you must recollect, I live out of the world ; and I must own, if Messrs. Macmillan will not think the confession rude, that, as far as I remember, I never before saw even the outside of their *Magazine*. And so of the Editor : when I saw his name on the cover, it conveyed to me no idea whatever. I am not defending myself, but merely stating what was the fact ; and as to the article, I said to myself, 'Here is a young scribe, who is making himself a cheap reputation by smart hits at safe objects'. . . .

The January number of the *Magazine* was sent to me, I know not by whom, friend or foe, with the passage on which I have animadverted, emphatically, not to say indignantly, scored against. Nor can there be a better proof that there was a call upon me to notice it, than the astounding fact that you can so calmly (excuse me) 'confess plainly' of yourself, as you do, 'that you had read the passage, and did not even think that I or any of my communion would think it unjust'. Most wonderful phenomenon ! . . .

I am, dear sir, yours faithfully,   JOHN H. NEWMAN

THOMAS WOOLNER

1825–1892

Woolner was one of the original Pre-Raphaelite Brotherhood and contributed to their magazine, *The Germ* (1850), a poem which Macmillans published as a book in 1863 — *My Beautiful Lady*. His fame rests on his sculpture. As a poet he received more encouragement than perhaps he merited from Thomas Carlyle and from Sir John Simeon (1815–70), scholar, country squire, M.P., and intimate friend of Tennyson.

29 Welbeck Street, W., 24 September 1863
My dear Macmillan,

I work as hard as I possibly can at my proofs ; but it is not to be expected that poetry can be corrected as easily and quickly as a prose article, for every syllable has to be studied not only with reference to its own especial meaning, and cadence to its particular verse, but also to all surrounding syllables a long way both before and after. It cannot be long ere it is completed now, I hope, as we are well into the last poem but one.

I can hardly expect my poem to delight everyone at once, for it is so wholly unlike anything else in tone and style and ideas that it would be odd if it should. But judging from what numbers of accomplished persons have said upon it I do not fear its ultimately making some way. Carlyle told me years ago that the public would be a long while making up its mind about me, but that it would do so eventually, and that there was no power on earth could keep me always hid from the world. And Sir John Simeon told me with reference to this poem that he was absolutely astonished from beginning to end at its extraordinary originality throughout every verse : well, if this is the case, I should be rash to expect that it should be at once taken in without discussion or comment. By degrees I hope that persons who love poetry proper and for its own sake will take an interest and like it. Anyway, if it be of no worth it will not be for want of having study bestowed upon it; for I should think there are not many modern poems of its size that have absorbed so much time and careful thinking — so that my conscience is at ease on the subject.

Yours ever,

THOS. WOOLNER

Eighteen years later Alexander Macmillan wrote to Woolner that he had seen in the press an announcement of 'a new volume by the author of *My Beautiful Lady*. The publisher of that poem has heard nothing of it. Is he to hear?' Eventually the new poem ran to a Prelude and twelve Books.

24 February 1881

When the poem is fit to be seen the publisher will be the first person to hear of it, but how it came to get into the papers that I am doing a poem I cannot conjecture.

The subject is *Pygmalion*, one of the most beautiful of all the old Greek stories, but which has not been in any way understood by mankind, which I attribute to the small knowledge of sculpture even men of widest culture possess. But we must manage to give them a lift on, at any rate, Pygmalion's story, and improve their education in this respect. The Poem will be in I think seven Books, and I am now in the Fourth.

Many thanks, wife and children very well; wife a bit of a cold. She was very pleased with the *Blake* you sent her. I need not ask how Mrs. Macmillan is, for I saw her the other day at Whistler's exhibition, looking as bright as I should like our days to look.

My Beautiful Lady, printed by Thomas Combe (1797–1872), printer to the Clarendon Press, had been published on half-profits. Woolner had made some £50 on the first two editions, but was in debt for £20 on the third. Macmillan suggested publishing *Pygmalion* on the same terms, but finally agreed on a one-sixth royalty on an edition of 1,500 copies.

4 August 1881

We had not discussed terms ; and I think the system of half profits for a first work not only fair but generous towards the author. But the case is different with a person whose name is established, for then the publisher has little or no risk. I will state the terms between a well-known house and a young friend, now becoming well known also.

His first book of poems on half profit system — very well satisfied, though he got nothing. His next book was a 750 edition. Publisher gave him nothing on the first 250 sold ; on all after he had 2s a copy. Nominal price of book 7s 6d, sold at 6s. He seemed very well satisfied with this arrangement. But I must mention he, in case of dead failure, was to be liable for a sum not exceeding £20.

Of course it would be a mistake to print so small an edition for *Pygmalion* as 750. We made a grave mistake in printing so small an edition of the *B. Lady* at first ; or rather dear old Combe made the mistake for us.

If I may judge from the inquiries I have endured for so many years for a new poem from India, Australia, Scotland and the North of England, I should fancy I may have a pretty large sale.

Of one thing I am certain : *Pygmalion* is quite a *new* poem, and totally unlike any other either in conception or workmanship ; because it contains a great variety of thoughts and emotions, and I have tried to make the language agree.

Of course I go into the matter thus closely because it is of considerable importance to me ; whereas to you in your vast business it is a mere trifle. This poem is the accumulation of nineteen years' thinking, and I naturally want to get as much out of it as I can, being, not a jolly bachelor whose hat covers his fortunes, but a poor grinding nigger with countless cords attached and depending on him.

COVENTRY PATMORE

1823–1896

Coventry Patmore was an assistant in the printed books department of the British Museum when Alexander Macmillan invited him — as Macmillan expressed it in a letter to James MacLehose — 'to do a *Children's Golden Treasury* on a new principle, avoiding entirely poems written *for* children, and selecting such poems from great poets as he finds children can enjoy'. The fee was £100, and *The Children's Garland from the Best Poets* appeared at Christmas 1861. For the title-page Thomas Woolner designed a vignette, though, as he told the publisher, he was 'not particularly fond of vignettes to new books': for later editions Woolner modified his engraving.

The reference to Macaulay's 'Armada' in 'the edition of 1842' must be a slip. *Lays of Ancient Rome* appeared in that year, but 'The Armada' was only added in the third edition of 1848.

British Museum, 7 November 1863

My dear Macmillan,

I send the *Garland* with a few small corrections. I have corrected Lord Macaulay's 'Armada' by the edition of 1842. I do not remember where I got my copy from at first; but there are so many differences that I suspect it must have been from another version of the *author's*, for some of the differences could not have arisen by any series of mistranscriptions.

I think you should agree to give me another £100 if another 5,000 copies are gone within seven years from the present time, and to let *that* be the final settlement. It is true I would once have taken £125; but it is also true that you would not give it — that is to say, that the book is a more fortunate speculation for *both* of us than we anticipated.

I wish Woolner would have the gauntlet and the bird

pecking the dumpling put out of the vignette. They make
too much of a *picture* and too little of a vignette. . . .

Ever truly yours,   COVENTRY PATMORE

Alexander Macmillan's next letter in the Macmillan file is, unfortunately, illegible. Patmore replied:

8 December 1863

Many thanks for acceding so good-humouredly to my 'taste'.
'What law regulates taste?' you say — a problem that will
outlast the squaring of the circle! You would not, however,
have chosen the right man to do your book unless, by nature
and cultivation, he happened to have a special knack of
smelling out the good from the bad. I certainly should not
have undertaken such a work if I had not been convinced
that I could do it better than any one who had not made this
sort of thing his speciality.

For a new edition of Patmore's long narrative poem *The Angel in the
House* (1866) Macmillans again wanted a title-page vignette. The
painting 'Psyché et l'Amour' by François Gérard (1770–1837) is in
the Louvre. (See plate facing page 56.) Charles Henry Jeens (d. 1879)
engraved several copper-plate vignettes from designs by Woolner and
others for the Golden Treasury Series. Alexander Macmillan regarded
him as 'really a crack man' and the equal of Raffaelo Morghen.

1 November 1865

I have found the design I wanted, extremely well engraved,
in the *Oeuvres du baron F. Gérard*, press-mark 1751.b. in the
library of the British Museum. It would certainly make a
most appropriate and attractive vignette, and I am anxious to
learn that Mr. Jeens will undertake it. The engraving is the

fifth plate in the second part of the work. Mr. J. must remember this, as there is another and inferior design of the same subject in the same volume. . . .

The one we want has the Psyche *seated* and Cupid about to kiss her forehead.

Again, unfortunately, Alexander's letter is irrecoverable, but it is evident that he rejected Patmore's Psyche. The book appeared with no vignette.

9 November 1865

I dare say you are right as to the shocking effect which that pure and lovely group would have on the sale of the *Angel*. The more I know of English chastity the more it reminds me of that of a saint of whom I was reading, the other day, in Butler's *Lives*, that he was so chaste that he could never remain in a room alone with his mother.

Perhaps you might get a little vignette done by Woolner — not in time for the Xmas sale, but for the greater part of the edition. I was thinking that Adam and Eve singing their morning hymn might do for a subject; but, alas, in those days there were no milliners or tailors, without whom the 'human form' is not 'divine' to 'English Families'.

Advertisements of *The Angel in the House* at first carried a quotation from Plato, which was later replaced by Patmore's lines:

Quit praise and blame, and, if you can,
Do, Critic, for the nonce enjoy.

On receiving the next letter Alexander Macmillan replied that he would have the offending lines on the placard pasted over with the former quotation from Plato.

Dr. William Bell Hunter (1834–94), hydropath and author of *Uses and Abuses of the Turkish Bath*, was a notorious self-advertiser.

'*Psyché et l'Amour*', *after François Gérard*
A rejected illustration

Vignettes
above: *The Golden Treasury*, 1861
below: The Golden Treasury Wordsworth, 1879

The Cedars, Epsom, 29 December 1866

My dear Macmillan,

As you were just leaving for the train this afternoon, when you showed me the advertising card of *The Angel in the House*, I had no opportunity of explaining to you the repugnance I felt at having the quotation you have made inserted in it. I have protested, as you may remember, against having my book advertised with the quotations from the recommendations of the reviewers ; but for an advertisement to go forth with an invitation, from my own pen, to 'Read this Poet', is what I cannot think of without shuddering.

In drawing up the card, you must have overlooked the fact that all readers of it will consider me, not you, as the Advertiser ; and that, were it to be hung up, as you proposed, at the railway bookstalls and elsewhere, I should be thought, by all persons who thought at all about it, to have out-Hunter'd Doctor Hunter himself in impudent self-puffery.

The sentence, as it stands in the book, is an aspiration put into the mouth of a fictitious person ; — even had it been a piece of sheer self-assertion it might have been excused by the customs of poetic licence. I am sure I need not point out to you how the bearing of the passage is changed, when it stands without its context, and in an advertising placard.

I am, my dear Macmillan, yours very truly,

COVENTRY PATMORE

SIR JOSEPH NOËL PATON

1821–1901

Paton was a successful painter of allegorical and historical subjects, with a particular gift for book illustration. His frontispiece to Charles Kingsley's *Water-Babies* in 1863 was engraved on wood by James Davis Cooper (1823–1904), and his title-page vignette to Mrs. Craik's *Fairy Book* of the same year was engraved on steel by C. H. Jeens.

33 George Square, Edinburgh, 12 February 1863

My dear Sir,

I have found it quite impracticable to snatch an earlier moment to acknowledge yours of the 6th, and in reply to say that I feel much flattered by Mr. Kingsley's expressed desire that I should design the frontispiece for his delicious fairy tale, *The Water-Babies* — which (being a sort of Water-Baby myself, having been once drowned outright, and three times all but) it is unnecessary to say I *have* '*dipt* into', and come out marvellously refreshed. And though my cup of occupation is already filled to the brim, I will contrive it shall contain this 'one drop more'. Will you kindly state the latest date you can afford to allow me? — as I should not like to do *this* 'job' in a hurry, if it can be avoided.

The first proof of 'The Sleeping Princess' I duly received — and spent the greater part of a day in correcting. For, though plausible enough *in effect*, it was utterly false to the original throughout : every trace of the delicacy of drawing and expression, by which I hoped to compensate for the absence of what is commonly called *effect*, having been ignored in a way by no means flattering to my vanity. But it must be said for the engraver that, in this respect of total incapacity to see, or, at least, of total inability to reproduce what is really worth reproducing in drawings of this description, he is not a whit worse than his brethren of the burin in general : as recently, to my sorrow and shame, I have had several painful proofs — to such an extent, indeed, that I had made up my mind not again to undertake any such designs, unless with the understanding that they were to be reproduced by *Photography*, as has been done with a rather careful and delicate drawing I made some time ago for a forthcoming book. Perhaps you will kindly turn over in your mind — and, should you think fit, consult Mr. Kingsley thereanent — the expediency of producing the Frontispiece to *The Water-Babies* in Photography. There is a thoroughly good Photographer here who, at my instigation, is turning his attention to this department. He was formerly a copper-plate printer ; and has some mode, not generally known, I believe, of fixing down photographs as firmly as india paper ; thereby removing one of the technical objections to their introduction in the midst of letterpress, i.e., their tendency to *peel off*.

In utmost haste, very faithfully yours,

J. NOËL PATON

RICHARD DODDRIDGE BLACKMORE

1825–1900

Blackmore had been barrister and schoolmaster before he became market-gardener and, in his fortieth year, novelist. Macmillans published his first novel, *Clara Vaughan*, in three volumes in 1864, and his second, *Cradock Nowell*, in *Macmillan's Magazine* in 1865–6. They lost him, for reasons implicit in these letters, before his third and most famous novel, *Lorna Doone* (1869).

In November 1863 Alexander Macmillan had told Blackmore that *Cassell's Illustrated Family Paper* — 'an inferior *Illustrated London News* ... perfectly respectable, no sort of prurience or nastiness about it' — was looking for 'a really first-class novel of the sensation kind, but without vulgarity'. The manuscript of *Clara Vaughan* was submitted to John Willis Clark (1833–1910), a fellow of Trinity College, Cambridge, who had lately joined Cassells as chief editor. Cassells haggled over terms, bowdlerized the text of the novel to suit their 'family' public, and serialized it under a title of their own choosing — *The Purpose of a Life* — in March–August 1864.

Many of Alexander Macmillan's letters to Blackmore are missing or undecipherable.

Teddington, 19 December 1863

My dear Sir,

I thank you most truly for your kind letter, and am willing to abide entirely by your decision, for you know of course tenfold what I do in the matter. My outgoings for the garden are so heavy (£15 per week on the average) that a good round sum will be most acceptable, for the market returns are ludicrous, and yet uncommonly tragic. Last week I was 1s worse than nothing for the expedition dispatched to Covent Garden.

So, if the conductors of Cassells think *Clara Vaughan* worth (subject to your primary rights) £250, and are ready to pay this at once, and if you *entirely approve* and do not consider your interest in the work affected, they shall have it piecemeal, while we keep it in the lump. Of course they will publish it anonymously, and with full cognizance of my prior and paramount engagement to you — and of course they will allow me to correct the press. Mr. Clark is welcome to my address, and it would give me *great pleasure* to see him here. I cannot well come to London just now, but I will not depart, in any wise, from the conditions specified. He will not think me curt or rude, I trust, though he may consider me exorbitant.

I am delighted that you liked the pears. When I came to think of it, I was ashamed of bringing you only three, without any explanation. . . . The sort is Knight's Monarch; they grow out of doors and on standards. I must get some more trees, if I can, and hope you will allow me the pleasure of sending you a couple if I succeed. Only, I should like to know whether you prefer wall or standard trees.

Believe me, dear sir, very truly yours,

RICHARD D. BLACKMORE

The 'men of a low order' in the next letter were the partners in Messrs. Cassell, Petter & Galpin. Mary Elizabeth Braddon (1837–1915), author of *Lady Audley's Secret* (1862) and *Henry Dunbar* (1864), was notorious for her 'sensational' plots and style.

31 December 1863

I cannot thank you enough for the trouble you have taken about my story *Clara Vaughan*; and I only regret that, through it, you have been brought into contact with men of a low order, utterly unworthy of a gentleman like Mr. Clark. For my part I am much relieved at being wholly quit of them. It may seem overweening of me, but I felt throughout as a father must, who prostitutes his daughter. Not that their paper is one of 'ill fame', but it rarely enters the hand of an educated person. And I believe that its owners are quite right (commercially) in declining the work. Miss Braddon's style is quite high enough for their readers. But I think it should be the object of all those popular journals to lift and educate their constituents; and with this in view the greatest writer might be proud of appearing there.

Herewith I return Mr. Clark's letter. To him individually I shall always be grateful. In my last I stated that I would not relax my terms. So the matter ends.

The printers [of Macmillans' edition] proceed very slowly; I do not doubt their being ready by the time you mention. Only for my own convenience, as my spring work begins in February, I wish they would march more evenly. Another thing — they won't keep to my pointing. Very likely they sometimes improve it, but more often they throw the whole sentence out of gear; for no compositor can know the writer's meaning so well as his pen does. There are clearly some very intelligent men upon it, and I should be sorry to lose (by the last remark) the use of their supervision. All I wish is that as a *general rule* they would observe my punctuation.

15 February 1864

My dear Mr. Macmillan,

Is it my *Clara Vaughan* which Cassell is announcing under the title of *The Purpose of a Life*? If not, they cannot keep time with me as expressed in the agreement. But if it be, they are acting amiss in two ways. First they should not (in common courtesy) change the title without my leave. Secondly, thereby they make me party to a trick upon their readers, which I consider very unworthy: the object being of course to prevent identification with the novel as published complete. I hope it may not be so: if it is I shall insist upon

advertising the alias, for I will have no complicity in anything
that savours of shuffling.

Very faithfully yours,   RICHARD D. BLACKMORE

2 March 1864

I am having a 'breeze' with Cassells. Being by nature the
most peaceable fellow going, I am of course always in
'breezes'. They have had the cheek to make seventy-two
alterations (every one of them for the worse) in their first
number of *C.V.*, converting Clara's hot strong English into
diluted and stale pig's wash. I can't stand it, and don't mean
to try ; so I have written to Mr. Clark either to cancel agreement, or to stick to it. *Omit* he may (under his proviso), but
insert he shall not. If you remember, I stipulated to that effect,
when we saw him. They actually reduce me to J. F. Smith's
and Cripney Grey's* style — I thought Mr. Clark had
more taste. Surely what you print is grammatical enough for
their pot-boys.

Their illustration is grand : the cobbler not bad at all ; but
the two detectives in *full Peeler uniform*, and the trees in
richest foliage *circa* 1 January ! A very mild winter no doubt,
in spite of the 'hard black frost', which must be improving
the constitution of that orange-tree (?) in the pot. And the
artist's idea of a pointed and elegant boot — but *ne sutor
ultra crepidam*, this is hypercriticism, and you have better
things to attend to.

23 May 1864

Mr. Mudie's note is very kind and explicit. Not even he can
force down the public gullet a morsel wrongly seasoned.

Nevertheless I believe that the drenching horn of advertisement may now be worked to some purpose. It — i.e., the

* Hack novelists whose latest serials were running in Cassell's *Illustrated Family
Paper* in 1864.

book — should, I think, be announced in all the weeklies (especially *Illustrated News*) and daily in *The Times* with an extract from *Examiner*. I have not seen it advertised one tenth as much as *Henry Dunbar*, a book which scarcely needs it during the present Braddonic furor.

If all these means fail, there is nothing more to be done. I can't tell why the folk won't call for it ; all who read are struck with it, even if they don't like it. And in Kingston (where I am quite unknown) it is always on the run. But from Oxford, Isle of Wight, Birmingham, Brighton, Taunton, Stow-on-the-Wold, Worcester and Richmond, I have received the same account that it is not to be got at the libraries. . . . My conviction is that the book is not advertised as it should be. I know that you mean to do all that is right. But your faith in the work has been shaken, naturally enough, by so many hostile reviews. So advertising seems 'throwing good money after bad'. I think otherwise : and if the proposition is allowable, I would gladly contribute £50 from my Cassell balance — the whole of which I *owe* to you. . . .

I am so loth to lose a year's concientious labour, and at the same time to damage my own repute for any future work, that if you think it would be of service I would quit the incognito, and attach my name in advertisement.* Not that my name is of any value, but that many will not read a work supposed to be by a woman. Moreover it might move some curiosity to see how a man can write in petticoats. But this as you think proper. 'Autobiography' — a word I detest — must be appended if this be done.

24 June 1864

Cradock Nowell languishes. Unsuccessful literature must go to the wall, when market-gardening produces £120 a week. And if I ever finish it, most likely I shall want to sell the

---

* *Clara Vaughan* was anonymous. The story was told in the first person as by the eponymous heroine.

copyright and have done with it. The first number (fair written) is at your service, but a mere brick from the house—for the plot (which is very peculiar) does not open more than an oyster-shell when the tenant takes suction. In *C.V.* I was too precipitate, jumping too high before I got into good harness action.

But come down and talk of these matters.

Twelve months later *Cradock Nowell* was in proof. Blackmore believed that he had succeeded in reducing it to 'a lame propriety'.

2 August 1865

I thank you for the cheque, receipt for which is enclosed.

Besides Mr. Masson's requirements, and my refinements to meet your taste, you chopped out of all shape two other sentences in my August number; and surely they were not objectionable to the very mildest society.

I must entreat you to let me have the last supervision of what is inserted. All my sentences are so cast, and turned in the brain-lathe afterwards, that they cannot be meddled with by any but the author without destroying the balance. One transposition has utterly ruined one of my most carefully written and phonoagogic paragraphs. You will think all this great prudery, just as I do your social exigencies : but by this time we can, I think, allow for one another.

When will you have the strawberries? Oh please to come and fetch them.

Late in 1865 David Masson, professor of English literature at University College, London, became professor of rhetoric and English literature at Edinburgh University. He did not give up the editorship of *Macmillan's Magazine* until 1868. His *British Novelists and their Styles* had appeared in 1859. Blackmore's 'Johnny Macraw' was not published in the magazine.

c

1 December 1865

If you are such an enemy to d—ns, why did you cut out my cut at the divines, who fight for eternal d—nation? It was all right in the proof, but disappeared *afterwards*, which is not fair. However I am very glad that on the whole you like the number. I assure you that storm was in my brain for a month. I forgot to tell Clark that La Constante is such a sweet little body, she only wants eighteen inches apart, instead of thirty like blustering Napier.

Last month I sent Mr. Masson a song called 'Johnny Macraw', a mere chit; but I wish he would send it back if he does not use it. I fear we shall lose him as editor. I have just read his work upon *British Novelists*, a piece of first-rate criticism.

Blackmore fretted under Masson's strictures, directed not only against his 'd—ns' but against the length of his novel, which bid fair to delay the opening of a serial by Henry Kingsley. He proposed that his own serial be discontinued. In the event *Cradock Nowell* was allowed to overlap for four months with Kingsley's *Silcote*.

25 January 1866

My dear Blackmore,

If the weakest must go to the wall, then it is we that must go to the wall; for indeed it would never do for us to break off a story in the middle, and the *Magazine* and Henry Kingsley must obey your will.

I honestly think that for your own sake as well as ours you are and have been wrong not to take advice. The faults which I have pointed out are felt as such by everybody I have talked to. Many excellent judges, without a word on my part, have said, 'What a pity that very able contributor of yours will mar his really fine qualities by such queernesses and coarsenesses'. . . .

Are you going to be up in town soon? If so, could you arrange to see me and let us talk it over?

Yours ever,   A. MACMILLAN

Mrs. Gaskell's *Sylvia's Lovers* had appeared in 1863 and Dickens's *Our Mutual Friend* in 1865.

Teddington, 27 January 1866

My dear Macmillan,

Yesterday I was at the Crystal Palace and saw a large section of 'good society' (in the reserve seats) applaud a performance of the coarsest, most indecent, and grossly lascivious order, called a 'pantomime'. Why did they do it? because they thought it was authorized by the opinions of others. Why do the self-same people condemn my physical allusions — none of which are immoral (even you cannot say that) — simply because I have no name, and they no pure perception. Prudery is self-conscious coarseness; a pretence to refinement, whose absence the pretender half suspects. Against this sham virginity of a prostituted age I shall always offend, as long as I can hold a pen, therefore I shall never be popular. So our fashionable ladies, taking their manners from men about town, their talk from livery stables, their air, hair and dress from kept women. Yet one of them would faint if my hero blows his nose. How can you fail to see the rottenness of such refinement?

Of course I do not pretend to say that all who are scandalized at me are so from their own indelicacy. Nothing of the kind. They have taken the tone of the age — that is all — in its false views of refinement; while they keep themselves perfectly pure from the corruption which engenders them. To me the fact that such false views are carried to their utmost extreme in America, where luxury and immorality are even in advance of our own, is one of no small significance.

I have just read *Sylvia's Lovers*. There are things in it far 'coarser' than any of my offences. Does anyone say a word against Mrs. Gaskell on that score? Of course not, because of her reputation. So again Dickens. None of my people were allowed to spit. In *Our Mutual Friend* there is mutual and monosyllabic expectoration, over and over again.

But though I shall never persuade you, of course — any more than you will me — I really think you have no right to complain of me after the exercise of your freely-granted power of excision. If anything remains unpleasant to the 'genteelest' taste, the fault surely lies with your editor.

Now for more practical matters. I will take *C.N.* in hand at once — though it is a great inconvenience to me, for my garden work is begun. I will omit all I can; and to do so, must rewrite great part of it. I cannot at this moment say how much it can be abridged, but after a week's work it will be in my power to tell you. I am extremely sorry to cause Mr. Kingsley any annoyance; but to him, whose fame is made, the question cannot be a quarter so serious as it is to me. I shall not have time to come to London, for I must mask very hard before 6 January. It is a dreadful plague and will spoil the story, but you must be obeyed. Only I *cannot* do it in the compass you first offered me. Twice I offered Mr. Masson to send the rest of my MS. for his examination, the whole of it having been finished, ere the first part appeared. Twice he answered neither letter (as an Irishman might say), and the consequence falls upon me. Still I would be loth to complain of him, for upon all other occasions I have found him most kind and courteous. May he ever prosper.

With kind regards to Mrs. Macmillan, very sincerely yours,   R. D. BLACKMORE

I want my 'Johnny Macraw'. I think *you* would sing it nicely. It is not at all bad rubbish.

2 March 1866

Your letter is very amusing. But surely you do not suppose
that because I object to a sham refinement, a perpetual con-
sciousness of sexuality, what in fact I may call a prurient
prudery, that I advocate savage nudity. All I say is 'let us not
conclude that our readers will be such sensualists as to turn to
evil mere incidental mention of a lady's back or bosom,
without even the slightest suggestion of voluptuous ideas'.

Moreover, having to deal with embodied human life, it is
almost essential (in order to attain any vivid effect) to allude
now and then to its outward manifestations. Surely this is a
question of art, and not a mere 'fighting for shadows'. As for
the ritualists (to whom you compare me, and whom I
heartily despise), they run into the very opposite extreme. I
contend for simplicity, they for trivial complexities.

However (as I have said so often) I am ready and glad to
defer entirely to your editor upon any physical questions,
only let me alter with my own hand, or at least approve his
alterations, instead of finding the form of my sentence
changed, and the melody of it destroyed, for some reason
which appears to me trivial.

There are nearly a dozen such changes in the March
number, and in each case they weaken the sentence. Meanwhile your other writers may allude to and describe things
ten times as bad. But I am now the dog with the ill name who
monopolizes the hanging. As long as Mr. Masson was my
Jack Ketch I never cried *measure 'e cord*, because I knew
his skill.

2 August 1866

Many thanks for your cheque and note.

I hope *C.N.* may do some good in spite of a little strong
language. In my own person I never swear, and even make
others swear as little as I can. The idyllic strain is, I fear,
already overworked. A romance of market-gardening would

almost involve 'cussing', but I think of having a shy at it, if I can overcome my repugnance to the strong language necessary. A book 'without a d——n in it' seems to suit people best : and perhaps you are right in your knowledge of their taste.

Either way and anyhow, I thank you for your friendliness, and feel that, while we differ about little questions of art, we entirely agree when the aspirate is added.

'LEWIS CARROLL'
Charles Lutwidge Dodgson
1832–1898

The story of the first edition of *Alice's Adventures in Wonderland* is well known. Printed at the author's charge by Thomas Combe, the university printer at Oxford, it was to have been issued by Macmillans in the summer of 1865, but before publication both Dodgson and the illustrator, (Sir) John Tenniel (1820–1914), expressed dissatisfaction with the reproduction of the drawings. Dodgson asked Macmillans to get an estimate for a new edition from Clay, Son & Taylor, and was told that 2000 copies would cost £240 to print. But what to do with the Oxford copies?

Croft Rectory, Darlington, 31 July 1865

Dear Sir,

Thanks for your letter with its alarming estimate — £100 more than it cost to print the book in Oxford. I rather doubt the wisdom of incurring such a large additional expense, but would like answers to the following questions.

1. What would be the cost of printing 1000, instead of 2000?

2. Would Mr. Clay print from the electrotypes (as I should certainly prefer)?

3. In case we have the first edition so printed, what should you advise me to do with regard to the 2000 printed at Oxford? The choice seems to lie between these courses :

(*a*) reserve them till next year, to 'sell in the provinces' (as has been suggested to me), or to send abroad, but keeping the price to 7*s* 6*d*.

(*b*) sell them at a reduced price (say 5*s*) as being

avowedly an inferior edition, stating in the advertisement what the two editions differ in.

(c) get Mr. Clay, or some experienced man, to look them over and select all such sheets as happen to be well printed — use these along with the London-printed copies and sell the rest as waste paper.

(d) sell the whole as waste paper.

In case (a) I should of course pay Mr. Combe's bill in full. In the other cases we should of course have to come to some other agreement. Of these four courses, (a) seems to me scarcely honest, and my own opinion inclines to (d). However, I should like to know what you think about it.

Believe me very truly yours,   C. L. DODGSON

Alexander Macmillan advised selling the Oxford copies as waste paper, 'or perhaps we might sell them a little above that to America. Shall we try?' In the event they were sold to Appleton & Co. of New York, and the book as finally issued in both countries was dated 1866.

In the next thirty years Macmillans published on commission almost all Dodgson's writings, fictional, poetical, pedagogical, satirical. *Alice* sold in tens of thousands. Lesser writings had little success, at least in America.

Christ Church, Oxford, 26 April 1871

Dear Mr. Macmillan,

The question of selling cheap copies in America is a wider one than I fancied, and had better be all settled at once.

1. *Alice* in French cost me in printing, etc., 2s 8d a copy. I see you have sold 22 in America at 2s 3d, the transaction bringing you 4s 10d as commission and involving a loss to me of 9s 2d.

2. *Phantasmagoria* cost me 2s 6d a copy. American sale, 59 at 1s 10d, your profits being 10s 5d, my loss £1 18s 0d.

3. *Determinants* cost me 6s a copy. American sale, 7 at 2s 6d, your profits being 1s 8d, and my loss £1 4s 6d.

Thus on the three transactions your entire profit was 16s 11d, while my loss was £3 11s 8d.

Your profits being so *very* small on the whole transaction, and my loss being so considerable in comparison, I feel no scruple in putting an end to *that* mode of sale altogether, and saying 'Sell none of my books, in America or elsewhere (unless printed cheap for the purpose), at a lower rate than in England.' And as to copies printed cheap, it is clear to me that we *must* have some other arrangement than the usual 10 per cent on the gross receipts. I don't want to take up literature in a money-making spirit, or be very anxious about making large profits, but selling it at a loss is another thing altogether, and an amusement I cannot well afford.

Yours very truly,   C. L. DODGSON

28 April 1871

Thanks for your letter. *One* good would certainly have followed a *viva voce* talk, that I should not have given you (as I fear I may now have done) an impression that I was in some sort finding fault with what has been done. I didn't mean *that* in the least. I began dealing with your house with full confidence in it in every way, and that confidence is undiminished. All my reasoning was to justify the course I wished pursued for the *future*. I *had* fully considered the argument you mention (that the books, at least the *Determinants*, wouldn't otherwise sell *at all*), and it doesn't alter my decision. My conclusion *may* be only sentimental, though I believe it may be defended on purely commercial grounds as well.

The argument you mention (that you get no profit till a sale has actually occurred) I admit as perfectly true, whether for you or for me, but I confess I *don't* see what it proves.

The illustrations in successive reprints of *Alice in Wonderland* continued to cause trouble, and *Through the Looking-Glass* fared little better. The latter, dated 1872, was in the bookshops well before Christmas of the previous year.

17 December 1871

I have a very important matter to write to you about. . . . I have been thinking a good deal about the pictures, and the best way to secure their being really artistically done. I have no doubt that what you told me of — the pressing between sheets of blank paper in order to dry for binding — is the real cause of all the 'inequality' which has so vexed Mr. Tenniel in the copies already done : indeed I can see for myself that several of the pictures have in this way quite lost all *brilliance* of effect.

I have now made up my mind that, whatever be the *commercial* consequences, we must have no more artistic 'fiascos', and I am stimulated to write *at once* about it by your alarming words of this morning — 'We are going on with another 6000 *as fast as possible*'. My decision is, we must have *no more hurry* : and *no more sheets must be pressed under blank paper*. It is my *particular desire* that all the sheets shall in future be 'stacked' and let to dry naturally. The result of this may possibly be that the 6000 will not be ready for sale till the end of January or even later. Very well : then fix that date in your advertisement : say that, 'Owing to the delay necessary to give the pictures their full artistic effect, no more copies can be delivered until the end of January.'

You will think me a lunatic for thus wishing to send away money from the doors, and will tell me perhaps that I shall thus lose thousands of would-be purchasers, who will not wait so long but will go and buy other Christmas books. I wish I could put into words how entirely such arguments go for nothing with me. As to how many copies we sell I care absolutely nothing : the one only thing I *do* care for is that all the copies that *are* sold shall be artistically first-rate.

I am afraid you will be able to urge that I am thus diminishing *your* profits as well as my own : but I must beg you to bear this for a little while. You will not lose in the long run, I think.

I have already had a bitter lesson in this matter with *Alice's Adventures*. With all my efforts to keep it up to a high artistic mark I was baffled at last by that sudden demand (which ought never to have been met!) which led to the working off of 3000 in a great hurry. The consequence was a blow to the artistic reputation of the book from which I doubt if it will *ever* quite recover : a general impression got abroad that 'the plates were failing, and the only chance to get a *good* copy was to find one of the earlier thousands'. How gladly I would sacrifice *double* the profit which that unfortunate 3000 brought in, if I could only annihilate them off the face of the earth!...

I have written at this length in order to set my reasons fully before you, and to show you how strongly I feel in the matter, and how entirely careless I am how it affects the profit. Indeed I consider the point as an essential one in our relations as publisher and author, and must beg you (with a view to a perfect understanding in the future) to give me your assurance in writing that '*No* copies, either of *Wonderland* or of the *Looking-Glass*, shall in future be dried by pressure under blank paper, but that they shall be stacked and let to dry naturally.'

Alexander Macmillan replied next day that he had ordered paper for another 12,000 copies 'to go on quietly'. They would be stacked, and could be drawn on as required. 'I see no other way of meeting your views and the public demand.'

At intervals over the years Dodgson complained that booksellers' profits were disproportionately large when compared with those of publisher and author. In 1876 he sent Macmillan an elaborate analysis of the profits from 40,000 copies of *Alice*, and proposed severely cutting booksellers' discounts in future. Macmillan's reply contained this characteristic paragraph:

Bedford Street, Covent Garden, 5 January 1877

Your natural desire to formulate by figures the respective share of profits all the parties concerned get is in effect impossible. You remember the old story of Robin Hood and someone else who tried to split the willow wand with him. The rival hits it on the side. Robin says, 'Well shot, but you did not allow for the wind.' This not allowing for the wind is the fault of all abstract calculators of mercantile results from Alnashar with his basket down to Ruskin with his *Fors* — and his fish.

Alnashar is in the *Arabian Nights*. Ruskin (*Fors Clavigera*, vol. vii, 1877) held all middlemen, rich or 'middling', to be parasites.

In December 1886 was published a facsimile edition of the manuscript of Lewis Carroll's first version of *Alice in Wonderland* under its original title, *Alice's Adventures Under Ground*.

23 January 1887

Dear Mr. Macmillan,

A letter which I received from Messrs. Burn & Co. on the 20th about *Alice Under Ground* contains a sentence I do not like *at all*. It is this : 'It (the book) was bound in a very great hurry.' This I suppose was done in order to get it out before Christmas.

I believe I have already expressed my wishes on this point, but, as I do not seem to have made them fully understood, I may as well repeat that I *do not care* in the least for any book of mine being brought out at any particular season : it matters nothing to me in what week, or month — I may even say year — the book appears. What *does* matter to me, very seriously, is that it should be done with all the leisure necessary to produce the *best* results that we can give the public for their money. You may say, 'the sale would have been less if it had been delayed.' By all means. *Let* it be less : I am quite willing it should be so.

I have laid it down as a fixed principle that I will give the public (profit or no profit) the *best* article I can : I consider that any 'very great hurry' involves very serious risk of the article *not* being the best I can give : and I shall be really much obliged if you will take measures to prevent any such hurry on future occasions.

Believe me very truly yours,   C. L. DODGSON

On the same subject a week later :

Please understand (that we may not quarrel about it when the time comes) that, if a similar thing happens in future, I will have no mercy at all, but shall come to town and myself examine the whole impression, and cancel all spoilt copies, and decline to reckon them as part of my order.

        Bedford Street, Covent Garden, 1 February 1887

Dear Mr. Dodgson,

  ... Burn is the finest binder in England and, we believe, unmatched by any other. ...

I hope there will be no shadow of further difficulty, but I repeat what I have said before, that I cordially sympathize with your enthusiasm for perfection.

Yours very truly,   GEO. LILLIE CRAIK

                     2 February 1887

Dear Mr. Craik,

  Thanks for your letter, and for taking in such good part my rather fierce letter. ...

CAROLINE NORTON
1808–1877

Poet, novelist and champion of women's rights, the Hon. Mrs. Norton was an intimate *confidante* of Lord Melbourne when he was Queen Victoria's first prime minister and closest personal adviser. Nearly thirty years later she sold the copyright of her novel *Old Sir Douglas* to Hurst & Blackett, who, while arranging to publish it themselves in three volumes (1867), resold the copyright to Macmillans. The novel was serialized in *Macmillan's Magazine* between January 1866 and October 1867, with several gaps while the author rewrote passages in response to the criticisms of the publisher and editor.

16 Bedford Street, W.C., 24 April 1866

Dear Madam,

You will perceive that we have not inserted the last chapter of this month's supply of your very beautiful novel which is charming us all. Pardon my saying that I think you can hardly have duly considered this chapter, as it has an air of personal pique that would be liable to very severe strictures, and I think most hurtful to yourself. The effect on the minds of all of us who read it was the same surprise and regret and a strong conviction that it would not do to put it in the *Magazine* under any possible circumstances. You must permit me to say so quite distinctly. There may be, I have no doubt there is, very much of pettiness about Court conduct, and kings and queens may be open to all sorts of reproach. But our Queen who whatever she is in herself (and we are as a nation very thankful for what she is — perhaps it may be for small mercies but still it is for *mercies*) is yet the person that does command our loyalty whatever that may mean. We certainly would incur deep blame, and as certainly would not

mend the ghost of a fault, either in her or in anyone surrounding her.

But I ought not to waste your time discussing these
general points, and must content myself with repeating my
extreme regret at reading the chapter 'Royal Idols', and
expressing my sincere hope that you will kindly leave it out
of the novel as it appears in the *Magazine*. Mr. Masson
telegraphed from Edinburgh to stop the insertion of the
chapter, which we had already resolved on here, and he quite
concurred in our decision that it would on no account do to
insert it. Pardon my repeating that much as I feel that it
would cause obloquy to us, I should regret much more what
I think it would bring on you.

The deeper my feeling of respect and admiration the
deeper is my sense of what this would do to impair that of
others.

I am, dear madam, most respectfully your faithful servant,

A. MACMILLAN

3 Chesterfield Street, 24 April 1866

Dear Sir,

I am really sorry to tell you — since you disapprove of the
tone taken — that the *main incidents* of my novel are bound
up in and dependent upon this view of court conduct; and
that beyond softening an expression, omitting a name, or
causing these opinions (which are not *given* as mine, but as
the opinions of *one of the characters in the book*) to be *disputed
and argued against* by *another* of the characters, I could make
no alteration whatever.

That they are my *deliberate* opinions, and neither new nor
the result of personal pique, you may judge by my being the
author of the very lines in the *John Bull* (to Lady Flora
Hastings) alluded to in the chapter you have omitted. These
lines were *published* without my consent being asked, and
without my knowledge; but they were *written* from feeling
and conviction.

Of course I cannot have a word to say as to what shall appear in the *Magazine* — and I can only regret the view taken by the Editor and yourself : but each of my novels has been written, not as a mere story but with a distinct purpose, and I cannot *unweave* my book because those who differ from me are startled at what one of the personages in it is made to say.

As to the effect of the book on general readers, if I did not expect it would have some influence, I should not take the trouble to write it. I do not expect to reform the Queen or the Court, but to show — as many writers are doing — the false importance set on decisions totally irrespective of knowledge or justice, merely because those decisions proceed from 'high places'.

The accident of knowing *daily* reports of the Queen and Court from the Prime Minister, after her accession, has at least enabled me to judge her character better than many other persons could possibly have an opportunity of doing : and if my life were to be prolonged some years I might possibly enable others also to judge, by publishing that journal.

As to any obloquy to me personally, I really should not feel the least hurt or mortified by it. I never cared for that, when I was writing my pamphlets in pursuit of what I believed to be justice, and I certainly should not care when I was merely propounding opinions of defective social government in a novel. I have no doubt thousands might think with me who would not have courage to own it. However that may be, I am compelled to repeat that it is not a question of omitting a *chapter* but omitting *the book*, if one main purpose of the book is objected to.

Meanwhile I would be glad of the return of the proofs I revised of the chapter 'Royal Idols' that I may look it over. 'Lorimer Boyd' is not intended either to be loyal, cheerful, or religious. Pray send me the chapter — and excuse the imperfect writing of this letter, which has been constantly interrupted by persons talking to me. I was anxious to answer your letter immediately — though I could not do so satisfactorily — or rather *because* I could not do so satisfactorily — and that leaves much to be thought of, before next month.

Believe me, dear sir, yours truly and obliged,

CAROLINE NORTON

In reply to a further letter from Macmillan Mrs. Norton wrote:

Saturday night

Dear Sir,

I am vexed to be obliged to reiterate that it is a question of omitting a *book* from your *Magazine* : not of omitting *chapters*.

I hope under all circumstances I should express myself courteously ; I respect you and your opinions — and I have a true respect also for Mr. Masson and his admirable writings : but no one can expect that, after more than thirty years' successful authorship both with my name and without it (a severer test of success), I should submit any work of mine to editorship ! nor am I in any way a party to this novel appearing in the *Magazine* — though I should have been happy to think you approved what I wrote. It cannot be too clearly understood that Mr. Masson can reject *in its entirety* the work I am bringing out, but not *modify* it — further than, as I wrote to you before, that I should be willing to make another of the imaginary personages contradict or debate the points involving what you consider blameable sentiments and opinions.

I cannot have my book published in a mutilated form.

Nor would it be *possible* to omit in the way you imagine. The ground-work of the story, the characters in the story, and the opinions advanced in it, are (as I have said) *warp and woof*, and not beads strung on a thread to be pulled off at pleasure.

It is perhaps scarcely worth while, after saying so much, to refer to the argument again that these censures of royalty are in the *mouth of one of the personages* — and no more to be taken as the Editor's or publisher's views, than the strong language used by the injured man in *Cradock Nowell** or any other story.

I will send back the portion returned to me, with such additions and alterations as may appear to me feasible. I fear they will not satisfy you or your Editor — if I am to judge by your letter — but I *can* only write with my own mind and hand — and it is easy, in that case, to put a stop to the coming out of the novel in numbers.

I am, dear sir, with regret for the occasion of writing, yours truly and obliged,   C. NORTON

3 Rosebery Crescent, Edinburgh, 4 May 1866

Dear Madam,

Mr. Macmillan has forwarded to me your letter to him respecting the chapter in your *Old Sir Douglas* which has caused us the misfortune of having to change for a moment our hitherto uniform delight in the progress of that beautiful story.

Allow me to assure you that nothing could have been farther from my thoughts than the notion that it would be tolerable or becoming in *me* to apply any process of editorship, in any ordinary sense of the word, to anything bearing your name or coming from your pen. Had I ever begun with the anticipation that I might have, as in other cases, to modify a phrase or correct a slight verbal slip, I should have been cured of this by the reading of the proofs as they successively came to me — in which I found myself admiring not only the story and the conception of the situations and characters but also the minute touches and details and the

---

* R. D. Blackmore's *Cradock Nowell* was appearing monthly in *Macmillan's Magazine*.

exact and artistic texture of the writing. So distinctly has this been the case (and I do not say it now for the first time), that, but for my formed habit of reading all proofs before final publication, and also my pleasure in each successive instalment of *Old Sir Douglas*, the last proofs, including that fatal chapter, might have gone to press in perfect confidence without my having seen them.

It was then in no mere exercise or presumption of Editorship — in short, on no literary ground whatsoever — that, when I did read that last chapter, I telegraphed to stop it until we could refer it to you. It came upon me, expecting nothing of the sort, but only another charming chapter in your story, as a painful surprise, a shock — a something the publication of which would be a calamitous impropriety in all concerned. All the reasons which you suggest for *our* caring nothing about the matter suggested themselves to me. Where you give your name and assume the responsibility an editor or publisher might, in almost any conceivable case, rest in that guarantee, even while he might feel a difference. Nor, in *Macmillan's Magazine*, should we be opposed to outspokenness, or to strength of opinion and language, as such, in an unpopular vein. Also I considered all you say as to the dramatic character of the language in the fatal chapter — as to its coming as dialogue in the mouths of characters in the story. But, all this and much more considered on one side, the conviction remained that we, as connected with *Macmillan's Magazine*, should be culpable, and should be held culpable, if, in whatever circumstances and under whatever name, that chapter appeared in its pages. 'Anything', I said to myself, 'anything from Mrs. Norton, but *this* !' This was the very case inconceivable beforehand. Here was what all the world would immediately denounce as an attack on the Queen — a flagrant act of disloyalty to a sovereign the public feeling towards whom is far deeper, tenderer and more personally respectful than could be any creation of mere custom. No editor or publisher, it seemed to me — no subject of her Majesty — could be concerned in the publication of such an invective, even though the concern were merely mechanical, without being justly held responsible ; nor could any plea of dramatic setting avail for the excuse of putting such language, or anything like it, in British print at the present moment.

Whatever your own views in the matter, I have not the least fear that you will receive this frank statement with serious displeasure. I only wish that I had the honour of such acquaintance with you, otherwise than through your writings, that I might venture to argue the matter more thoroughly. But I have no right to enter on that side of the argument which might consist in an earnest discussion with you of the tenability of your opinion or of the advisability, from your own point of view, of sending it forth. I confine myself to a statement of our own position in the matter — unless I may add, as one of your readers, that it seems to me the story would suffer nothing, and the development of your conception of the characters would suffer nothing, by the excision of this bit of dialogue, the outcry against which would be so wide, keen, and vehement.

Mr. Macmillan tells me that you are to send a modified version of the chapter. I shall anxiously expect it, in the sincere hope that, on reconsideration, your kindness may have induced you to accommodate this difficulty to what you may regard as our weakness, and that we may go on delighting the public with Old Sir Douglas and the group around him.

Believe me, dear madam, with great respect, yours,

DAVID MASSON

When Macmillans published a cheap edition of *Old Sir Douglas* in 1868 Mrs. Norton was surprised — 'Is the copyright passed on to you ?' Three years later, in the course of an acrimonious correspondence in *The Times*, she accused Baron Tauchnitz of Leipzig of having pirated her novels on the Continent: in fact she had parted with her foreign rights 'in America and elsewhere', and Hurst & Blackett and Macmillans had jointly sold *Old Sir Douglas* to Tauchnitz. Writing to Alexander Macmillan, Mrs. Norton charged Mr. Hurst with sharp practice and Sydney Williams, Tauchnitz's London agent, with 'unmitigated falsehood' couched in 'insolent and offensive' language: Macmillans and 'the good baron' she exonerated.

Keir, Dunblane, N.B., 2 November 1871

I shall be really very much vexed if anything occurs to alter the sort of feeling I have for years entertained (and which is evidenced in my occasional correspondence) with respect to yourself.

If you have had any communication with Mr. Williams, and have read my first letter (dictated to my granddaughter) to that person, you will have seen there that I state that I corrected the sheets in your *Magazine* (*though I did not like novels in a serial form*) because of *my personal esteem and respect* for you. And it was only the other day that I spoke of sending something for the *Magazine* again, as I have felt better since I have been in Scotland this year than for a long time past, since my accident.

My unlucky absence from London prevents my referring to any papers. I can only assure you that I had an understanding with *Mr. Hurst* that I should have right of *translation and foreign copyright* for *Old Sir Douglas*. . . .

I cannot but think, under the circumstances, you are *bound* (in courtesy and gentlemanlike feeling) to write a brief letter in my behalf to *The Times* as the closing note of this disagreeable correspondence. Of course I know, as between publishing firms and houses of business, your reply must be a guarded one ; but I expect so much *as a matter of honourable dealing*, whatever the confusion may be between my personal understanding with Mr. Hurst and your interpretation of the word 'elsewhere' in the agreement. . . .

Mr. Williams talks of the 'honour of Baron Tauchnitz'.
Have I then no reputation to sustain of honourable dealing?

Drayton Manor, Tamworth, 10 December 1871

With regard to *Old Sir Douglas*, if you will say what you
think fair for the copyright (at the expiration of six months or
so from the present time) I would consider about resuming
it. I should make some additions, as I have always thought
the *plan* deteriorated by the changes I interpolated in obedi-
ence to Mr. Masson's opinion.

CHARLOTTE MARY YONGE

1823–1901

and

FRANCES MARTIN

1832–1922

In 1865 Alexander Macmillan projected a series of children's books, to be published in monthly parts under the general title of 'The Sunday Library for Household Reading'. It was to start with the topography and history of the Bible lands. He invited first Miss Yonge, and later Miss Martin, to edit it. Macmillans had already published several of Miss Yonge's books, including *The Daisy Chain* and *The Heir of Redclyffe*, and both ladies regularly read educational and devotional books for the firm. Miss Yonge edited for over forty years the *Monthly Packet*, a periodical 'designed to imbue young people, especially young women, with the principles of the Oxford Movement' (*D.N.B.*). Miss Martin was the founder of the College for Working Women (now the Frances Martin College) in London.

Among books in the Sunday Library were *Nations Around* by Annie Keary (1825–79), author of *Heroes of Asgard* and other children's books; Charlotte M. Yonge's *Pupils of St. John the Divine* and *Pioneers and Founders; England's Antiphon*, by the Scottish poet and novelist George Macdonald (1824–1905); and others by Charles Kingsley, Tom Hughes, Archdeacon Farrar and Mrs. Oliphant.

Elderfield, Otterbourne, Winchester, 10 February 1865
Dear Mr. Macmillan,
    I think such a Sunday Library would be extremely valuable : the S.P.C.K. have attempted the like but their way of taking slices bodily from travellers' descriptions does not

answer at all in exciting children's interest, especially those for whom the S.P.C.K. design them. I think Miss Keary would do the adjoining nations beautifully, and what I myself could best do would, I think, be the intermediate space between the Old and New Testaments. But in the matter of editorship, which you kindly propose to me, I should like quite to understand the sort of management and control it would involve — whether such as I have been used to give to the *Monthly Packet*, where I have been used to admit nothing that I do not quite go along with.

I imagine that this is not what you mean ; and in that case, I am in doubt whether I could exactly be the ostensible editor in thorough fairness to those who take my name as a pledge for the strict line of distinctly Anglican orthodoxy.

On the other hand, if I were to have the power of judging and pruning, literary standing and experience do indeed enable me to drive my magazine team, they chiefly consisting of novices and ladies ; and not often of a clergyman, except of the same way of thinking as myself. But I have had a little experience of getting into that said web of mine a fly that I did not quite trust, and yet was too big for me easily to deal with, and I think it might be the same with some of the contributors who would arise in a series like this. The doubtful matters and controversies most perilous just now lie in such shades of tone that it would require a real divine to judge of the safety of other people's writings, on such delicate subjects as early Scripture history has become.

I doubt if I could safely undertake it. Writing a book or two for a series is so different from being in any way responsible for the whole. One book I should like to do if it would come into your series would be a history of the Prayer Book, in a way I have never yet seen it attempted. . . .

Yours very truly,   C. M. YONGE

To counterbalance Miss Yonge's High Church views Miss Martin invokes the presbyterian Dr. James Donaldson (1831–1915), whose volume on *The Apostolic Fathers* Macmillans had recently published, and the evangelical Canon John Cale Miller (1814–80), author of *Bible Inspiration Vindicated*.

Canal Cottage, Bude, 19 July 1867

Dear Mr. Macmillan,

I enclose my letter to Miss Yonge, and will you send it on if you think well, but if not will you tell me what had better be done?

I have read her proofs again and the fact is that she is writing a Sunday Story Book (of which there are thousands) and she will not have the story broken up. It is very prettily told and no doubt will be very taking. Miss Yonge believes everything that she wishes to believe and gives you no hint that there are grounds for doubting it. I suppose by the time we get to Ignatius we shall receive his celebrated 'Be ye subject to the bishop as to Jesus Christ' and 'Follow your bishop as Jesus Christ the Father, the presbytery as the Apostles : reverence the deacons' as the ordinance of God, as undoubted Apostolical utterances.

Please don't think I am in a bad temper — because I am not — but it has always seemed to me unfair to children or anyone else to make them out a coherent story of materials which one knows to be untrustworthy or doubtful. The information which Papias gives about the four Marys is interesting, but, as you see, Donaldson says there is 'unfortunately' no testimony as to its genuineness — and it is from him that we get the testimony as to the relationship of John to Christ.

I have not written at all to Miss Yonge on these points because she would naturally be annoyed at my criticisms. I think it will be much better to get her to abridge as much as possible the earlier and more dangerous part and then to tell her own story.

I do hope it will all go on smoothly, and it really does not trouble me a bit if you think I can manage discreetly and not do or say anything that shall give needless pain or annoyance. . . .

I think *England's Antiphon* looks very well. . . .

Very truly yours,   FRANCES MARTIN

[Undated]

[Miss Yonge] persists in 'not understanding' more resolutely than any one whom I have ever known. . . . I can only imagine her to be so bored by my letters that she does not read them. . . . Miss Yonge does not seem to me to use an author fairly : her object is not to show the man's mind and soul, and help us to understand him, but to strengthen and confirm her own views and deduce her own opinions.

29 July 1867

I have received Miss Yonge's sheets. She has omitted a few passages — and I suppose that is all we can get her to do. She writes to suggest that she shall finish the whole before sending any more copy and I am sure that is wise, for it must be very difficult to have the first chapters in type before the last are written. Some modification would almost certainly be needed. But I will enclose Miss Yonge's note and will not answer until I hear from you. She has struck out one of her pleasant descriptions, that of the lake Gennesaret and Galilee, which I shall ask her to re-insert. That is not at all the kind of thing we want abridged. And I shall try for a modification of 'really cleansing baptism' and the 'divinely inspired' messages in the epistles. . . .

If we could get Dr. Miller of Greenwich to join or to take an interest in it we should be sure of almost the whole Evangelical body. Shall I try?

CHRISTINA GEORGINA ROSSETTI

1830–1894

Christina Rossetti's letters to Alexander Macmillan, all most business-like, are full of humour and good humour. 'I don't know whom to bore, so I arbitrarily select you'; 'Your visit will always be a favour — mine to your office (where I have never yet been) looks a little formidable. . . . I fear the "formidableness" of your office may rather seem to you laziness in myself: but pray wink at so subtle a distinction'. She seldom failed to send her publishers Christmas and Easter greetings.

Her first book, *Goblin Market and Other Poems*, with frontispiece, title-page and binding designed by her brother Dante Gabriel* was published by Macmillans in 1862 (see plate facing page 96). In the previous October Macmillan had written to the brother:

I took the liberty of reading *Goblin Market* aloud to a number of people belonging to a small working-men's society here. They seemed at first to wonder whether I was making fun of them; by degrees they got as still as death, and when I finished there was a tremendous burst of applause. I wish Miss Rossetti could have heard it.

There was no call for a reprint of *Goblin Market* for three years, whereas *A Chaplet of Verses* by Adelaide Procter (1825–64) and the *Poems* of Jean Ingelow (1820–97), both published elsewhere at about the same time, had had immediate success. Christina's second volume, *The Prince's Progress*, did not appear until 1866.

* For Laurence Housman's illustrations to *Goblin Market*, and the author's criticism of them, see pages 238 and 240 below.

45 Upper Albany Street, N.W., 1 December 1863
My dear Mr. Macmillan,

I enclose my receipt and many thanks for the cheque —
and many more thanks for the kind words of encouragement
you give me. Miss Procter I am not afraid of : but Miss
Ingelow (judging by extracts ; I have not yet seen the actual
volume) would be a formidable rival to most men, and
to any woman. Indeed I have been bewailing that she did not
publish with you.

Few things within the range of probability would give me
greater pleasure than to see in print my second volume : but
I am sadly convinced that I have not by me materials, equal
both in quantity and quality, to what are already before the
public. And, if one conviction can go beyond another, I am
yet more firmly convinced that my system of not writing
against the grain is the right one, at any rate as concerns
myself. Had a second edition of *Goblin Market* been called
for, one considerably augmented would have been at once
feasible : but a second volume must I fear stand over to the
indefinite future.

Yours very truly,   CHRISTINA G. ROSSETTI

In February 1874 Christina submitted the manuscript of a children's
book called *Nowhere*, published later that year as *Speaking Likenesses*
because 'my small heroines perpetually encounter "speaking (literally
speaking) likenesses" or embodiments or caricatures of themselves or
their faults. This premised, I think the title boasts of some point and
neatness'. The illustrator was Arthur Hughes (1832–1915), an early
adherent of the Pre-Raphaelite movement. The title of the last illustration reads 'Maggie drinks tea and eats buttered toast with Granny'.
The modifications suggested by Christina in the next letter, written in
the autumn of 1874, were not made.

56 Euston Square, N.W., Friday evening
Dear Mr. Macmillan,

Thank you cordially for my book which pleases me much,

and of which your gift of six copies was most welcome. I only hope the public appetite will not be satisfied with six or sixty, but crave on for 600 or 6000 at least !

But Gabriel writes me that I ought to beg a *cancel* of the *title-page* ; and though I don't know how to ask this of you, I will own that 'with pictures thereof' is so different from the 'with (so many) illustrations' which I had thought of, that I feel uneasiness at the different form being read as my own. I don't think 'thereof' happy in this particular context. Then the *List of Illustrations* treats my subjects as I should not have treated them : the word 'fairy' I should altogether have excluded as not appropriate to my story — I should have aimed at greater neatness and brevity — and not least I should (as who would not ?) have described the *last* on the list in other terms. In short, I am now deploring that the *Title-page* and *List of Illustrations* were not shown me in proof, even if in the first instance I was not called upon to supply the latter.

What shall we do ? Cannot something be done to remedy these oversights and soothe my anxiety ?

Do please reassure, yours in trouble,

CHRISTINA G. ROSSETTI

In 1881 Macmillan accepted *A Pageant and Other Poems*.

30 Torrington Square, W.C., 20 April 1881

Thank you for welcoming my offered MS., and I hope and dare say we shall come to one mind.

But copyright is my hobby : with it I cannot part. If it is of any value I think I have the first claim upon it, and if it is of none it may gracefully be left to me !

So, you see, I cannot proceed to sign the proposed form, either for my old volume or for my new. Please write me back something that may help matters forward. I am, thank you, so wonderfully stronger than I used to be that I could easily call at the office and talk the business over with you : but I think one often gets on better and keeps more to one's point in a letter.

Three days later :

Your assurance that I do not lose copyright reconciles me to the form for both volumes. So please send me such a form as you propose, either for each edition or for all editions as you like best. I see with satisfaction that you erase the clause about *corrections*, so trust I may improve my text as often as I please : will it not be so? There remains really nothing to discuss verbally : I hope I worried you less than I worried myself by misunderstanding business terms. My brother's wife has just presented us all with *twins* ! so the minutest prospective gains become of double value, and I cling to my dear copyright more than ever — if possible and so to say.

DANTE GABRIEL ROSSETTI

1828–1882

Rossetti illustrated books and designed bindings for Macmillans, but his poems were published elsewhere. In 1864 he recommended Swinburne's *Chastelard* to Alexander Macmillan. When he wrote of Swinburne's work 'best adapted to come first before the public' he had no doubt forgotten Swinburne's verse-plays, *The Queen Mother and Rosamond*, dedicated to himself and published in 1860.

16 Cheyne Walk, Chelsea, March 1864

My dear Macmillan,

I have been wishing to write to you respecting the poems of my friend Mr. Swinburne, of which you have I think already heard something both from me and others. They are still unpublished, their author being more apt to write new ones than to think of the old. I hardly know how to give you an adequate idea of what not I alone, but many excellent judges who have seen them, think of their astonishing beauty. They inspire a certainty that Swinburne, who is still very young, is destined to take in his own generation the acknowledged place which Tennyson holds among *his* contemporaries.

I should like you much to be the first to have submitted to you the work which both Swinburne and I think the best adapted to come first before the public It is a tragedy on the subject of Chastelard and Mary Queen of Scots. If you have time at present for consideration of it, will you let me know, and it shall be sent to you at once.

With kind remembrances, I am, my dear Macmillan, ever yours truly,   D. G. ROSSETTI

Macmillan's private opinion was that Swinburne's interpretation of Mary Queen of Scots was 'carried to characteristically hideous exaggeration', but he gave the poem a fair trial before rejecting it. The 'minor poems' which he asked to see (parts at least of *Poems and Ballads*, 1866) were submitted by Rossetti and also duly rejected.

16 Bedford Street, W.C., 3 June 1864

My dear Rossetti,

I wanted very much to have read Swinburne's poem again carefully, and if possible aloud to my wife and sister-in-law. I certainly thought it a work of genius, but some parts of it were very *queer* — very. Whether the public could be expected to like them was doubtful. I will try to test it, in the way I have indicated, soon. Do you think he would send me the minor poems to look at? I could perhaps judge better of what a volume would be like.

Yours ever, A. MACMILLAN

Rossetti designed the title-page, frontispiece and binding of his sister's *The Prince's Progress*, 1866 (see plate facing page 97). He was baptized Gabriel Charles Dante, and his family and friends called him Gabriel. Although he preferred to reverse his initials, Macmillan's mistake, referred to in the next letter, is understandable.

4 April 1865

My dear Macmillan,

With this I post to you (by book post) the MS. of *The Prince's Progress and other poems*. Christina is anxious to get on with the printing immediately as it is not unlikely she may be going to Italy in May and would like to see all the proofs before then. I wish you'd always send a proof to me at the same time as to her, and not print off till *both* are returned to you. I'll see to my two drawings as soon as possible.

Pray pardon my oblivious alarm about the binding. On seeing it I saw it was improved and even guessed I must have

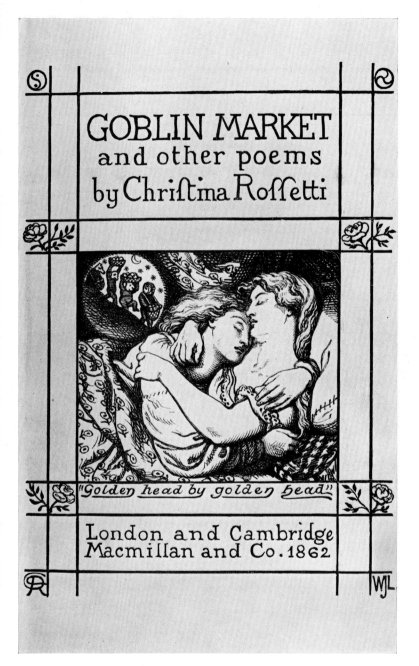

GOBLIN MARKET
and other poems
by Christina Rossetti

"Golden head by golden head"

London and Cambridge
Macmillan and Co. 1862

Title-page by D. G. Rossetti

Binding by D. G. Rossetti 1866

had a hand in it, though many things meanwhile had so put
the matter out of my mind that I can't even recall it now. As
for the colour it's 'dreffle', but never mind.

By the by you always reverse my signature in advertisements. Will you oblige me by henceforth printing it as when
I am (and when am I not?), sincerely yours,

D. G. ROSSETTI

I 2

Of 1,000 copies of the second edition of Christina's *Goblin Market*
printed in 1865, 450 remained unsold in 1870.

Rossetti was working on his biggest canvas, 'Dante's Dream', now in
the Walker Art Gallery, Liverpool. What Alexander Macmillan had
said about 'fame in the next generation' can only be surmised. There is
no evidence, apart from this letter, to suggest that George Grove may
have turned down a contribution offered by William Morris to
Macmillan's Magazine.

30 December 1870

Dear Macmillan,

As there are so many *Goblin Markets*, will you kindly send
me one. My messenger must have spoken to someone who
didn't know, as he was certainly told that both books were
out of print and reprinting. He is much too unimaginative to
have conceived the idea.

I shall be very glad to see yourself, son, and all friends,
some time in March, but till then shall be completely boxed
up with a big picture I am doing. It and I have now been
tugging against each other for some months, but I mean to
get it under by then. By the by, my dear Macmillan, it is all
very well talking about 'Fame in the next generation', but
why does your magazine resolutely ignore the best things
going? It's no business and no meaning of mine to speak for
myself — let anyone do that who pleases — but why in the

D

world has Morris been left in the lurch till now? I don't know who your present editor is, but I may assure him that it is of no use sulking over good work. There is some credit in acknowledging it at first; and it has to be acknowledged at last without credit at all. So for my New Year's gift of plain speech to your publication.

To yourself and to yours come all good and seasonable wishes, from yours always,　　　　D. G. ROSSETTI

WILLIAM MICHAEL ROSSETTI

1829–1919

W. M. Rossetti has been described as 'the publicity agent of the Pre-Raphaelite Brotherhood'. In 1866 he published a spirited defence of Swinburne ('my Swinburne volume') against the charge of being an exponent of 'the fleshly school' of poetry; and in the following year Macmillans issued a collection of his articles on the Pre-Raphaelites and others, *Fine Art, Chiefly Contemporary* ('the present reissue').

166 Albany Street, N.W., 11 June 1867

Dear Macmillan,

Thanks for the copies received early this afternoon. The book looks a very creditable one to your firm so far as its outer man is concerned. I hope its inner man may be found proportional.

You seem to have sent the book to a very fair number of papers. The only other papers — which however I must leave entirely to your decision — that occur to my mind are the following:

1. The *London Review*. I scarcely know whether it is now of sufficient importance. It was very civil to my Swinburne volume, and has been drawn upon in the present reissue.

2. The *Chronicle* (24 Tavistock Street). This is the only paper I am now writing in. So far as I have observed, it gets from circulating libraries all the books it reviews; and I don't know whether or not its policy would be to notice a contributor, even were his work forwarded. It is a very creditable paper, newly started. I cannot vouch for its circulation.

3. *Edinburgh Courant*. There have been, and as far as I know still are, two leading writers on this paper, friends of

mine, and previous publications in our family have been well received in the *Courant*.

4. *Fraser*. This is freely drawn on in the reissue, and I think it more likely than not that the book would receive a review. Can't say however — nor do I know whether there is any occasion to *send* it.

5. *Westminster Review*. I know the gentleman who does a large proportion of the quarterly notice of books, and have little doubt he would mention the book if it comes before him : maybe this will be equally the case whether or not the book is sent.

With thanks for all your attention to this venture, yours always truly,   W. M. ROSSETTI

Rossetti, a contributor to *Macmillan's Magazine*, found — or fancied — himself insulted in an article by Harry Quilter (1851–1907) in the issue for September 1880. Quilter had written, 'The temptation, of course, was very great for Mr. W. M. Rossetti to write complimentary criticism of Mr. Swinburne', and 'We know that . . . one Rossetti wrote poems and painted pictures, and the other wrote criticism on them, and so influenced both arts'.

The following are extracts from two letters to George Grove (1812–92), editor of *Macmillan's*, best remembered for his *Dictionary of Music and Musicians* (four volumes, 1878–89). Grove first counter-proposed that a remonstrance would come better from a third party, but later published Rossetti's 'remarks' and Quilter's reply in the magazine for November.

5 Endsleigh Gardens, N.W., 10 September 1880

Mr. Quilter's article contains a great deal of matter which I should suppose to be distasteful to the parties concerned, and open to confutation : with this however I have nothing to do. I am myself mentioned only twice, and in each instance I consider the mention to be invidious, and (seemingly) even unfair or incorrect. I always object to seeing in print a wrong statement of *fact* concerning myself, while as to critical opinion of my performances I take the good and the bad with equal placidity.

My own opinion is that the enclosed remarks of mine ought in fairness to be printed in the magazine, along with any answer which Mr. Q. may furnish thereto. If you think otherwise, this will of course not be done : but I should like Mr. Q. to see my remarks, and should suppose that he will not neglect to send me a reply to them.

20 September 1880

As to your suggestion of a general counter-statement from one of the persons chiefly concerned — such as Swinburne, Morris, or my brother — I can only say that I have not as yet had any communication with any of these persons on the subject : don't know whether any of them have read the article, or how they take it. My own concern was simply to repel mis-statement or unfounded insinuation concerning myself, and I should not wish to put myself forward as inter-mediary with any one else — certainly not with my brother, nor yet with Morris. As to Swinburne, it so happens that I shall be seeing him on Friday, and if the conversation should lead to it, I would not mind putting him in possession of your views — but this would depend on chances of the moment. Mr. Quilter may perhaps be a much more eminent personage in the world of letters than I have at present any idea of — his name not having been known to me (I think) until I saw it appended to the *Macmillan* article ; but as yet my impres-sion is that Swinburne might hardly consider him a foeman worthy of his steel. This may all be my ignorance.

MATTHEW ARNOLD

1822–1888

The professor of poetry at Oxford came to Macmillans through their *Magazine*. He collected some of his lectures and magazine contributions in the first series of his *Essays in Criticism* (1865), and from then on the firm became his regular publishers, issuing his *New Poems* in 1867.

'Young Lytton', later first Earl of Lytton (1831–91), was the son of Bulwer-Lytton, the novelist: a rising diplomatist, later viceroy of India, he too was making a reputation with novels and verses, under the pseudonym of 'Owen Meredith'; he had collaborated as poet with the Hon. Julian Fane (1827–70), also a member of the diplomatic service.

The poem which was to conclude Arnold's *New Poems* was 'Obermann Once More'.

Athenaeum Club, Pall Mall, S.W., 13 March 1867

My dear Macmillan,

I hoped to have been able to come and see you, but time fails me. It was very kind of you to communicate young Lytton's civilities ; I had heard from Fane and from Browning of his liking my poems. I hope if he is in England for any time I shall make his aquaintance ; he has an undeniable dash of genius, but as in his father it is flavoured with a gust of theatricality, gas light and orange peel.

I have nearly done a poem I want to conclude my new volume with, and then everything for this volume will be finished and off my mind, down even to the four lines of introduction.

Ever yours sincerely,   MATTHEW ARNOLD

Arnold affected distaste for publicity. To Alexander Macmillan, 25 February 1865: 'Pray do not, in advertising my book, put the newspaper panegyrics at the bottom. I have an inexpressible dislike to it.' But he appreciated 'virtuous discrimination'. George Richmond (1809–96) perhaps had in mind the lines in Arnold's 'Epilogue to Lessing's Laocoon' describing 'the painter's sphere':

> *In outward semblance he must give*
> *A moment's life of things that live;*
> *Then let him choose his moment well,*
> *With power divine its story tell!*

The Provost of Oriel was Edward Hawkins (1789–1882), to whom Arnold wished to give a copy of his *Schools and Universities on the Continent* (1868).

Norwich, 21 May 1868

My dear Macmillan,

Richmond, the painter and R.A., goes about with four lines of mine about painting in his pocket, and tells everybody that he and the Royal Acadamy have at last got a perfect motto, which they have long been seeking in vain. Virtuous discrimination of this kind should be encouraged, so I want you to send him my new edition. And it would be very kind if you would send my School Report to the old Provost of Oriel, my father's friend and head of my own college, who I hear would like to have it. . . .

Ever most sincerely yours,   MATTHEW ARNOLD

Poems by Matthew Arnold in two volumes ('Narrative and Elegaic' and 'Dramatic and Lyric'), without 'new edition' on the title-pages, appeared in June 1869. The suggestion that 'Arnolds are legion' was an exaggeration, echoing Matthew Arnold's irritation at having been confused in the public mind with (Sir) Edwin Arnold (1832–1904): Matthew's first collection of *Poems* (1853) had been reviewed together with Edwin's *Poems, Narrative and Lyrical* of the same year, and now the former's new collection was being announced at the same time as the latter's *The Poets of Greece*. The two Arnolds were unrelated.

Saffron Walden, 11 May 1869

Nine o'clock at night, and instead of passing the flowing bowl at the Garrick I am in a dismal class-room examining pupil teachers. I write a line to say that it occurs to me there is no mention of a *new edition* on my title-pages. Perhaps this is better so ; but consider whether in advertising you would not say something about its being a new edition — or the first collected edition, or something of that sort. About a third of the poems have been absolutely out of print since the end of 1862 ; another third belong to the *New Poems* which you published ; the remainder belong to the first series of my *Poems*, of which the third edition went out of print last year. Now you have the facts — manipulate them as you think proper.

I think on the back of the book should be put, on one panel, *Matthew Arnold's Poems*, on another panel *Narrative and Elegiac*, or *Dramatic and Lyric*, as the case may be. It must not be *Arnold's Poems* because the Arnolds are legion ; and I like *Matthew Arnold's Poems* better than *Poems by Matthew Arnold*. I am now all but clear of the printers, I much like the style in which they have done the book. The poems, as a body of doctrine, gain greatly by their new and regular classification, I think.

I return to Harrow on Thursday.

In 1867 Arnold had contracted to edit a *Guide to Greek Poetry*. Among many reasons for delay was the appearance of Edwin Arnold's book on the same subject, and in the end Matthew Arnold never finished his guide.

His little book on *Isaiah xl–lxvi, A Bible Reading for Schools*, appeared in 1872 and was twice expanded, under different titles, in 1875 and 1883.

Harrow, 27 April 1872

I have been for some time meaning to repay you the £150 you advanced me for the Greek poetry book. I find that you paid the money on the 27th of November 1867 : so I send you a cheque for £172 1*s* 8*d* which represents the principal with interest at five per cent from that day till the present.

It is more satisfactory to me to do this, because I cannot see my way to promptly finishing the Greek poetry book. You have always been very good natured about the delay, but it has gone on too long. I think Edwin Arnold's book gave me a coolness for going on with the project at present, though some day I hope to carry it through, and indeed a good deal is done. But it is a work which will gain by being done slowly and not under pressure ; and I think of it as a work which may be done as one grows old and when one's spirits for other work are not what they were.

I have carried the Isaiah through the press at last, though Clay is very slow and, what is worse, irregular. George Smith's people are much more satisfactory to print with. However on Monday I hope to see my last revise and to dismiss the little book. It should be out soon. That earlier or later it will come into general use I have little doubt. It is possible, however, it may meet with opposition at first. I must come and talk to you about the terms of publication, and I have several further projects about the book to com-municate to you. I shall not publish it on the half-profits system : I should like best the *royalty* plan, but if *you* do not like *that*, I shall publish, I think, on my own account, as I did my poems originally : that is, you will publish the book on commission. But I will come and see you early in next week. As to advertising, the first advertisement should be in the *weekly* papers, the *Saturday*, *Athenaeum*, etc. and I do not wish this to appear till the book can be announced to be published *at the end of the week following*.

In 1879 Arnold was editing *Poems of Wordsworth* for the Golden Treasury series. It appeared in September, with a vignette by C. H. Jeens after an engraving by Thomas Goff Lupton of the portrait of Wordsworth (in the National Portrait Gallery) by Benjamin Robert Haydon (see plate facing page 57).

Pains Hill Cottage, Cobham, Surrey, 30 June 1879

Amid the many worries and disappointments of life, it is a treat to come across anything so satisfactory as Jeens's work. It is better than I had even ventured to expect : for there is something not quite *right* about the picture, fine as it is. Your criticism is just, but I should be content to leave it to Jeens to say whether on looking carefully at his work he thinks he can mend it : I would not prescribe to him to lighten this or deepen the other, for one never knows what may come of that. I had thought of the vignette as a round, with the date of W.'s birth and death along the lower sides of the circle ; but I don't know whether it will be found possible to manage this.

Of all the dawdles I have ever met with, your Edinburgh printers are the worst. When do you propose to have the book out? They are not half through with it. Why do you use these provincial and imperfectly awakened people?

I was sorry to miss you the other day, very.

FRANCIS TURNER PALGRAVE

1824–1897

Palgrave's letters to Macmillans concerning his most famous book, *The Golden Treasury* (1861), have not survived. Among his other books published by the firm were an edition of Shakespeare's *Songs and Sonnets* (1865) and *Essays on Art* (1866).

In 1869 Macmillans were planning the first collected edition of Matthew Arnold's *Poems* in two volumes. This appeared without vignettes on the title-pages, and without the omissions and additions here proposed by Palgrave. M. H. N. Story-Maskelyne (1823–1911), mineralogist and M.P., was a well-known collector of antique engraved gems.

5 York Gate, N.W., 5 April 1869

Dear Macmillan,

Will you kindly forward a copy of my *Essays on Art* — a defunct work which cumbers your magazine — to Rev. J. Gaffney, Clontarf, Dublin, by book post.

I am very glad to hear of the proposed collected edition of M. Arnold's poems. I have sent him a little list of *omittenda* and *addenda*, which may be of use when it happens to confirm his own judgment. I am for leaving out most of 'Tristram' and 'Brou', as rather insipid and like exercises in poetry rather than poems, and for inserting several pieces (chiefly choral) from 'Merope'. Matt's style lends itself easily to such extracts — a fact which, by the by, raises the question whether he preserves sufficient plastic *unity* in his larger pieces.

I mean to propose to him to put a gem on each of the title pages (I assume two vols.) so as to give his book an air of 'distinction', 'noble style', etc., and, for one, I shall offer him

(if you don't object) the *Muse* Jeens did for my Shakespeare
Sonnets and which certainly can't be worn out by overprint-
ing. For the other, Maskelyne will lend him a fine thing,
which may again employ our excellent engraver, whose work
I never hear mentioned without laudation.

Ever truly yours,   F. T. PALGRAVE

In 1877 Palgrave edited for the Golden Treasury series *Chrysomela*,
a selection of the lyrics of Robert Herrick, dedicated 'to the Lady
Beatrix Maud Cecil' — who was nineteen years of age — and adorned
with a vignette of an antique gem. Macmillans had previously published Palgrave's own *Hymns* (1867) and *Lyrical Poems* (1871). He
was elected professor of poetry at Oxford in 1885.

Charles Patrick O'Conor contributed patriotic poems to the
Irishman and rustic verse to the *Kentish Mercury*.

15 Chester Terrace, N.W., 26 February 1877

Please send, paid per book post, a copy of my *Poems* and
Hymns to C. O'Conor Esq., May Cottage, 2 Berthon Street,
Deptford. He represents himself as a poor poet and begs for
the above. May he only not make a return in kind!

The Herrick affair is happily at its last revise. Before it is
issued, I should like to see the title *with the gem*, to judge of
the effect.

You will see that I dedicate to a girl, which has a pretty
look in such a case. But the fact has forced me to change at
the last two or three pieces in which the Muse unloosed her
zone a little too freely for maiden grace.

I wish much to reprint the *Hymns*, adding a few written
since and omitting the 'Reign of Law' which is not a hymn
and has been printed in my other book. But I fear it will
be long before even the expenses of the present edition are
covered. I hope the Herrick may do better : and that it will
now *soon* be advertised and out : as the preface may serve to
help me in my candidature for the Oxford poetry professorship which is vacant this year.

WILLIAM BARNES

1801–1886

Barnes was rector of Came, Dorset. Between 1844 and 1862 his three volumes of *Poems of Rural Life in the Dorset Dialect* ('hwomely rhymes') were published by George Russell Smith, of Soho Square. Supposing 'that, for common English poetry, yours is a better house than a more philological and antiquarian one', Barnes took his next volume, *Poems of Rural Life in Common English*, 1868, to Macmillans.

The first poem in the book begins

> *The long-lighted days begin to shrink,*
> *And flowers are thin in meads among*
> *The late-shooting grass, that shines along*
> *Brook upon brook, and brink by brink.*

Came Rectory, 2 June 1868

Dear Sirs,

I thank you for the notices which you have sent me of my poems. I suppose I ought to deem myself very lucky that I have so far fared pretty well under the ordeal of my judges of the press.

The trick of verse to which the *Scotsman* objects (the repetitive words as in the last lines of those of the first poem) happen not to be an invention of mine. It is found in a convivial song of Hafiz, the Persian poet, which is even now, as I am told by men who can speak from good knowledge, one of the most popular songs among the Persians, who therefore have not, in more than three hundred years, ceased to sing them.

tazah ba taza, nao ba nao.

fresh upon fresh, and new by new.

I should of course be glad to hear that you are not sorry to have undertaken the publication of my homely poems, and that you believe the copies will in time go off.

I am, dear gentlemen, yours truly,   WM BARNES

ALFRED TENNYSON
Lord Tennyson
1809–1892

None of Tennyson's letters to Alexander Macmillan survived in the firm's archives, though there are copies of many long and lively letters from the publisher to the poet laureate. Macmillan so admired *The Idylls of the King* that he first thought of naming *Macmillan's Magazine* after Arthur's *Round Table*. In the third issue, in January 1860, he printed Tennyson's 'Sea Dreams' as 'an Idyll', having secured the author's permission to do so.

The first two letters printed,* and that reproduced on page 113, concern the poem 'Lucretius' which appeared in *Macmillan's Magazine* and in *Every Saturday* (New York) in May 1868. George Grove gradually took over the editorship of *Macmillan's* from David Masson in the early months of that year. Negotiations for the American publication of the poem were conducted with James Thomas Fields (1817–81) of Messrs. Ticknor & Fields, of Boston.

Grove had returned from a visit to Tennyson at Farringford, and had reported to his brother-in-law, G. G. Bradley:

A.T. has been pleased to promise me 'Lucretius' for *Macmillan's*. The subject is not pleasant, but it is a grand poem : one of the grandest of all his works.

The passage to which most exception was taken (and which was later restored) read:

* The letters to Grove are printed by courtesy of the Berg Collection, New York Public Library, and the letter to Macmillan is reproduced by courtesy of Mr. W. S. G. Macmillan. The last-mentioned refers to James Bertrand Payne (1833–1898), manager of Edward Moxon & Co., then Tennyson's publishers.

And here an Oread — how the sun delights
To glance and shift about her slippery sides,
And rosy knees and supple roundedness,
And budded bosom-peaks — who this way runs . . .

This was abbreviated by Tennyson for *Macmillan's* as:

And here an Oread — and this way she runs.

Farringford, Freshwater, Isle of Wight, February 1868

My dear Grove,

The lawyer's opinion has not arrived but if it can be depended on there would seem no good reason why 'Lucretius' should not appear in *Macmillan's*.

In that case (I send you Ticknor & Fields' letter) perhaps it would be as well not to let it appear before April, as that would accommodate the American publishers. Then it should be printed first and sent to me to correct, and afterwards dispatched to Boston. The firm has been immensely liberal to Dickens, giving him £2,000 for some slight essays in their publications, and I suppose would also give me something.

The passage in that foolish book of Büchner's (and we have looked all over the book to find it) wouldn't do as a motto.

Yours always,

A. TENNYSON

I think 'flying by' is the best reading : fame goes clanging overhead like a great bird — fainter and fainter, till the cry dies away.

My wife is copying 'Lucretius'. As there is only one MS. it is thought better not to trust that to the post.

There are a few slight errors in the copy — *she* says she does not think it will shock people.

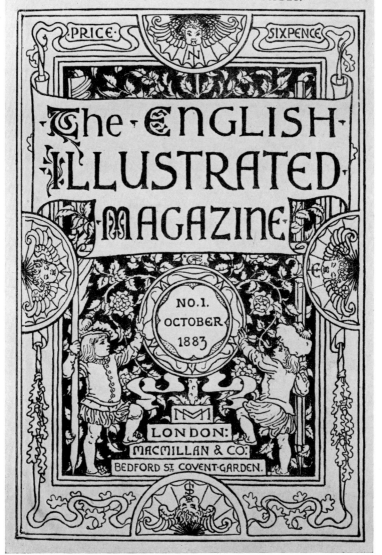

PRICE· ·SIXPENCE

The· ENGLISH·
·ILLUSTRATED·
·Magazine·

NO. I.
·OCTOBER·
1883

LONDON:
·MACMILLAN & CO·
BEDFORD St COVENT·GARDEN·

I stop in the
Creed — As you go
with her ref. ?

My dear Mr Macmillan

I had rather if you have no objection
see my directions once again. If you don't
publish before May {have you decided upon
it?} there will be ample time to send it out
to ~~send it out~~ to Fields.

Payne has put me into a great perplexity
by advertising the Standard Edition in his
tremendous style — before any agreement
was signed & before I had made up my
mind as to whether I would have one at all.
I expect now that if I do not publish
this edition (and I have little desire
to do it) the sale of the ~~other~~ old one
will fall off in expectation of this

Yours ever
A Tennyson

3 March 1868

My dear Grove,

'To peer behind the laurels' is to me the least decorous passage in the poem: I have altered it

> ... do I wish —
> What? that the bush were leafless, or etc. ....

then

> I know you careless, yet behold, to you ...

'backward' instead of 'backwards'. I never put an unnecessary S.

'hand' for 'hands' is the printer's, not mine.

Pray let this be sent off by the next American mail, I believe on Thursday, or Fields will say it has come too late.

With respect to the Oread please yourself but send the full passage to America — they are not so squeamish as we are.

Yours, my dear Grove, in great haste,   A. TENNYSON

'Kypris' for 'Kupris', 'anew' for 'afresh'.

3 Rosebery Crescent, Edinburgh, 27 March 1868

My dear Macmillan,

... About that 'Lucretius' matter, which Grove asked me to write to you about, here is my opinion.

Decidedly I think the briefer form of the passage the better of the two — and this not only on account of what that blatant beast, the public, might say about the longer form of the passage ; but also because my own taste objects to at least one of the expressions in that longer form, and thinks it not good enough, not new enough, not poetical enough for Tennyson. 'Budded bosom-peaks' seems to me too hackneyed and too physically-harsh an indelicacy to come from Tennyson, even though he gives it to the mouth of Lucretius mad with a love-drug. Unless the phrase could be enriched and subtilized, I would have it left out altogether, even if there were no chance of a row about it from Mrs. Grundy. Also I would vote for omitting 'supple roundedness', as, though innocent enough, not new enough, and rather insipid. But I would keep in the 'slippery sides' and 'rosy knees' — to which, I think, in such a poem, there can be no objection special to that passage. Indeed it seems to me that some flash of the figure of the running Oread, more than is given in the abbreviated form of the passage, is necessary for the full effect of what is to follow, and therefore that one or two of the phrases of description should be left in. In short, could there not be an intermediate form of the passage between the longer and the shorter, keeping the 'slippery sides', etc., but omitting the 'peaks'?

The poem is a most powerful one — a strong rendering of a high and difficult idea throughout, and with passages of large force. But I dare say it will not pass without yelping on various sides.

Ever yours affectionately,   DAVID MASSON

Tennyson's verse-play *The Cup* was produced in London in July 1881 with some success, though it failed to please William Archer (1856–1924), the rising young dramatic critic of *The World*. His prose-drama *The Promise of May*, which ran for five weeks in 1882, was taken to be an attack on the socialist free-thinker Charles Bradlaugh (1833–91). Apparently the play was hooted down also by *aficionados* of Sir Francis Cowley Burnand (1836–1917), farce-writer and editor of *Punch*. Both plays were later published by Macmillans, who took over all Tennyson's books in 1884. From about this time the poet entrusted most of his business correspondence to his son Hallam (1852–1928), the second Lord Tennyson.

Archer seems not to have reviewed *The Promise of May*.

Aldworth, Haslemere, Surrey, 16 November 1882

My dear Mr. Grove,

Who is *Archer* who has written *English Dramatists of To-day*? The man seems to have some idea of what drama should be, but I do not know why he hates *The Cup* so much. Can you not get him to write something in your magazine on *The Promise of May*? It is a beautiful play, and the actors believe it will be successful, in spite of dramatic critics. Do go and see it. We have had delightful letters about its *great merit* from the most cultivated in London. The Bradlaughites and perhaps Burnandites tried to hoot it down first night, and such was the brutal temper of the mob that they smashed the pit doors to atoms. When are you coming to see us? Tell anyone, who only saw the play first night, to go to it again now that it has fair play.

Yours ever,

HALLAM TENNYSON

If Archer does review, tell him that my father has been reading his book, and does not like it altogether but thinks he is on the right tack and wishes there were more critics like him, with good sense of their own and independent judgment.

JOHN RICHARD GREEN

1837–1883

At the age of thirty, owing to ill-health and doctrinal doubt, Green resigned his cure of souls at St. Philip's, Stepney, and turned to journalism and history. Fame was to come to him with his *Short History of the English People* (1874).

1 Manchester Square, W., December 1869

My dear Macmillan,

I have taken a day or two to think over the proposal I made to you on Saturday. The plan of the book is this. I propose to condense into a volume of 600 pages the history of the English people which I contemplated undertaking on a far larger scale. The work would serve as a school-manual for the higher forms, and as a handbook for the universities, while in a more general sense it might I think supply a want in our literature — that of a book in which the great lines of our history should be fixed with precision and which might serve as an introduction to its more detailed study.

The book would be strictly a history of *England*, in which foreign wars and outer events would occupy a far more subordinate position than they generally do, and in which the main attention would be directed to the growth, political, social, religious, intellectual, of the people itself. Thus men like Aidan and Bede would claim more space than the wars of the Anglo-Saxon kingdoms; and Spencer, Shakspere, and Bacon would stand as prominently forward as the defeat of the Armada or the death of Strafford.

The style of such a book, from its very brevity, ought to be more picturesque — in the true sense of the term — than if it were on a larger scale. I should especially avoid cramming pages with details. Minor events could easily be grouped with their dates at the end of the chapters, as Michelet has done in his admirable *Précis.**

The work would consist of twelve chapters, broken into four distinct books, the first embracing the period from the landing of the English to the acceptance of the Charter and the death of Simon de Montfort ; the second the period of the rise and decay of Feudalism, from Edward the First to the reign of Henry the Eighth ; the third the successive ages of the Revival of Letters, the Reformation, and the Puritan Rebellion ; the fourth the different phases of the Revolution which had been silently going on from the Restoration to the Reform Bill of 1830. Each book would comprise three chapters of some 50 pages each — the first, for instance, describing in Cap. I, England before the Conquest, Cap. II, England under Foreign Kings, Cap. III, England and the Charter.

For a single chapter I may take that on the Reformation which would begin with the death of Thomas, Lord Cromwell, and end with the defeat of the Armada. It would open with a sketch of the early Protestants, poor artisans despised by the literary men and statesmen of the past age, suddenly lifted into power and using it unwisely under Edward VI, purified by the persecutions of Mary, and still stunned and conscious how hard the struggle must be confiding in the merely political Elizabeth. In that pause I should introduce the revival of our literature as it is embodied (with all the spirit of the age that was passing away) in Spencer. Then, how silently the new zeal of the Papacy and the new fervour of Protestantism prepared to clash in Jesuit and Puritan, how the English Buccaneers suddenly flung a new force of war into Protestant hands, how the Armada ruined not merely Catholicism but the temporizing system of English statesmanship, how Elizabeth was 'left alone in her realm'.

* Jules Michelet, *Précis de l'histoire moderne* (1840). Macmillans published an English translation in 1875.

And in the new pause before the coming Rebellion I would watch the highest expression of English letters in Shakspere.

I wish for *no plates or maps*. In a volume of this sort they would be useless.

If such a work is worth anything to you it is of course worth a good deal; and for myself I must consider it as representing not merely a year's good work but the result of ten years' reading and thought. I do not think £450 an excessive sum for the copyright; but of this you are of course a better judge than I, and I am sure, my dear Macmillan, that there will be no disappointment on my part if you feel yourself unable to pursue the negotiation any further. I will only say frankly that I would rather publish the book with you than with any other London house.

Believe me, very faithfully yours,   J. R. GREEN

P.S. You will remember what I said about the necessity for payment on delivery of the successive chapters in MS.

Alexander Macmillan's response was to offer Green £350 in instalments before publication, and a further £100 after the sale of 2,000 copies: a royalty agreement was substituted later.

Green was a favourite of the circle surrounding Macmillan. Other members of the circle were Stopford Augustus Brooke (1832–1916), chaplain-in-ordinary to Queen Victoria; the Rev. Brooke Lambert (1834–1901), pupil of F. D. Maurice and social reformer; Charles John Clay (1827–1905), partner in Richard Clay & Sons, printers to Cambridge University; the historians Freeman, Bryce and Stubbs; and Richard Chenevix Trench (1807–86), archbishop of Dublin and the author of some forty books and pamphlets, theological and poetical, in Macmillans' list.

27 September 1871

My dear Macmillan,

Lambert and Clay and I are anxious about Green's affairs.

You see, for absolute want of money, he is forced to give his time, which is wanted for his history, to writing petty articles in the *Saturday*. He is without any cure or stipend. And if he had enough to take him abroad and keep him there without his being compelled to produce two articles a week, he could finish his history and when he returned be, I hope, well enough to take some well paid post.

We propose then to get up among his friends a sufficient sum to give him. Are you inclined to join? And as you know Freeman, Stubbs and Bryce, are you inclined to write and mention the matter to them? They would, I am sure, help and get help from his historical friends. We propose that it should be done with the greatest privacy — only by personal letters. We propose that no names should be given, but when the sum is collected, that it be handed over in a lump to Green.

Lambert has written to the archbishop — we three give ten guineas apiece. If G. got a hundred pounds, it would be enough. Would you be the centre and receive the cash? And when it is collected send it to Green?

Yours ever sincerely,　　　　　　　　S. A. BROOKE

Torquay

My dear Brooke,

It will be a very great pleasure for me to co-operate in the good work for dear Green, whom I feel for as a son or brother. I will most readily give my ten guineas and receive the money and pay it over to him, if you think that best. But I would on the whole rather avoid asking others like Freeman, Stubbs, or Bryce. You will probably see reasons why I should not, and the same reasons seem to me to weigh against my being the almoner, though if you and Clay and others think I should, I will bow to your judgment. I am down here for a little rest, which I need, but Craik my partner knows my mind and feels as I do and will co-operate with

you in any way he can and you deem best. I cannot say with
what satisfaction I will help this good enterprise, and if you
think my being the centre is the best, by all means make me
so. Of course, it should be wholly *private* application —
personal where possible. I think Craik might ask Bryce.

Ever sincerely yours,   A. MACMILLAN

The publication of the *Short History* in 1874 helped to relieve
Green's financial straits: the book sold 35,000 copies in eighteen
months, and was expanded into four volumes in 1877–80.

Macmillan found plenty of work for Green, and employed him
from 1875 as editor of a new series of literary and historical primers.
Green however, who knew that his illness was incurable, was not
always happy either about his own competence as an editor or about
his publisher's motive, in which he scented charity. In 1877 Macmillan
wrote:

I can assure you that hardly any enterprise we have ever been
engaged in has been more satisfactory to me personally, and
no less to other members of the firm, than your primers.
Believe me, my dear Green, that you are loved and honoured
and trusted among us all in a very high degree, and we count
all that you do with and for us among our most precious
work.

In January 1883, learning that Green, at forty-five, was dying of
consumption at Mentone, Macmillan changed his holiday plans in
order to be near him. He wrote to Trench:

6 April 1883

Dear Archbishop of Dublin,
    ... My wife and I spent the last five weeks of dear Green's
life at Mentone and were seeing him, of course, every day.

He could rarely bear more than a few minutes' talk at a time, but every utterance was as clear and vivid as it ever was. When one went up in the morning — our hotel was only five minutes' walk from their pleasant little villa — he had read the little local paper that gave all the telegrams, and with that marvellous power he had of catching the *vital part* in whatever came before him could tell you all you could learn of importance in the longer, later papers. Thanks greatly to the absolute self-sacrifice of his noble, tender, wise wife, he had little, if any, actual suffering, and the natural sense of decaying physical power was borne with admirable patience. I think he had grown in moral sweetness of late years, and one saw its results in those last weeks. . . .

Ever your Grace's faithful servant,

ALEX. MACMILLAN

EDWARD AUGUSTUS FREEMAN

1823–1892

Who is Freeman? What a question! He is a country gentleman living in Somerset. I believe as a matter of fact he really
knows more about history generally than any man living. I
will take an even wager that he can abuse any one who
differs from him or who commits what he thinks is a historical blunder more intensely than any one I know. . . .
Seriously he is a very able accomplished cantankerous yet
substantially good-tempered fellow.

Alexander Macmillan was writing to the editor of a quarterly
magazine to whom he had sent for review the first of the six volumes
of Freeman's *History of the Norman Conquest* (Oxford, 1867–79).
Freeman later became regius professor of modern history at Oxford.

In 1871 Freeman was invited by George Grove to contribute to
Macmillan's Magazine a paper on the work of William Stubbs (1825–
1901), then regius professor and later bishop of Oxford. The paper,
'The Use of Historical Documents', was rejected by *Macmillan's*
and published in the *Fortnightly Review* (September 1871), edited by
John Morley.

Freeman was an avowed φρουδοκτόνος — or slayer of Froude,
rival historian of England. The other persons mentioned in these
letters are Dean Stanley, James Bryce and John Richard Green.

Macmillan's Magazine, Lower Sydenham, S.E.,

17 August 1871

My dear Freeman,

. . . I am sorry we differ so radically about personalities —
to me the paper seems more or less permeated with them —

you assume throughout that because, in your opinion, Froude is inaccurate, therefore he is so of design and malice, and is an impostor. A kind of Procrustean rule that is intolerable — at any rate cannot be allowed in *Macmillan's Magazine* as long as I am editor.

I am sure you will pardon my saying that I think this line of conduct always more or less likely to defeat itself. In this particular instance I know that my sympathies for Froude and Stanley have been very much quickened and increased by the strong personal animosity displayed in the articles on them in the *Saturday* — attributed wrongly or rightly to you — and I am sure that the same thing has happened to hundreds of others. It is intolerable that scholars and gentlemen are to be browbeaten and abused because they hold their own opinion on certain points.

With regard to this article I should very much regret not having it because half of it seems to me so very good, and because I respect Stubbs and wish the world to know how good and great he is, but the portions of which I complain must come out.

I am just off to the Continent. Yours very truly,

G. GROVE

16 Bedford Street, W.C., 19 August 1871

My dear Freeman,

. . . I am terribly anxious that you should do the article on Stubbs. He is a *great* man, and what I want is to do him a service. The Froude part of what you sent will only do harm. The question is not about Froude's being right or wrong, but as to the wisdom in your own cause — which is that of Stubbs, Bryce, Green, and all you love and admire — of that ceaseless nagging. I know that all those I have named agree with me on this point — that it hurts what you aim at. . . .

Yours ever faithfully,   A. MACMILLAN

Somerleaze, Wells, Somerset, 20 August 1871

My dear Macmillan,

... I enclose a letter from Grove,* which I cannot but call impertinent. He does right to say whether he will take an article or not, but he need not take upon him to lecture me in a way which shows his own ignorance. No man's life offers more room for personality than Froude's, but there is none in the article — nothing but a fair comparison between the right way of using documents and the wrong. Grove evidently does not know that there is such a thing as truth. He thinks that every protest in its name is a sign of 'personal animosity', as if Froude or Stanley were of any consequence to me personally. He thinks that careless and culpable blundering is matter of 'opinion'. As for what 'permeated' may mean — that I leave to the editor of the *Daily Telegraph*. The man is simply insolent. I am ready to bear anything from you, but no more dealings with him.

As for the article, when it came back I sent it to Morley, who is much more likely to understand it than Grove. What becomes of it must depend on his answer: but I stick to Herbert of Bosham's rule, *Ne mutilet*. ...

Yours ever,   EDWARD A. FREEMAN

In 1872 Freeman's *General Sketch of European History* appeared as the first volume of Macmillans' Historical Course for Schools, of which he was general editor. The most troublesome of the contributors to the series was Charlotte M. Yonge — 'Aunt Charlotte', as he liked to call her. (It was the name she had adopted for a series of children's books for another publisher.) Her *History of France* — 'Little France' or 'Petty France' to Freeman — took four years in the writing, proofing and rewriting.

20 August 1877

My dear Craik,

You must really think very seriously about Little France.

* The letter of 17 August printed above.

I had hoped on Saturday that I had got to the end of it : but it has now begun again in the middle, in a fearful state, almost rewritten on the proof, which puts my eyes out if I try to read it. And it is so wretchedly done — naturally I feel that most at the beginning and the end, the part that I have worked at and the part that I can remember. In a great deal of the middle part I have no doubt that she knows the mere run of the story much better than I do ; but she never catches any of the points, never brings out the great landmarks, all on, on, on, and such sentences — O how long! All political matters are simply confused ; she seems to understand nothing. The plebiscite of 1870 was to make the 'Empire' hereditary, and that kind of thing. I do my best to lick it into some kind of shape, but it is but an Aaron's calf that comes out. What is to be done? I shall be thoroughly ashamed to see my name as editor of such stuff — specially as she has made no attempt to do what all the others have done, to work on the lines of my *General Sketch* — and I should think all the others will be ashamed of their yoke-fellow. And all the time she is so good, a perfect saint for taking reproof. . . .

Yours very truly,   EDWARD A. FREEMAN

Palermo, 10 November 1877

My dear Macmillan,

I have sent off the rest of the latter part of Aunt Charlotte. . . . If you think I have changed too much, ask Johnny [Green] or Jack [Morley] or anybody. You would hardly have wished me to keep these propositions :

1st. That the last tyrant, L.N.B. (not the old boy),* being elected President, called himself First Consul.

2nd. That Wörth (spelled in some odd way) was the first engagement in 1870.

3rd. That Thiers was the son of the beloved Queen Louise of Prussia.

* I.e., Louis-Napoleon Bonaparte, not Napoleon I.

4th. That the Duke of Orleans's horses ran away, leaving two infant sons.

The first of these errors I take on myself to denounce : the fourth, which may or may not be an error, I leave to such as be learned in the pedigrees of horses. . . .

Yours ever,   EDWARD A. FREEMAN

In the next extract, Clay is Macmillans' printer.

Somerleaze, Wells, 25 July 1878

I rejoice to say that I have done Petty France, as far as the revision of Aunt Charlotte's text is concerned, and that the last portion is going off Clayward. But then, as I told you a week ago, Clay would seem to be even mire where no ground is : nothing comes back from it, however much goes into it. It is a horrid bore of them, as I am longing to get rid of the thing altogether. . . .

You must seriously think of me when you settle about royalties with Aunt Charlotte. It is no light work that I have done — almost as much work as writing the book, and much less interesting. And after all I do not venture to say that it is good or accurate, only less shamefully bad and inaccurate that it was aforetime. You can't make — Stubbs could not make — a silk purse out of a sow's ear. It is longer than it should be, for there were so many absolutely needful things — generally *all the needful things* — to be put in, while I did not like to cut out anything that I could anyhow keep. . . . But she is a good creature, and takes kicking better than any living soul — or body.

ANTHONY TROLLOPE
1815–1882

Trollope's only connexion as a novelist with Macmillans — he also wrote the Thackeray volume in English Men of Letters — was over his late, and unusually short, novel *Sir Harry Hotspur of Humblethwaite*, which was serialized in *Macmillan's Magazine* in 1870. Macmillans had bought all rights in this book, which they had hoped to publish in two volumes: a single volume would be less profitable. When Trollope refused to lengthen it, they sold the first-edition rights to Hurst & Blackett, of Great Marlborough Street.*

Waltham House, Waltham Cross, 18 October 1870

My dear Mr. Macmillan,

I am sorry that anything to do with my tale should be less advantageous to you than you had expected. But the fact is that as one pound of tea won't make two by any variance in packing the article — so neither will a one-volumed tale make two volumes. You will say that in one case the quantity is fixed, and in the other not. But in regard to the latter article the quantity is too well and too nearly fixed to admit of such violent stretching. The real pound may be, and often is, lessened by an ounce in the packing; — but to make two pounds out of one is more than can be done even in Marlbro' Street. I am quite sure that you agree with me.

You tell me that the trials of authors have their mitigations. I have had none to complain of, but what have come from a dull brain and relaxed application.

Yours always faithfully,   ANTHONY TROLLOPE

* Text from B. A. Booth (ed.), *The Letters of Anthony Trollope*, Oxford, 1951.

THOMAS HARDY
1840–1928

Hardy's relations with Macmillans are described in Charles Morgan's *The House of Macmillan*. Morgan quoted liberally from the early letters between the novelist and Alexander Macmillan, and from John Morley's reports on the two novels — Hardy's first two, *The Poor Man and the Lady* (never published) and *Desperate Remedies* (1871) — which the firm rejected. Briefly, both Macmillan and Morley saw promise in Hardy and encouraged him to continue writing. A misunderstanding seems to have led to his taking his third novel, *Under the Greenwood Tree*, elsewhere.

Hardy's first letter was not printed by Morgan. It was precisely his treatment of 'the upper classes of society' that Alexander Macmillan most disliked. ('I don't know what opportunities you have had of seeing the class you deal with. . . . It is inconceivable to me that any considerable number of human beings — God's creatures — could be so bad without going to utter wreck in a week.')

Horace Mosley Moule (b. 1832), Dorset man and London journalist, was Hardy's close friend and patron up to the time of his suicide in 1873.

Bockhampton, Dorchester, 25 July 1868

Sir,

In writing the novel I wish to lay before you — *The Poor Man and the Lady* (sent by today's post) — the following considerations had place.

That the upper classes of society have been induced to read, before any, books in which *they themselves* are painted by a comparative outsider.

That, in works of such a kind, unmitigated utterances of strong feeling against the class to which these readers belong

E

may lead them to throw down a volume in disgust; whilst the very same feelings inserted edgewise so to say — half concealed beneath ambiguous expressions, or at any rate written as if they were not the chief aims of the book (even though they may be) — become the most attractive remarks of all.

That, nowadays, discussions on the questions of manners, rising in the world, etc. (the main incidents of the novel), have grown to be particularly absorbing.

That as a rule no fiction will considerably interest readers poor or rich unless the passion of love forms a prominent feature in the thread of the story.

That novelty of *position* and *view*, in relation to a known subject, is more taking among the readers of light literature than even absolute novelty of subject.

Hence the book took its shape, rightly or wrongly.

Mr. Moule has very kindly written me a letter of introduction, which accompanies my own, and, I believe, sufficiently explains other points.

I am, sir, your obedient servant,   THOMAS HARDY

Hardy's reputation was established by 1886 when Macmillans secured *The Mayor of Casterbridge* for their newly launched Colonial Library and, more important, *The Woodlanders* both for *Macmillan's Magazine* and as a three-decker (1887). The latter novel was not to everybody's taste, a fact that no doubt influenced the magazine's rejection of Hardy's next novel, *Tess of the d'Urbervilles*.

                    The Vicarage, Crewkerne, 9 April 1887
Sir,
    I fear you will think I am taking a liberty, but I cannot forbear expressing the regret felt by myself and other mothers that you should have admitted such a story as *The Woodlanders* into your *Magazine*. We have hitherto felt that

Macmillan's might be put without any hesitation into the hands of our daughters, and it has been with both surprise and sorrow that I have seen such a story in it. I feel sure that it must have been through some oversight that this has happened.

A story which can hinge on conjugal infidelity, can describe coarse flirtations, and can end in pronouncing a married woman's avowed lover to be a 'good man who did good things', is certainly not fit to be printed in a high-toned periodical and to be put into the hands of pure-minded English girls. I regret much having to make this protest but I cannot apologize for doing so.

Believe me, sir, yours faithfully,   ELIZABETH HOLME

In 1888 Macmillans published *Wessex Tales*, and five years later Hardy wished to withdraw this and *The Woodlanders* in order that his regular publishers, Osgood, McIlvaine, should include them in a collected edition. Macmillans objected that he had no right to do so. Hardy riposted:

70 Hamilton Terrace, N.W., 8 June 1893

Mr. F. Macmillan appears to take an erroneous view of the arrangement between us, and I think it best, in order to prevent misapprehension, to say that the licence I granted you was revocable at will, of which he seems to be unaware.

12 June 1893

Dear Sirs,

I regret to learn from your letter of a debt against *The Woodlanders* and *Wessex Tales* of nearly £200, which I am quite unable to understand in the face of the sales as rendered, and the now well-known cost of production.

I can assure you that you are mistaken in supposing me to

have used in any agreement words empowering you to continue the publication of those books during the term of copyright, as I understand you to assert. So far from it I have, ever since producing my first or second novel, carefully avoided selling a copyright from the very consideration that the present contingency of having to collect my writings might arise.

Yours faithfully,   THOMAS HARDY

Macmillans continued to 'resist to the utmost' the author's 'claim to treat us as tenants-at-will'. Nevertheless, as they wrote on 14 June:

We are prepared to meet you, as we have no wish to be disobliging, and we therefore write to say that we are willing to hand over to you the stereotype plates and sheet stock of these two books for the sum of £250, but only on condition that your present claim is withdrawn, that it is distinctly understood that our right in the books is undisputed, and that we do not surrender them on compulsion.

Harmony was quickly re-established. A few months later Macmillans contracted to add a dozen Hardy titles, including the repudiated *Tess*, to their Colonial Library. Soon after the turn of the century Hardy transferred all his books to the firm.

Hardy's return to Macmillans, marked by the appearance of *The Dynasts, Part First*, in 1904, is well documented in Charles Morgan's book. By October 1907 he was able to submit 'the Third and last Part of *The Dynasts*, which will at least give you the satisfaction of being the end of what I believe to be the longest English drama in existence. . . . Next year', he remarked, 'it will be forty years since I sent my first MS. to your house!' He was to send MSS. for another twenty years.

The volume to which the next letter refers was *Time's Laughing-stocks* (1909), in which the poem 'Panthera', a legend of the Crucifixion, was included. The named persons were John Bagnell Bury (1861–1927), regius professor of modern history at Cambridge; Sir George Walter Prothero (1848–1922), editor of the *Quarterly Review* and co-editor of the *Cambridge Modern History*; and Canon Thomas Kelly Cheyne (1841–1915), Oriel professor of the interpretation of scripture at Oxford, an advanced and somewhat erratic theologian.

Private   Max Gate, Dorchester, 18 September 1909
My dear Macmillan,

I was going to include in the new volume among the rest of the poems the legendary one I enclose. It has been read by Professor Bury of King's, Cambridge, who says by all means print it — in which opinion a lady of light and learning in University circles also coincides. Another literary friend — a Rationalist reviewer — says include it : but two others (one a reviewer) advise me not to print it, though they, like the rest, call it a poem of great interest. I had a good mind to ask another friend, Prothero, editor of the *Quarterly*, but he may not be in London just now.

My own feeling was that, as there are some poems in the collection quite of an opposite kind — quite 'churchy' in fact — this would contrast well with them, and excite no bad feeling.

But I should like you or your cousin, or any trusty reader at hand for subjects of this kind, to decide whether to include it or not. To divines of the Higher Criticism, Dr. Cheyne for instance, there is, of course, no harm in it at all, the legend being well-known to such scholars — but I do not want to provoke acrimony amongst well-meaning but narrower minded people for the sake of one poem, good or bad. On the other hand I do not want to leave out a piece which may be liked by advanced readers, and may possibly start a good wholesome controversy : poetry, as you know, is sadly in need of some stimulus to set it going.

You understand these practical matters better than I, so will you say frankly what you think. It comes near the end of the book, so there is time to settle the question before the printers get to it.

Sincerely yours,

THOMAS HARDY

P.S. I have omitted to mention the rather important detail that since the objectors read it I have rewritten the poem, and made the events a possibly erroneous fantasy of the narrator — which I think removes all objection. However, you decide.

JOHN ADDINGTON SYMONDS

1840–1893

A brilliant pupil of Master Jowett at Balliol, where he gained a first class in classics and won the Newdigate (*The Escorial*, 1860) and the university essay prize (*The Renaissance*, 1863), Symonds never fulfilled his promise. The book he is offering to Alexander Macmillan, *Renaissance in Italy*, turned out to be less a 'history of Italian literature' than a series of impressionistic sketches. It was published in seven volumes by Smith, Elder in 1875–86.

Frederic William Henry Myers (1843–1901), the poet, and Henry Sidgwick (1838–1900), the philosopher, were both distinguished classical scholars at Cambridge before both becoming pioneers of 'psychical research'. Myers's projected book on French literature was not written.

7 Victoria Square, Clifton, Bristol, 21 January 1871

My dear Mr. Macmillan,

I am going to trouble you with a question which is of great importance to me. I am engaged in studying for and in writing a history of Italian Literature, in the course of which I hope to take into account the arts of Italy, the manners of the people, etc., so as to make my book as far as in me lies a history of the Italian genius in its several phases. The scale on which I contemplate to write the book will probably oblige me to extend it to five volumes. As yet I have only rough hewn a portion of my matter. Getting the whole into shape must be the work of years.

Now comes my question to you. The fact that I am engaged on this book has become known, partly through Mr. Jowett who is kindly interested in it, partly through Mr. Myers who once entertained a similar project, through Mr.

Sidgwick, and other friends of mine. In consequence of this I have been asked whether I would announce my project to the public.

I feel as if I could hardly take this step — which, while it might prevent the rising up of some rivals, might incite others perhaps to preoccupy the public mind on the same subject — without consulting someone of experience. Now I have had recourse to you for this reason principally, that I had hoped, when my work was more mature, to submit it to your judgment and ask you first whether you would care to undertake the publication of it.

I feel it is premature to put *this* question to you, though there is no one whom I would rather choose as publisher of my book if it sees the light : but I think that I cannot, with this wish in my mind, ask the advice of any other experienced person on the minor question of the expediency of inserting an advertisement in the columns of the *Academy*.

If you will give me your counsel I shall feel very greatly obliged to you. I need not repeat that it would be a pleasure to me to know that you would entertain the notion of publishing the book provided it is finished and approved of in due course.

I hope that you and Mrs. Macmillan and all your family are well. I have not forgotten the pleasant night I spent at your house.

I am most truly yours,   J. A. SYMONDS

16, Bedford Street, W.C., 24 January 1871

Dear Mr. Symonds,

I am very glad to know that you are at work on the subject of Italian culture. It is a large and fine one, though of course it can hardly ever be made very popular. But in this as in most things the *manner* will have a great deal to do with it. In spite of Socrates's denunciation of cookery, as an injurious form of flattery, modern medicine recognizes that the way your food is prepared has a good deal to do, not only with the delight which accompanies its consumption, but also with the facility and efficacy of its digestion. Mental food does not differ much in this.

I should have been a little afraid of the five volumes as being more than people will be likely to buy on one subject. But some day when you are in town, you must come down and let me know your ideas on the subject. In the mean time I may express my sincere wish that we should be its publishers, both for the sake of the subject and of the author. When it is farther advanced I should very much like to see some of it and then we could perhaps discuss the question of terms. As to making any announcement I think this could be done well enough through the 'gossip' column of the *Athenaeum*. I enclose a sort of paragraph that might do the work you want of making it known that you are engaged in the enterprise. I don't think there is much danger of its exciting rivalry. If you will make any modification in it and return it I will take care that it appears soon. This costs nothing and does not commit you to much. I did the same for Mr. Frederic Myers's proposed book on French literature.

I shall be very glad if when you next come to London you can arrange to spend a night or two at my house, or at least dine with me.

With kind regards, yours very truly,

ALEX. MACMILLAN

ANDREW CECIL BRADLEY

1851–1935

Bradley, later professor of poetry at Oxford and the foremost Shake-spearean critic of his day, was an undergraduate when he submitted a volume of verse to Macmillans. It was rejected on the advice of a reader who found the verses 'extremely musical, graceful and sweet, but defective in thought', with echoes of 'Swinburne (without the erotics) and Tennyson (without the weight)'. Bradley's much older half-brother, George Granville Bradley (1821–1903), was at the time Master of University College; his sister Harriet was married to George Grove.

Balliol College, Oxford, 26 November 1871

Sir,

You may know if not my name, yet the name borne by me, from my sharing it with my brother, the Rev. G. G. Bradley, and from my connexion with my brother-in-law, Mr. Grove. I have been urged by friends, and I wish myself, to publish some poems, and I have been advised to send them for your inspection, in the hope that you may consent to publish them on such an arrangement as would take some part of the risk from my shoulders, that condition being necessary to my design of making them public. The poems I send today: and there are some remarks I wish to make about them before they come under your notice.

The poems are arranged in chronological order, for the reason that there is so much change in the subjects and treatment that the book would in this way take an almost biographical form, and I confess one of my reasons for wishing to publish them is the belief that those poems which come near the end of the volume might be of service as well as a pleasure to persons who go through some such experience as is there portrayed. I say this in order to guard the poems from producing the impression which the first half alone might produce, that of being a mere collection of sentimental songs.

If the poems were published, I should probably wish to add some two or three pieces on a Future Life and on the Spiritual Conception of Love.

With this preface, and hoping you may look on the proposition I make in a favourable light, I am your obedient servant,   A. C. BRADLEY

Bradley's long review of Browning's *The Inn Album* appeared in *Macmillan's Magazine* in February 1876. Among other modifications suggested by Grove, Bradley omitted a quotation from, or allusion to, 'The Cock and the Bull', the parody of Browning in *Fly Leaves* (1872) by Charles Stuart Calverley.

Thursday [1875]

Dear G.,

One line in great haste. I was a good deal disturbed by your letter, as disrespect to B. was certainly the last thing that I should have wished to show, and it bothered me to find that, so unexpectedly to me, I turned out to have written too sharply. However I have thought over it all and I think it is inevitable — and we probably differ about what a critic ought to do. I think I should never choose to review a book I thought bad (I do distinctly think this a bad poem, for Browning) *proprio motu* — but if one does, I think one is bound to convey one's idea of it as a whole though one may wish to bring its good points into prominence. That is what I have tried to do, and I think the article (though it is certainly not well written) conveys my meaning.

Apart from any possible duty to the public, or possible

use to the poet, I shouldn't like anybody to think I thought it a good poem. And if you praise such a poem or are enthusiastic over it, what are you to do to good poetry? I think criticism ought to try and form a judgment on a poem, independent of the opinion of the moment, and of the sensitiveness of the author — if it thinks it necessary to notice bad poems at all. Otherwise I see no use in it. It is bound to be respectful to the *author* — and that I think I am — and more than respectful. I don't think it is fair to look upon such expressions as 'extreme improbability' etc. as applying to the poet : one has to do simply with his poem and not him. And I was rather aghast to see the words you don't like. I'm afraid that kind of thing can't be mended. One can't be expected to say in criticism only what one could say without embarrassment to the author face to face, and yet I should not hesitate (and have not) to say things quite as strong to my own friends about their poems, and feel sure I should not be hurt if it were done to me. But I think we must look at the matter with different eyes. Of course I can't think of the effect on Browning — though I should think very little of him if he were hurt by such criticism — because I don't know him.

'Improbability' would be enough, and 'inpoetical' without the 'thoroughly', but, though I can't remember where 'fatally' and 'mistake' occur, I really don't see what one can say else. It never occurred to me anybody could mind them and I no more hesitated over them than I would to say that *Love's Labour's Lost* is tedious, or the cannons in *Paradise Lost* comic, or *The Excursion* often dull, or *The Revolt of Islam* extremely ill constructed — and yet compared with any one of them it is o. Out with the reference to Calverley by all means. I put in no quotations for space sake, but no doubt it would be improved by them. I quite feel the truth of what you say of it. I'm very glad you like it on the whole, very glad — I hope you won't doubt that because of the above. But want of respect or appreciation to a poet — that's a vice I didn't suspect myself of and too horrid a one, and now I am uneasy if it should really be so.

But what I meant to say when I began is that I hope you won't think twice of chucking it into the wastepaper-basket, if you would feel it at all unpleasant to Browning to publish it in what he knows to be your magazine. I can quite understand and am not such a fool as to rate it at the price of any possibility of unpleasantness or uneasiness to you.

Otherwise I'm more than willing to change anything I can without altering the impression I want to produce. If I were to write of it exactly as I think, it would be very different. But I should be very uncomfortable if I thought you were putting any pressure on your own inclination about it for my sake. . . .

Ever yours affectionately,   A. C. BRADLEY

WALTER HORATIO PATER

1839–1894

Offering Macmillans his first book, *Studies in the History of the Renaissance*, Pater, a young Oxford don, had precise, aesthetic, but slightly antiquarian ideas about its appearance.

Brasenose, 2 November 1872

Dear Mr. Macmillan,

... I like the look of the page very much, but not altogether the paper. It has occurred to me that the old-fashioned binding in pasteboard with paper back and printed label, usual, I think, about thirty years ago, but not yet gone quite out of use, would be an economical and very pretty binding for my book. It would, I am sure, be much approved of by many persons of taste, among whom the sale of the book would probably in the first instance be. I have just had in my hands an old book so bound, the pasteboard covers of a greyish blue, and the paper back olive green ; nothing could be prettier or more simple ; and I should be very glad if you could indulge me in this particular.

I do not know whether without adding to the expense of publication the present paper might be changed for paper with rough edges and showing the watermark ; but suppose not....

Very sincerely yours,   W. H. PATER

Alexander Macmillan replied that a return to boards-and-label, besides being unpractical, was 'like a recurrence to the *fig-leaf*'. Pater wrote :

11 November 1872

I was disappointed at the contents of your letter, as the cover I wished for had occurred to me as a way of giving my book the artistic appearance which I am sure is necessary for it, without the expense and trouble of an unusual form of binding. I fancy that if I saw you I could persuade you to think the old-fashioned binding in boards as pretty as it seems to me. The objection as to its liability to be soiled might be met by the paper wrapper for packing, now not uncommon. Something not quite in the ordinary way is, I must repeat, very necessary in a volume the contents of which are so unpretending as mine, and which is intended in the first instance for a comparatively small section of readers. For a book on art to be bound quite in the ordinary way is, it seems to me, behind the times; and the difficulty of getting a book bound in cloth so as to be at all artistic, and indeed not quite the other way, is very great. I prefer in all cases the paper label, as the lettering is necessarily clumsy on a cloth binding, especially when, as in this case, the volume is a thin one.

Macmillan's reply follows. *Olrig Grange*, 1872, was a poem by 'Hermann Knott' (Walter Chalmers Smith, 1824–1908); the 'intimate friend of Mr. Burne Jones' has not been identified.

Bedford Street, Covent Garden, 12 November 1872

Dear Mr. Pater,

I don't think you would convince me that paper covers are more beautiful than cloth, and they certainly are very much less useful. I am speaking with recent experience when I say that it would interfere with the sale of the book, as booksellers won't keep them — even with the paper cover. My friend, Mr. MacLehose, of Glasgow, published *Olrig Grange* in this fashion at first, and has been obliged to abandon it for cloth. He still uses paper labels — and gives a duplicate label to be stuck on when the old gets dirty ! This is droll, to say the least of it. The bookseller or possessor has to remove the old one and get paste — which he possibly has not at hand — and repaste the clean one on. The *recurrence* has nothing admirable in it to me.

The use of inferior, unuseful materials cannot be needful to the realization of any art which is of much value — at least I cannot see how. Gold lettering on cloth was an immense advance on the old paper boards, and was welcomed as such. I remember the period of change. I still possess books which are done up in smooth cloth with paper labels, and value them historically — just as I would value Adam's original fig-leaf, if I could find it.

But I will most gladly cede my tastes to yours as far as possible. I send you by this post a book in a style of binding which I devised for the author, and which he liked. His tastes were 'artistic'. He is an intimate friend of Mr. Burne Jones and others who think in that line. Also the paper of the book is made to imitate the old wire-wove paper, which can only now be got in this mock rib, which is really rather pleasant to my own eye. If you like the paper, please let me know at once, as it will have to be made on purpose. Perhaps we can meditate on the binding a little further.

Yours very truly,   A. MACMILLAN

A compromise was reached. The book appeared, in February 1873, in a cloth binding of an unusual shade of green of Pater's choosing.

EDWIN ABBOTT ABBOTT

1838–1926

Headmaster of the City of London School, the Rev. Edwin Abbott was, for his period, an unorthodox schoolmaster and a heterodox Christian. He was, however, more widely appreciated in orthodox circles than at times he feared. The book here described, *Philochristus, Memoirs of a Disciple of the Lord*, was published anonymously by Macmillans in 1878: it cost the author neither his headmastership nor his office as select preacher at Oxford.

Macmillans had published a number of theological works by the Rev. John Llewelyn Davies (1826–1916), as well as the anonymous *Ecce Homo, a Survey of the Life and Work of Jesus Christ* (1866) by Sir John Robert Seeley (1834–95). *The Life of Christ* by the Rev. Frederic William Farrar (1831–1903), then headmaster of Marlborough, was announced for publication by Cassells at the time of the following letter.

Private   32 Abbey Road, N.W., 6 January 1874

Dear Macmillan,

. . . Today I've finished a work half fiction, half religious — memoirs written by a disciple of Jesus, who was with him from the first. Of course I think it is good : but that is not much to the purpose. However it is full of incident and picture, and one of my friends tells me it is 'deeply interesting', and another (Ll. Davies) that what he has seen of it, the first 200 pages, is 'charming'. What I now want to ask you is when shall I publish it? I think November. I have carefully compared it with *Ecce Homo* and find it would take half as much again of space as that, with same print and page. It is 664 pages of letter paper, or thereabouts, say 650.

I shall publish it anonymously, but shall carefully let it be known that I am the author : for there are reasons why (though I may not like to be abused by *name* in the religious papers) I have no right to shirk the odium of heterodoxy, for the book is heterodox.

I do not think it can possibly be published this season (let alone Farrar's *Life*) and have no wish for it : for, hurrier as I usually am, I hate hurry about such a work as this. It is the result of years of labour and, if I have any chance of being remembered for a generation, this is my only chance. . . .

Yours very truly,   EDWIN A. ABBOTT

23 January 1877

On the eve of publishing this new book of mine I feel an increasing fear that I shall expose myself to a great deal of obloquy and, not improbably — but this must be quite private, for, if my fear were known, it might realize itself — lose my present post at the City School. I frankly confess that, if I did not think it cowardly and wrong to shrink back, I should do so and should willingly throw away the money spent in printing the book. However, as I *do* think it wrong to go back, go on I must. But this fear of mine will necessarily influence our arrangements as to terms of publication. If I do not lose my present position I shall be quite willing — supposing you to be willing — that the book should be published on our usual terms, half-profits, you taking risk. But if I lose my post I shall have next to nothing to live on and no other post that I can easily think of to which I could turn. In that case I should be obliged to think, I won't say of £. *s. d.*, but of *d*. In short every penny would be of importance to me.

Now of course I could not be turned out of my present post for this book without attracting a great deal of attention to the book and making it commercially a great success. Therefore I wish to publish thus — I will take all risk, pay all bills, and receive all profits, paying you the usual commission. (As to the advertising, I should like very little of it ; the *Record* and the *Literary Churchman* and probably even the *Guardian* will soon advertise me enough by attacking the book. You probably have a stated charge for the advertisement appearing in your catalogue. That of course I must pay, and a week or so in a few of the best papers. But I do *not* want the book freely advertised. I want to avoid the appearance of puffing it, and I wish to appear as unobtrusive and inoffensive as possible. I am quite sure the Oxford people will want to strike me off the list of select preachers to which I have just been appointed — and that will be advertisement enough at Oxford.) But *if* I am not turned out of my present post owing to this book, then I should be quite willing (if you desired it) to go on the supposition that we had agreed on the half-profits system, and to refund (if it came to refunding) such amounts as would reduce our arrangement to the half-profit system.

I think, in spite of parentheses, this letter will be clear to you. I will call soon, if you agree to this, to talk about cover, etc. But it will be as well that you should have this letter from me and that I should have something in writing from you, besides a mere conversation. I have struck out almost all the 'Dreams' and 'Visions'. Write me a line as soon as possible : for I expect the whole to be in pages by Friday and ready for printing off next week.

WILLIAM H. STONE

1830–1891

Dr. Stone contributed articles to *Grove's Dictionary of Music and Musicians* both before and after the encounter with George Lillie Craik here described.

14 Dean's Yard, Westminster, 21 October 1874

Gentlemen,

On Tuesday last I called, by appointment, on Mr. G. Grove at your house of business ; entering by the side door, which, I believe, bears the number of your printed letter-paper, and by which I have always been admitted.

On the staircase I met a gentleman, who stated he was a partner in the firm. He asked me if I knew the door was private. I replied that I did not. He said it gave trouble to the housekeeper (whom by the way I have never seen), and that he must request me to enter by the shop. I asked the clerk who let me in to explain, but as he took no notice of that, and as his manner was offensive, I said I should be happy to enter by any door, or even by the window, if that would satisfy him. He replied he 'must insist on my entering by the shop'. On this I told him I should leave, but not to return.

After mature deliberation, I cannot, with self-respect, allow such a matter to pass. I must therefore ask for some explanation and apology, or request to be allowed to withdraw from my unsolicited engagements with Mr. Grove.

I feel sure it is the wish, and the interest, of so honourable a firm as yours to treat with courtesy a person of at least equal standing and education as themselves. At any rate my perfect innocence of any intention to trespass ought to have been sufficient to protect me. I prefer writing directly to you, instead of to Mr. Grove, because from him I have always received the utmost kindness and consideration. He, as well as the clerk who was present, can I think corroborate my account of what occurred just outside the door of his room.

I remain, Gentlemen,
Your obedient Servant,
WILLIAM H. STONE, M.A. OXON., F.R.C.P.,
Physician to St. Thomas's Hospital.

SIR RICHARD CLAVERHOUSE JEBB

1841–1905

In 1876 Jebb was professor of Greek at Glasgow University, and much admired as a scholar by Alexander Macmillan. John Pentland Mahaffy (1839–1919) was professor of ancient history at Trinity College, Dublin, and a friend of Alexander's son George. Both professors had been commissioned to write volumes in Macmillan's series of literary and historical primers, edited by J. R. Green — Mahaffy on *Old Greek Life* and Jebb on *Greek Literature*. Macmillans were about to publish the two volumes of Jebb's *Attic Orators from Antiphon to Isaeos*.

Glasgow, 19 January 1876

My dear Macmillan,

I do hope I am in time to have the advertisement sheet — which I saw for the first time this morning — removed from the end of my second volume. To my thinking, it is grievously out of place in a book of this kind. If, however, you insist on it, at least do me this favour. Remove Prof. Mahaffy's book from the list. I must absolutely decline to have my book made a vehicle for advertising a book which I believe is more calculated to destroy the study of Greek literature at the very root than any other I have ever read. Of its merits in other respects I am not called upon to say anything. But, as far as it deals with Greek *literature*, it is simply 'impudently absurd', as Mr. Matthew Arnold renders the French *saugrenu*. Excuse my freedom of speech, but I feel strongly on this point.

In haste, ever yours,   R. C. JEBB

Attic Orators was reviewed anonymously in the *Spectator* of 25 March.

27 March 1876

You see Mahaffy has wreaked his spite in the *Spectator*. I do
not think it will do me lasting harm. His venom is a little too
evident, and the abuse is too coarse. But I hope that your
eyes are now opened to the real character of the man. There
is not a single statement of his which I could not blow to the
winds. But silence is wisest, and I shall say nothing. That is
my present resolve, at least.

Write, please, and tell me what you think. Tell me, too, if
you can, how far the attack has been noticed by people likely
to feel any interest in the subject, and how. It is a hard fight,
for anyone who stands nearly alone, as I do: and when
impudent assertion, and coarse invective, are allowed to avail
against the conscientious work of years....

There is one point on which I cannot help adding a word.
The internal evidence for Mahaffy's personal authorship of
the attack is *conclusive*. Now I naturally feel an exceedingly
strong repugnance to being associated with a series to which
he contributes: and I want to know whether Green would
wish *both* our primers to appear under his editorship after
what has passed.

Although Jebb had judged that 'silence is wisest', he could not
remain silent in the face of a review that appeared in the *Academy* over
Mahaffy's signature. In the next six months he prepared a sixty-page
pamphlet, *Some Remarks on an article by the Rev. Prof. J. P. Mahaffy
in the 'Academy' on 1 April* 1876. Macmillan tried to dissuade him
from publishing this. It would, he wrote on 2 October:

only be opening a most irritating and endless controversy.
Whatever injustices have been done against you will most
certainly die out if you leave them alone. But it is absolutely
certain that your pamphlet or paper will be answered again
and with greater animus, and time and temper and labour,
all in your case of the highest value, will be wasted.

Macmillan was right. He published Jebb's pamphlet, Mahaffy issued a *Reply to the 'Remarks' of Mr. Jebb*, and Jebb concluded the immediate controversy with *A Rejoinder to Prof. Mahaffy's 'Reply'* (1877). Even so, Jebb smouldered — and soldiered — on.

22 December 1878

The point which I was more particularly desirous to learn with regard to the sale of my *Attic Orators*, and on which your letter does not inform me, is whether the annual sale, however small, has been continuous, or has ceased altogether. The subject of course precluded the prospect of a vulgar popularity. But if an overwhelming preponderance of favourable judgments in the press ought to count, then, I think, the book had every claim to a success in its own way. The elaborate lying of Mr. Mahaffy, and the ravings of two drunken schoolmasters, cannot have done any appreciable harm, I should think. I exposed Mr. Mahaffy in a way from which his reputation will not recover. The *Saturday Review*, *Athenaeum*, *Westminster Review*, *Edinburgh Review*, *Macmillan's Magazine*, *Times*, and many others were decisively or cordially favourable. If, then, the enterprise was what you term 'problematical', this epithet must refer to the nature of the subject, not to the quality of the work.

Will you allow me to remark that I do not see how the book can have any chance unless its existence is at least known? But it does not appear in your list of classical works, and though, when I pointed this out more than a year ago, its insertion was promised, the list appears again this year without it. . . .

Meanwhile, I can only say that the books published for me by your firm are those which I regard as my best work, and that I doubt whether the personal enmity to which they have been so exceptionally exposed will eventually hinder them from obtaining such a modest rank as they claim.

In 1880 Macmillans invited Jebb to write a history of Greek literature. He replied by drawing their attention to some observations in the *Athenaeum* on his contributions to the subject in the *Encyclo-paedia Britannica*.

3 St. Peter's Terrace, Cambridge, 3 September 1880

I may be wrong: but I have little doubt as to the author-ship. As to the *animus*, no reader will have any.

If my conjecture — which rests on evidence which would satisfy most juries — is correct, then, I think, it ought to convince impartial observers that I am pursued by a steady animosity. The assertions are either false (as about ostracism) or irrelevant.

It may perhaps interest you to know that an important weekly review once sent me a work of the writer to whom (rightly or otherwise) I ascribe this latest attack. I returned it, stating that I had had a controversy with the author which made me feel that it would not be honourable to review him, as I could not trust myself to do so with that detachment from prejudice which I desired.

It is for my publishers, I think, to weigh the practical aspect of these facts. It is now clear that anything which I may publish will be exposed to unscrupulous and specious — because careful — attacks from the same quarter. They have been, from the first, entirely unprovoked: but it is not in my power to avert a malevolence excited by mere envy.

It is evident that they are calculated to injure, more or less, the sale of my books. I should wish you, then, to consider this point simply as one of business. It is one of those which have to be taken into the calculation. I am so as-tonished by the gross unfairness — the positive untruth — of the statements in this article, that I am painfully alive to the risk which you, as well as myself, would incur by pub-lishing anything of mine meant for general use.

WILLIAM EWART GLADSTONE

1809–1898

Gladstone's first contribution to Homeric scholarship was *Studies in Homer and the Homeric Age* (three volumes, Oxford, 1858). Eleven years later Macmillans published his *Juventus Mundi, the Gods and Men of the Heroic Age*, and in 1876 his *Homeric Synchronism*. He found in the monthly magazines a convenient forum for his views on a variety of subjects, especially during a political lull. After the defeat of his policy over the Russo-Turkish war ('the Eastern Question') in 1877 he published articles on Borneo in *The Contemporary* in July and on 'The Dominions of Odysseus' in *Macmillan's* in October.

Hawarden Castle, 17 August 1877

Dear Mr. Grove,

I received with concern your expression of disappointment about my article on Borneo.

Under cover of our 'neutrality' about the Eastern Question, I have during the last fortnight again turned a portion of my time to Homeric studies : and have arrived at a determined view, after many years of study, of a question debated for at least two millenniums : namely the geography of the dominions of Odysseus. My material is all ready for writing a paper upon it, and I am happy to place it at your disposal for any number after September.

It may be quite unsuited to your magazine, in which case I hope you will make no scruple of declining it : but I am sure you will interpret my offer as a sign of a desire to meet your wish and to pay due respect to the periodical which bears the name of our esteemed friend Mr. Macmillan.

Believe me always faithfully yours, W. E. GLADSTONE

Alexander Macmillan sent Gladstone in 1886 copies of the *Odyssey*, books i–xii, in a verse translation by the Earl of Carnarvon (1831–90), Conservative statesman and president of the Society of Antiquaries; *Neaera*, a tale of ancient Rome, by John W. Graham; and *Sir Percival*, a novel by J. H. Shorthouse. Alexander Macmillan was for twenty years official publisher to the University of Oxford, and would therefore stock, among other Clarendon Press books, Henry Dunbar's *Concordance to the Odyssey and Hymns of Homer*, 1880.

4 November 1886

Dear Mr. Macmillan,

I saw with much pleasure that Lord Carnarvon had become a translator of the *Odyssey*, and thought it did him much honour. I now thank you very much for the book, which arrived this morning ; and I shall have the opportunity of profiting by his labours as I had to begin the poem today — for about the twenty-fifth time, as I guess. The fact is that I give all such time as I can to the study of the text with a view to my work on the Olympian religion, which I am not without hope of licking into shape during the approaching winter.

Let me also thank you for *Neaera*, which I have just begun and find every inducement to go through with. But I was interrupted in order to read Mr. Shorthouse's book. I find it a beautiful tale, of a tone nobly high, and indicating in some respects, as compared with *John Inglesant*, social growth and a more practised hand. I hope it will have a wide circulation. Lord Rosebery liked it very much. So does my daughter Mrs. Drew, who is still an invalid but now, thank God, able to read.

If you keep the concordance to the *Odyssey* (Oxford), would you kindly send me one and put it in my account. (I cannot quite forgive the Delegates for putting the Hymns into it. They might as well have put Quintus Calaber.)

Yours sincerely,   **W. E. GLADSTONE**

Margaret Lee (1845–1914) published a number of novels in the United States, including *Divorce* (1882). Macmillans brought out *Divorce* (as *Faithful and Unfaithful*) in London, at 3*s* 6*d*, within a month of the next letter. In the *Nineteenth Century* (edited by James Thomas Knowles, 1831–1908) in February 1889 Gladstone wrote that Miss Lee 'has indicated her belief in a certain old-fashioned doctrine that the path of suffering may not be the path of duty only, but likewise the path of glory and of triumph for our race'.

Lucerne, 20 December 1888

Dear Mr. Macmillan,

By the joint action of my daughter Mrs. Drew and myself, a *short* novel termed *Divorce* will reach you by the post about the same time with this letter, and is hereby tendered to you with the unconditional permission of the authoress for publication.

She is an American lady, a Miss Lee. Any *terms* of publication would be between you and her; that is to say I conceive they would be such as you might freely grant her.

My daughter read the book and formed an opinion, in which I concur, that its publication would be useful — useful, I think, under two aspects. First it exhibits on one side American social life at work; secondly in connection with the great Marriage controversy, the greatest of all controversies. The book takes the strict side. This the title does not quite convey : with leave, it is to be altered, perhaps to this — *Divorce, or Faithful and Unfaithful*. You, if we go on, might be able to suggest something better.

Finally : I have arranged with Mr. Knowles that I am to write him a short letter on the book which will almost certainly appear in his January number. . . .

If you take up the matter, please to proceed as rapidly as possible. If you do not, then (as it would hardly be in Mr. Murray's line) I should think Mr. Kegan Paul as likely as any one to deal with it. But if I waited for your answer to write to him from Naples (Rocca Bella, Posillipo, 22 December), it would entail a week's delay which under the circumstances would be bad. Would it be rude to him if, this being so, I asked you to send on to him the book and this note?

As regards the risk of this (I suppose) 3s or 4s book, I would freely take it, but for the circumstance that this would entail on me rather too close a responsibility for every phrase in the book.

Believe me, most faithfully yours,   W. E. GLADSTONE

Robbery Under Arms in the postcard reproduced above is the novel by 'Rolf Boldrewood' (see page 210).

ROBERT LOUIS STEVENSON
1850–1894

and

WILLIAM ERNEST HENLEY
1849–1903

Henley, cripple and minor poet, destined to become a major editor of literary magazines, was a patient in the Edinburgh Infirmary when Stevenson was first introduced to him by Leslie Stephen (1832–1904), editor of the *Cornhill*, in 1875. Neither Henley nor Stevenson had so far published a book, though both had written for magazines.

Having kept them in proof for several months (the 'evil' for which the author returned 'good'), George Grove published Stevenson's essays on John Knox in *Macmillan's Magazine* for September and October 1875. Henley's sonnet sequence, 'Notes on the Firth', appeared in the October number: his *rondeaux* celebrating tobacco were rejected.

Swanston, Lothianburn, Edinburgh, July 1875

Dear Mr. Grove,

Will you allow me to recommend you the accompanying sonnets. They are by Mr. Henley, who wrote the 'Hospital Outlines' in this month's *Cornhill* — poems which have made a great sensation here, where the portraits are easily recognized; and though these have not the same extrinsic interest, they seem to me better as workmanship and more agreeable altogether. Henley is a singularly fine fellow, whose constancy under great trouble is as remarkable as his verse. Let me add that he is not the richest person in the world ; so (should these sonnets suit you for the magazine) an early publication will be of great service to him.

Talking of early publication, and thus not unnaturally thinking of poor John Knox, it occurs to me that I am returning good for evil. And I believe, when you have read the sonnets, you will think so too.

Yours very truly,   ROBERT LOUIS STEVENSON

4 Straiton Place, Portobello, Edinburgh, 3 August 1875

Dear Sir,

Mr. Stevenson has handed me your letter. In reply to it I beg to assure you that William Ernest Henley is by no means a *nom-de-plume*, but the name by which I am, and have been always, known to all those who know me.

I shall be very glad of a proof at your earliest convenience. I am conscious of several little roughnesses in the sonnets which I am anxious to smooth away if I can. I need not say that I shall be grateful for any remarks you may be pleased to make to this end.

I do not know whether it is a usual thing, or whether I am committing a breach of etiquette — if I am, pray excuse me therefor. But it would be most convenient for me to receive at once whatever will in course of time be due to me on account of the sonnets. If you could send it to me, you would oblige me very much.

I am, dear sir, very obediently yours,   W. E. HENLEY

7 September 1875

Your kindly reception of my 'Notes on the Firth' has emboldened me to seek your approbation for the enclosed MS., to which I venture to direct your attention, with the hope that its contents may be found worthy of the place in *Macmillan's Magazine*.

In these songs I have endeavoured to say all the good I

could of Tobacco, a subject that has always seemed to me more deserving than fortunate. With the exception of a little sonnet of Baudelaire's (not one of his best), and a more ambitious little poem by Soulary, I know of no other attempts in the same direction. I have chosen a structure, which, though common enough in French, has not received any attention whatever from English versifiers. I speak of course with all submission, but I am bound to say that, so far as I know, the Rondeau of Voiture and Musset has been seldom, if ever, attempted in English. I hope you will like my own adaptations of it.

I have been so long shut out from life and the world that I have altogether forgotten the tone of the *Magazine*. I trust that in adventuring these songs, I am not going astray.

I have one other remark to make : the songs were written, and are intended to be printed, as a suite, one number explaining the other. If you accept them, therefore, I should like you to accept them *en masse*. As I send them they form part of a book I hope to see one day in print ; my hope is of the vaguest, but I do not want to break with any part of it till I must.

JOHN MORLEY
Lord Morley
1838–1923

Morley's connexion with Macmillans lasted from the 1860s, when he was a freelance journalist, to the first world war, when he was a cabinet minister. One of Alexander and Frederick Macmillan's most valued readers and advisers, he edited both the English Men of Letters series and, for eighteen months in 1883–5, *Macmillan's Magazine*.

The first group of letters belongs to the gestation period of English Men of Letters, as yet unnamed. In the event Froude was diverted from Giraldus Cambrensis to *Bunyan* (1880).

17 Broadwater Down, Tunbridge Wells, 5 October 1877

My dear Macmillan,

. . . Please let me have a dozen more prospectuses.

Froude will write *Giraldus Cambrensis*, he says, if I like. If I insist on some other subject, then he would have to take time to reflect, etc. — but if *Giraldus*, then he could do it easily and speedily. His letter is interesting. I will bring it on Tuesday. I hope I have not done wrong in taking a twelfth-century man : he says it will be pleasant and amusing. Indeed there is some advantage in having one faraway man of this sort. It makes the series look more comprehensive. And Froude's name is very valuable, of course. . . .

The highest respectability and the highest capacity — an impossible union, O my dear Macmillan. But I accept your doctrine, all the same.

Ever yours affectionately,   J. MORLEY

F

Pitfield, Farnham, 2 November 1877

My dear Craik,

On turning the matter over in my mind, and calculating the time which the series will take in the shape of endless correspondence, when the printing begins, I have concluded that I ought to have £250, instead of £200. The £250 from 1 July '78 to 1 July '79 to be set against royalties accruing *after* July '79, *unless* recouped by royalties within the year. That is, you will repay yourselves the second year's advance outside that year as well as inside. The first year's advance to be absolute.

You will have at least four books out by May. . . . The second year, ending July '79, ought to bring eight more. Supposing all to go well, and 5,000 copies to be sold of each, my share would equal £372. I don't believe therefore that you would run much risk of losing the difference between the £400 that you propose, and the £500 that I propose, as my payment for the two years.

In my judgment the title ought to be $\begin{cases} \text{Studies} \\ \text{Sketches of Great} \\ \text{Lives} \end{cases}$

English Authors, or Great English Authors alone, but my preference is for the first, with the word Lives.

Ever yours,   J. M.

Alexander Macmillan was active in seeking contributors to the new series. Having failed to persuade Matthew Arnold to write on Shakespeare* he approached George Eliot (Mrs. George Lewes), who, as he wrote to tell Morley, had invited him to luncheon to discuss the proposal.

7 November 1877

My dear Macmillan,

Your news is good news indeed, and I feel rather ashamed

* Twenty-five years elapsed before a volume on Shakespeare was commissioned from Walter Raleigh (page 250 below).

that you have forestalled me. If Mrs. Lewes won't do it, perhaps Lewes himself would. If you think it desirable that I should write a line to them before your interview, please telegraph to me tomorrow at Tongham, and then I will write so that Lewes has my letter on Friday morning.

You might mention the difficulty of title. I am more and more averse to Men of Letters. To call Bunyan or Burns — to say nothing of Shakespeare or Bacon — by that title is certainly not good. . . .

Ever yours,   J. MORLEY

Of course we could not press Mrs. Lewes for time, but it would be worth much silver and gold to us if she could start the series — say in April. I'm so afraid of all the flatter ones coming first and dulling the impression.

Bedford Street, Covent Garden, 9 November 1877
My dear Morley,

I have just come back from a very pleasant interview with George Eliot. She did not say *no*, and promised to think it over and write us. The scheme evidently interests her. She repeated what Lewes told me was her feeling, that she has a dread of coming forward in her own person and passing judgment on authors, and spoke, as you — or even I — might speak, with aversion of the habit of mind that leads people to pass off as sort of *final utterances* the feelings and thoughts which come to you in reading an author. She quoted a passage from Sainte-Beuve which she thought should be the motto of such a series as we propose. I cannot give you the French — she is to send it — but the effect of it was that the business of a true critic was to appreciate, not *fix the doom* of an author. When you see it I have no doubt you will at once adopt it, and if we can't get her to contribute a book it will be something at least to have a motto from her.

But I am by no means hopeless about the book. Lewes

came with me to the door and said it was a great thing to have got her to consent to think of it. I asked if I might tell you to write to her and she said she would be glad to hear from you. But I think it would be well that we should have our talk on Monday before you do write. My own feeling is that when you write you should name the sum we are willing to give her. It is clear that our *Prima Donna* must be paid on a different scale from the others — whether three or four times we must consider and consult.

Lewes is very friendly but I hardly gathered that he expects to be asked. But I will tell you all that passed when I see you on Monday. We clearly are not *shut out*.

Ever yours,   ALEX. MACMILLAN

George Eliot's quotation from Sainte-Beuve was 'La critique pour moi (comme pour Monsieur Joubert) c'est le plaisir de connaître les esprits, non de les régenter'. The motto was not adopted, nor did George Eliot finally consent to write the book.

Next day Macmillan wrote to say that both Mr. and Mrs. Lewes thought 'English Men of Letters' a good title. 'Also it has come to my mind that Carlyle applies it in his *Hero-Worship* to Johnson, Rousseau and *Burns*.' Morley in the next letter refers to his namesake Henry Morley (1822–94), professor of English literature at University College, London, and a prolific *vulgarisateur*, who edited ten volumes of *English Writers* between 1864 and 1894.

4 Chesham Place, Brighton, 18 November 1877

I think the 20th is the day for the advertisement : so here it is.

I submit as possible titles :

1. Great Men of Letters
2. English Men of Letters
3. Short Books on English Authors
4. Masters of Literature

With any one of them I should be perfectly content —
with preference for 3, and next to 3, and *nearly* equal, I
should like 2. (But it is very like H. Morley.) So choose.

19 November 1877

I am well satisfied with the title as it now stands. You will
find, by the way, that Carlyle in the Hero lecture expressly
says that the Man of Letters is only a hundred years old.
However, it will do well enough.

Morley's official *Life of William Ewart Gladstone* was published
by Macmillans in 1903. His attitude to the Grand Old Man had
changed with the years. When first invited by Alexander Macmillan
to meet Gladstone, J. R. Green and the Dean of St. Paul's at dinner
he had replied:

20 September 1877

I will dine with you on Thursday at the Garrick at seven with
much pleasure.
    N.B. Gladstone has nothing to say to men like you and me
— but it is interesting to see the kind of men whom the
world thinks great. Foolish world !

Four years later, when his second Irish Land Bill was before
parliament, Gladstone paid a call on Macmillan, who wrote to Morley,
'What a man he is! He spoke of the Lords and the Parnellites without
a touch of bitterness. . . .' Morley replied:

19 August 1881

I'm very interested in your account of Gladstone. He is
magnificent, and what I admire as much as anything is the
tact and compromise with which he has dealt with the Lords.
I've never been an *idolater* at that shrine, but I do honour
him at this moment more than I can say.

THOMAS HENRY HUXLEY
1825–1895

Several of Huxley's scientific articles first appeared in *Nature* or in *Macmillan's Magazine*, and the firm published a number of his books from 1866 onwards. The immediate success of John Morley's English Men of Letters, launched in May 1878, led to the following letter. Huxley's 'idea' was no more successful then General Trochu's plan to save beleaguered Paris in 1870: no English Men of Science materialized. Huxley did, however, contribute the volume on David Hume to Morley's series.

Sir Henry Enfield Roscoe (1833–1915), another Macmillan author and contributor to *Nature*, was professor of chemistry at Owens College, Manchester.

4 Marlborough Place, 4 November 1878
My dear Macmillan,

Like Trochu I have an idea — and talking it over with Roscoe at Manchester yesterday he thought it good and helped in developing it.

To wit: a series of small books like John Morley's by various hands (selected by your humble servant as editor — who will do some hisself — and bullied or wheedled into writing) intituled 'English Men of Science'. If you are inclined to think the proposition worth your while, I will come and talk over the thing from a financial point of view in a day or two. Meanwhile here's a draft of a prospectus.

Ever yours very truly,   T. H. HUXLEY

English Men of Science

Among the many peculiarities of the national character, one of the most singular is a certain pride in the assumed incapacity of the English mind for abstract or speculative inquiries. Nevertheless it may be safely affirmed that no modern nation can show a more remarkable muster-roll of great names in philosophy and in physical science ; nor point to more important contributions towards the foundations of the scientific conception of Nature than those made by Englishmen.

It seems desirable to spread the knowledge of this truth beyond the few students of the history of science, and bring the evidence on which it rests within reach of the general public, by the publication of a series of small but carefully written books, each devoted to some one Englishman or small group of Englishmen by whose means one or more branches of science have been notably advanced, and comprising a biography, a statement of the man's work and its relation to earlier, and its influence on later, scientific thought.

There follows a list of thirty-one individual scientists, from Roger Bacon to Charles Darwin, with a suggestion for two composite volumes, one on early Astronomers Royal and one on mathematicians.

HENRY JAMES
1843–1916

Four books by James, including *The American*, had appeared in the
United States before he made his first approach to a London publisher.
George Washburn Smalley (1833–1916) was the chief European
correspondent of the *New York Tribune*.

3 Bolton Street, Piccadilly, 7 August 1877

Dear Sirs,

It was mentioned to me some time since by my friend and
countryman Mr. J. W. Smalley that you had inquired my
address of him with some apparent intention of making a
proposal to me with regard to the simultaneous issue here of
a novel of mine lately published in Boston by Messrs. Osgood
& Co., viz. *The American*. As, in fact, I did not hear from you,
I supposed that you had subsequently decided otherwise : but
the circumstance I mention gives me a certain ground for
myself making you a proposal. I am disposed to collect into
a volume a series of papers published during the last four or
five years in American periodicals (the *North American
Review*, the *Galaxy*, the *Nation*, etc.) upon French writers.
I should like to publish the book in England ; I have taken,
and propose to take, no steps with regard to its appearing in
America. It would consist of some thirteen or fourteen
articles, of various lengths, and would make a volume, I
should say, of about 325 (largely-printed) pages. It would
treat of writers of the day, and I should call it *French Poets
and Novelists*. . . .

Should you feel disposed to undertake the publication of
such a volume as I speak of? I shall be glad to hear what
your inclination may be.

I remain, dear sirs, respectfully yours, HENRY JAMES

Macmillans published *French Poets and Novelists* in February 1878 and *The American* in March 1879. Meanwhile Frederick Macmillan had suggested that James should send his next novel, *The Europeans*, to the editor of *Macmillan's Magazine*.

Ventnor, Isle of Wight, 24 April 1878

My dear Mr. Grove,

Your note has just been forwarded to me here. I shall be very happy to come and see you on Monday next, and give you what information I can about my projected novel, of which Frederick Macmillan spoke to you. I say 'what information I can' for I have not yet the MS. in any state to show. I can, however, tell you definitely what the thing is about and show you some of it some time hence. But I confess frankly that if you broke down in the middle of *The American* I fear that there is a danger of the present story finding little more favour with you. Still, I hasten to add that I think I may claim for it that it is a stronger work than *The American*. As regards the latter I venture to recommend you, since you express a disposition to do so, to have, as they say, another 'try' at it. Perhaps it will go more smoothly. At any rate I will, gladly, call on you on Monday.

Very truly yours,   HENRY JAMES

The Europeans was published not in the magazine but in two volumes in September 1878.

May 1878

Dear Macmillan,

I meant to have written you yesterday that I am very glad you undertake the book. As regards the profits, I am afraid there is not much danger of their being 'enormous', exactly : but even if they are only moderate, it will be a beginning of my appearance before the British Public as a novelist — as *the* novelist of the future, destined to extract from the B.P. eventually (both for himself and his publishers) a colossal fortune ! You shall have the rest of the copy the moment it arrives and proofsheets shall receive the promptest attention. Kind regards in St. John's Wood, and a *bon voyage* for Étretat.

Yours very truly,   H. JAMES

Macmillans published almost all James's books in London between 1878 and 1893, and most of them in New York between 1886 and 1898, but there was no fortune in them for either novelist or publisher.

34 De Vere Gardens, W., 24 March 1890

Dear Macmillan,

The very long novel (*The Tragic Muse*) which, ever since January 1889, I have been contributing to the *Atlantic Monthly* is to terminate there in May. When it was a question of arranging for it two years ago I found it indispensable to meet Houghton, Mifflin's conditions that *they* should publish the book in the U.S. The terms they offered me for the serial were so much better on this condition that I couldn't afford not to agree to them, even though they constituted an implication that such tales as I shall hereafter publish in the *Atlantic* shall also come, as books, to its proprietors. The *Atlantic*, on this basis, is more hospitable and remunerative to me than any other periodical appears anxious to be on any other. I thought it injudicious to appeal to you, as an alternative, for other conditions ; but I have all along taken for granted, not fallaciously, I trust, that in England you will still be glad to issue the book. I have just got the revised copy all ready to send you if you will have it. Will you let me know your ideas about it ? I must frankly add that the book is, I fear, almost formidably long — it is to make (probably) two volumes even in the U.S. At the same time I think it only fair to add that it is, in my opinion — and I believe in those of such 'admirers' as Providence has vouchsafed me — the best of my productions. (This, I suppose, however, will strike you as what 'we all' say.) It is altogether, in subject, a matter of English life.

Ever yours,   HENRY JAMES

Frederick Macmillan replied:

26 March 1890

The commercial result of the last few books we have published for you has been anything but satisfactory. At the same time we like to be your publishers and are anxious to fall in with your wishes about terms so far as we can prudently do so. I propose therefore that, in order to meet your views as to immediate payment, we should pay you 'down' a sum equal to two-thirds of the estimated profits of an edition of 500 copies. I cannot say offhand how much this would come to, but it would not be less than £70.

28 March 1890

My dear Macmillan,
    I thank you for your note and the offer of £70. Don't, however, think my pretensions monstrous if I say that, in spite of what you tell me of the poor success of my recent books, I still do desire to get a larger sum, and have determined to take what steps I can in this direction. These steps I know will carry me away from you, but it comes over me that that is after all better, even with a due and grateful recognition of the readiness you express to go on with me, unprofitable as I am. I say it is 'better', because I had far rather that in these circumstances you should *not* go on with me. I would rather not be published at all than be published and not pay — other people at least. The latter alternative

makes me uncomfortable and the former makes me, of the two, feel least like a failure ; the failure that, at this time of day, it is too humiliating to consent to be without trying, at least, as they say in America, to 'know more about it'. Unless I can put the matter on a more remunerative footing all round I shall give up my English 'market' — heaven save the market ! — and confine myself to my American. But I must experiment a bit first — and to experiment is of course to say farewell to you. Farewell then, my dear Macmillan, with great regret — but with the sustaining cheer of all the links in the chain that remain still unbroken.

Yours ever,   HENRY JAMES

The farewell was not final. James's literary agent persuaded Macmillan to buy a five years' lease of *The Tragic Muse* for £250. At the end of five years the publishers were more than £170 down on the transaction.

In 1903 Macmillans commissioned from James a book on London. He described it as 'romantical-psychological-pictorial-social', but it was never written: nor was the 'longish novel', mentioned in the next letter. The volume of 'Impressions' was *The American Scene* (Chapman & Hall, 1907). The collective — or 'New York' — edition of James's novels was later published in London by Macmillans.

Lamb House, Rye, Sussex, 5 April 1908

My dear Macmillan,

...As for the other and much greater question, the 'London' book, I don't wonder at your inquiry; only do wonder, rather, that some thunderbolt of reprobation hasn't descended on me long before this. I have expected it very often, and crouched and grovelled, burying my head in the sand, whenever I could fancy the faintest distant mutter. How can I tell you coherently, or inspire you with any patience to hear, what a long train of fatality and difficulty and practical deterrence, has attended my connection with that (none the less cherished and unrelinquished) promise. Things kept going damnably against my performance of it, going practically, I mean, and perversely and pertinaciously, from very soon after my making it to you : this frustration and delay took the form of my having to keep as hard as possible at (more or less immediately productive) fiction, which I had near chances to serialize, and which, with my lean ability to do but one good job at once, took all my weeks and months and — I blush red to write the word ! — years, wretched years ! Then came the immense distraction of my going for a year to America — which raised an enormous barrier, that of a different, an opposite association and interest ; and from which I returned saddled, inevitably, with too portentous complications : very good in themselves, but awful from the point of view of buckling down to a book about London and putting it through.

One of these engagements was to begin immediately (immediately, that is, after I had written a great fat book of Impressions, the first of two volumes of such, the second of which will now, however, not appear) the publication of an elaborately revised and retouched and embellished and copiously prefaced and introduced Collective, and *selective*, Edition of my productions, in twenty-four volumes — which I have been putting through, and which has proved a task of the most arduous sort, such as I can't but be glad of, but such as I at the same time wouldn't have had the courage to undertake had I measured all the job was to cost me. It is still going on, my own part of it, though I draw to a close. The beautiful volumes have begun successively to appear in New York — though arrangements for them here have been difficult, complicated and delayed. I mention all this to account for my burdened and tied-up and apparently (in respect to 'London') thankless and perfidious state. The worst is, however, that the Edition represents but half the burden I assumed in respect to New York : I came away pledged to supply two novels for serialization — and even the first of these (with which alone, perhaps, however, I shall be able to get off) has been most inconveniently and disgracefully delayed. The Edition has smothered me, in other words, like an enormous feather-bed — and I have scarce breathed outside of it : indeed either outside or in !

This is my sorry tale, and I scarce expect you to be able to take it for anything but a virtual, though deeply unintentional and most rueful, trifling with your honourable hopes ! The case remains that, all the while, I haven't, for myself, 'gone back' on the idea of the book at all, but have kept it constantly in view, making a great deal of preparation for it. I have been able fortunately to read a great deal (I've even bought a good many books), and roamed and poked and pried about in town when I have had leisure moments on being 'up'. I feel still strongly that I should like to do it ; I feel that having known the subject, having sounded and cared for it, on certain sides, so well and so long, I shall quite have lost one of the opportunities of my life if I don't do it. But there remain the fact that I have absolutely to finish both my Edition and a longish Novel first ; and that I am perfectly conscious of my little right to expect of you more waiting and postponing. If any other idea — by which I mean if any other image of 'attractive' authorship — for getting the book done should hover before you, you certainly owe me no consideration ; and I shouldn't look to you for any but definite notice ! I hope still it won't come to that, and I feel that if I once clear away my Novel (the first to be done — I can manage for the time with that) the ground will be more disencumbered than it has been for a long time, and a good deal of additional reading which I want to put in will have been managed.

Don't answer this on the spot, but let me come to see you the next time I'm in town, when there are various other things I shall be able to say to you that may mitigate a little the disgrace, and still keep alive a little the hope, of yours ever faithfully,   HENRY JAMES

OSCAR WILDE

1854–1900

In 1877 Wilde travelled to Italy and Greece in a party which included Professor Mahaffy and George Macmillan. Two years later Macmillan was a founder-member of the Society for the Promotion of Hellenic Studies.

In spite of encouragement from Macmillan, Wilde did not contribute the proposed volumes to the firm's recently launched Classical Series for Colleges and Schools.

> St. Stephen's Club, Westminster, 22 March 1879
>
> Dear Macmillan,
>
> I was very glad to get your note and to see that the Society is to be set on foot : I have every confidence in its success. . . .
>
> Nothing would please me more than to engage in literary work for your house. I have looked forward to this opporunity for some time.
>
> Herodotos I should like to translate very much indeed — selections, that is — and I feel sure that the wonderful picturesqueness of his writings, as well as the pathos and tenderness of some of his stories, would command a great many readers. It is a work I should enjoy doing, and should engage to have it done by 1 September next.
>
> I do not know how many Greek plays you intend publishing, but I have been working at Euripides a good deal lately and should of all things wish to edit either the *Mad Hercules* or the *Phoenissae*, plays with which I am well acquainted. I think I see what style of editing is required completely. . . .
>
> Believe me, very truly yours,   OSCAR WILDE

In 1887 Cassells invited Wilde to take over the editorship of the *Lady's World*. At the suggestion of Mrs. Craik (Dinah Maria Mulock, 1826–87, wife of the Macmillans' partner George Lillie Craik and author of *John Halifax, Gentleman*) the title was altered to the *Woman's World*: she died suddenly on 12 October.

Wilde reviewed *Ismay's Children*, an anonymous novel by May Hartley, in the *Woman's World* in December 1887, and *Hithersea Mere* by Lady Augusta Noel in January 1888.

16 Tite Street, Chelsea, S.W., October 1887

Dear George,

I am going to make literary criticism one of the features of the *Woman's World*, and to give special prominence to books written by women. Should you care to send me any books of the kind I will see that they are duly noticed, Lady Augusta Noel's novel, for instance, or Mrs. Hartley's last book.

How sad Mrs. Craik's death is — I was very shocked to hear of it, as I had heard from her only a few days before her death.

Believe me, sincerely yours,   OSCAR WILDE

'London Models', the article Wilde sent to J. W. Comyns Carr (1849–1916), editor of the *English Illustrated Magazine*, in 1886, was not printed there until January 1889. The fairy story which he reclaimed from Carr was first published, by David Nutt, in *The Happy Prince and Other Tales* in May 1888.

Coaching Days and Ways, by W. Outram Tristram, was being serialized in the *English Illustrated*.

January 1889

My dear George,

Thank you for your letter and its enclosure, for which I send receipt.

The article was written in March 1886, at Carr's request, and I could not get a proof of it till last June. Finally in November last I wrote to Carr to say that I was going to publish it in my own magazine, and I am afraid that its appearance in the *Eng. Ill.* is entirely due to that terrible threat. For an article written on commission it was certainly kept too long. I am however very pleased that it has been so popular as I hear it is.

My little story of 'The Happy Prince', which perhaps you have read, languished in the MS. chest of the same magazine for eighteen months, but I finally got it back. I fear I must take to writing on Coaching Days! This is the only subject that ensures publication.

Sincerely yours,   OSCAR WILDE

ALBERT VENN DICEY

1835–1922

In 1860 Dicey won the Arnold history prize at Oxford with his essay on *The Privy Council*. Three years later James Bryce won the same prize with *The Holy Roman Empire*. Both essays were published by Messrs. T. & G. Shrimpton in Oxford at the time, and were later reprinted by Macmillans in London.

Private　　　　　　2 Brick Court, Temple, 20 May 1881
Dear Mr. Macmillan,
　　　　　　Essay on the Privy Council
　　I am very glad to accept your offer and put the publication of the second edition of my essay into your hands on the terms you propose. I enclose a copy of my letter to Shrimpton that you may see exactly how matters stand. It would have been a great advantage to me and perhaps no loss to you could I have entered into arrangements with you twenty years ago, instead of with Shrimpton.

　　I am sorry to say that much as I should like to re-touch and expand the essay it is quite impossible for me to do so. My time is too fully occupied for a work which if done satisfactorily would take months, and my knowledge of the subject is less than it was twenty years ago. I shall therefore be able to correct the press but must otherwise leave the essay just as it is. I regret this the less because nothing short of re-writing the whole would turn what I think a not discreditable performance for a young man of twenty-five into the sort of book which I ought to produce at my present time of life. As to shape and type I shall trust to your judgment ; the more nearly you can make it look like B's *Holy*

Roman Empire the better. The essay will at any rate gain credit from its good company.

Since writing the above I have had information on which I can I think rely that Shrimpton, who stated to me on Wednesday 11th that the first edition was sold out, have themselves during the last two months surreptitiously printed additional copies. I should be glad to see you any time next week that we might talk over this affair. I will call some time on Monday or Tuesday between one and three if you are to be found in at those hours.

Yours very truly,   A. V. DICEY

Messrs. Shrimpton & Son, Oxford.
Gentlemen,
                Essay on the Privy Council
I absolutely deny any claim to ownership or copyright in my book on your part and I further decline to accept the proposal made to me by you on Wednesday 11th that the first edition having as you informed me been sold out I should allow you to publish a second in consideration of a payment of £10. I have placed the publication of the second edition in the hands of Messrs. Macmillan & Co.

On one matter of fact you are under a misconception. I did not in 1860 receive £10 or any sum from you but paid you £10 as part of the expense of printing. My only doubt is whether there was not some idea of our sharing the profits of the 500 copies to be printed. On neither part was there any arrangement made or proposed about the publication of further editions.

I registered the essay in my own name years ago at Stationers' Hall.

Yours faithfully,   A. V. DICEY

Dicey, a practising barrister, became Vinerian professor of English law at Oxford in 1882. Macmillans published his lectures on *The Law of the Constitution* (1885) and on *Law and Public Opinion in the Nine-teenth Century* (1905). To the latter work Dicey added a new intro-duction in 1914. Robert Erskine Childers (1870–1922) had a few years earlier espoused the cause of Irish home rule which was ulti-mately to lead to his execution as a traitor. Asquith's Home Rule Bill was passed in September 1914.

24 February 1914

Dear Sir Frederick Macmillan,

Introduction to Law and Opinion

. . . Thank you much for your letter received this morning. I wish I were sure that I could startle the public half as much as I have been startled myself by noting the extraordinary rapid progress of unsystematic socialism. The alarming feature in the case is this : the mass of the country and certainly of the richer classes, are not really inclined towards socialism, but our party system gives for the moment an excessive power to an energetic party who can command a considerable number of votes. I have no belief myself that England will in the long run be converted into a socialistic state. The rich and the educated will somehow or other get the upper hand, but I fear dreadfully long contests and dangerous experiments which may undermine the power of the United Kingdom and possibly ruin the British Empire, that is to say the greatest and freest state which has ever existed.

Yours sincerely,   A. V. DICEY

30 March 1914

I am afraid that in the midst of the present political excite-ment a review of legislation during the last fourteen years will fall flat, still the changes of law and of sentiment since the beginning of this century have been so extraordinary that they ought to excite attention. The last claim of trade unionists that soldiers should never be employed to put down the violence of men on strike would be amusing from its absurdity did it not represent a morbid condition of feeling which may become very dangerous. As to Ireland I am more and more convinced of the truth of the doctrine which I have preached in season and out of season for thirty years, that any plan of Home Rule would be more injurious to England than Irish independence. Every one must see now that if Ireland were as independent as say Belgium, the men of Ulster would probably govern the rest of the country. If any experiment short of independence or, what is far better, the maintenance of the Union with Great Britain is to be tried, I am convinced that colonial independence as in New Zealand is the most hopeful among dangerous experiments ; and in this I am certain from his books that Mr. Childers agrees with me though, why I know not, he gives a reluctant support to the present Home Rule Bill.

THOMAS EDWARD BROWN
1830–1897

The Rev. Thomas Brown, a schoolmaster, best remembered for 'A garden is a lovesome thing, Got wot', contributed a number of racy 'fo'c's'le yarns' in Manx dialect to the *Isle of Man Times*. The first of these, 'Betsy Lee', was subsequently published by Macmillans in 1873, but when a collection of five was mooted seven years later,* George Craik proposed modifications — in the interest of what the poet called 'Methodism and Macmillanism'. The narrator and principal character in these poems, Tom Baynes, is a hard-living, hard-swearing Manx fisherman, a character so close to Brown's heart that he once wrote, 'He simply is I. . . . When I am alone I think and speak to myself always as Tom Baynes.'

Brown wrote to Alexander Macmillan:

34 Clifton College, Bristol, 29 December 1880

Dear Sir,

. . . Mr. Craik wrote to me about my 'poems'. I asked him to mark the passages that *bored* him as being tedious, super-fluous, and flat. No doubt he has been too busy to return to the matter. Meantime I have been cutting out at a great rate. My poor Tom Baynes will now appear in the character of a castrato, more musical, I hope, certainly less formidable, and less vigorous. Somehow I don't seem to care much about him. Tom ought to swear, and that hugely — I have not left him a single oath: he ought to handle scripture with a fine freedom — I have stopped 'his allowance' of texts.

I don't know whether you are familiar with Crabbe's *Tales* : there is one about a poor old sailor who gets 'done to death' by the gentility of an awful sister-in-law and the

* *Fo'c's'le Yarns*, Macmillan, 1881; second edition, 1889.

cowardice of a sneaking brother. My old salt is very nearly in the same case.

Truly yours,   T. E. BROWN

The allusion in the last paragraph above is to 'The Brothers' in George Crabbe's *Tales in Verse* (1812).

In 1886 the publishers Swan Sonnenschein & Co. approached Brown about his poem 'The Doctor', which they had heard of in circumstances related in the next letter. The persons mentioned by Brown are the Rev. J. M. Wilson (1836–1931), another Manxman and Clifton schoolmaster; Professor Friedrich Max Müller (1823–1900), the eminent orientalist and philologist;* William Wetmore Story (1819–95), an American sculptor domiciled in Italy; and Victoria, British Princess Royal, wife of the future Kaiser Friedrich III — distinguished company for Tom Baynes. Brown consulted Macmillans before agreeing to Swan Sonnenschein's terms.

7 October 1886

I had better give you a brief history of this little book. I wrote it about twelve years ago, and it appeared in the *Isle of Man Times* (newspaper), and of course was unknown beyond the island. Then the newspaper people printed me some fifty copies, which I distributed among friends ; and so the whole thing was at an end.

Last year my colleague, Mr. Wilson, read 'The Doctor' to a set of people at the Malaga Hotel. Among these were Professor Max Müller and Mr. Story the sculptor. Mrs. Story wrote to me for a copy, and Professor Max Müller, going on to Venice, met there the Crown Princess of Germany, and read 'The Doctor' to her. She asked for a copy, and I sent her one. Lastly, Professor Max Müller mentions 'The

* Macmillans had published several mathematical textbooks and sermons by Archdeacon Wilson, and also Max Müller's English translation of Kant's *Kritik*, 1881.

Doctor', in terms of extravagant eulogy, in the *Pall Mall* (some nonsense about 'best books', the sort of fussy rubbish the *Pall Mall* occasionally goes in for).

Now there you have all I know. It does seem on the cards that the book might have some sale, but of course I don't forget, nor will you, the Davidian 'Put not your trust in princes' — might we not add 'professors'?

In 1888, when Macmillans wished to reprint *Fo'c's'le Yarns*, Brown stipulated that some of the cuts in the first edition should be restored, to which the publishers agreed. He sent a copy of the private off-print of 'Tommy Big-eyes' from the *Isle of Man Times* (the 'green book') containing the text before emasculation. His 'Cain' is a Methodist preacher suspected of wife-murder. 'Holy Willie's Prayer' is Burns's satire against a self-righteous Kirk elder.

16 November 1888

The first alteration I propose is in *Betsy Lee*. I wish to restore the original motive as given in your 1873 edition. I think this restoration is quite necessary. The toning down of this passage was due to a well meant desire and a modest ambition to get *Betsy Lee* admitted as a 'drawing-room book'. This it signally failed to become, and it must steer out into the open sea of literature. Let it wear its true colours.

The substitutions and insertions in 'Tommy Big-eyes' amount to a considerable addition. The longest insertion, that from the green book, pp. 59–70, is decidedly the most characteristic passage in the poem. I omitted it chiefly, if I remember, at the instance of Mr. Craik, who objected to it, I think, only on the ground of length. Possibly the 'drawing-room' theory came in here too a little. However, I am most desirous to have this passage printed. My 'Cain', without it, is not worked up to anything like the pitch of grotesque horror that I contemplate. What I have in view is the tremendous picture in 'Holy Willie's Prayer' — *longissimo intervallo*, of course, and fairly accommodated, I think, to the chaster ears of our 'very particular' nineteenth century. The Methodist Consistory, with the speeches of the 'Shuperintandin' and Cain is, I submit, above the average of what passes for humour.

ALFRED AUSTIN
1835–1913

Austin had found other publishers for half a dozen volumes of narrative verse and poetical drama, and three novels, before Macmillans
accepted *Savonarola, a Tragedy*, in 1881. The Lord Lytton in the first
of these letters was the poet 'Owen Meredith', son of the Lord Lytton
(Bulwer-Lytton the novelist) mentioned later.

Swinford House, Ashford, Kent, 12 December 1881
My dear Mr. Macmillan,

I enclose a letter which I think will interest you. It is from
Lord Lytton, chiefly on *Savonarola*, but concluding with a
private matter.

I do not know — and I do not ask — how you are 'doing'
with the volume. But I shall be quite prepared to hear, very
indifferently. I think you will find there is some truth in
what I said to you one day, that just as in the early part of the
century Tory reviewers could see no merit in Liberal poets,
so the Liberal reviewers of these days are not very anxious to
recognize, or at least to proclaim, merit in Tory poets. To me
this is a matter of no consequence, but I hope it does not
disappoint you. You have been so kind, and have taken so
much interest in *Savonarola*, that I am sure you are anxious
justice should be done it. One thing, however, you must
allow me to say : your house shall not be a loser, financially,
by any unpopularity or unworthiness of mine.

Believe me, yours very sincerely,   ALFRED AUSTIN

Alexander Macmillan wrote next day that *Savonarola* (which had
been out for two months) had sold 160 copies in England and 23 in
America : 60 copies had been given away. He added :

Your political theory is wholly contrary to my experience. Surely Lord Beaconsfield, the first Lord Lytton and Sir Walter Scott were well known Tories, and this fact did not injure their popularity. Who thinks of, or cares for, Tennyson's opinion on political matters?

Austin replied:

16 December 1881

I cannot help thinking the instances you adduce rather corroborate than shake my theory. Scott was a Tory in Tory days. His fame as a novelist he acquired at first anonymously ; nor was it till late in his career, till he was too notorious to be injured by neglect or depreciation, that his Toryism was made patent. Lord Beaconsfield again was too notorious, as a public man and *member of Parliament*, to be touched in that way. But I can scarcely doubt that *Lothair* and *Endymion* would have been more admired by Liberal critics had the author been a Liberal, and less by Tories had he not been a Tory. The late Lord Lytton began life as a Liberal ; but after he was a Conservative he more than once published anonymously in order to trick the critics whose motives he so well understood. Moreover, I could not mention a man of letters who, in my opinion, despite his notoriety (every successful *novelist* acquires *that*), was so insufficiently appreciated by critics generally as Bulwer-Lytton. He had grave faults of taste and style. But, take him *all round*, was he not the most considerable English man of letters since Scott?

Mr. Tennyson has had what some people would call the sagacity to wrap up his political opinions in lavender, and has never yet cared to seem to be on the losing side. I happen to know that he strongly disapproved of the Bulgarian Atrocity agitation, for he loves his country. But he took precious good care not to irritate anybody by saying so publicly.

All this, of course, is very unimportant, except as a curiosity of human nature, whose foibles always fail and are defeated in the end. An entire generation was robbed of the pleasure of reading Shelley because Tory criticism was in the ascendant, and he was a 'Republican' and an 'Atheist'. I fear the world wags so. Some people are annoyed by it, some shocked, some amused. The last is the proper way of looking at it.

But, again I say, though I may be wrong, I think my theory, and, if I may venture to say so, my facts, throw some light upon the figures you kindly send me. They are not brilliant. But wherever the cause lies, it is mine, and mine only. Do you, however, think it is wise to desist from advertising *Savonarola* altogether? You know best. But I venture to ask the question.

When Tennyson died in 1892, Gladstone being then prime minister, there was no obvious successor to the poet-laureateship. Lord Salisbury's choice in 1896 of Alfred Austin, who had had more success as a Conservative party journalist than as a poet, was much criticized at the time and has found little commendation since. Austin however took his office, as he took his poetry, seriously. He dutifully sent *vers d'occasion* to *The Times*, and was resentful when *Literature* (the forerunner of *The Times Literary Supplement*) reviewed unfavourably his prose story *Lamia's Winter Quarters*.

Sir Francis Jeune (Baron St. Helier, 1843–1905) was a distinguished judge who had been an unsuccessful Conservative parliamentary candidate.

Hotel Bristol, Naples, 28 January 1898

I should like someone — you, if you like, or, if you think it better, Sir Francis Jeune (whom, in that case, you might ask to do so ; but I can see no reason why *you* should not do so, anonymously, of course) — to write some such letter as the enclosed to *Literature*, headed 'The Laureateship and its Duties'. And, if you like, you might perhaps add something to the effect that whether the author of 'Victoria 1837–1897', 'Three Sonnets written in Mid-Channel' and 'Pax Britannica', published the other day in *The Times*, has or has not the note of Tyrtaeus, which its reviewer seems disposed to question, everybody must judge for himself.

Again, I can only say that I have but you to put straight things which many others are continually trying to put crooked. . . .

[Enclosure]

In its review of *Lamia's Winter Quarters*, *Literature* has given fresh and wider currency to the prevailing belief that Poets Laureate are 'compelled by official duty' to write on certain themes, and on certain occasions, whether they feel a spontaneous impulse to do so, or not. It is much to be desired that this misconception of the position and duty of the Laureate should once for all be dispelled. When Southey was appointed to the office, it was well understood that any supposed existing obligation of the kind was to fall into desuetude, and I do not think I am committing any breach of confidence or etiquette in adding that the present Poet Laureate has been heard to say that, on his nomination, it was graciously intimated to him by the Sovereign that he would know when best, and how best, to give expression to national sentiment. I am quite certain, moreover, that he is the last person in the world to write on ceremonial compulsion.

GEORGE BERNARD SHAW

1856–1950

Shaw was a novelist before he became a playwright. His first novel, *Immaturity*, was rejected by seven publishers, Macmillans among them, in 1879–80, and did not finally appear until 1930 when Shaw was his own publisher. Of the other four 'novels of his nonage', *The Irrational Knot, Cashel Byron's Profession* and *An Unsocial Socialist* were successively refused by Macmillans in circumstances fully described by Charles Morgan in *The House of Macmillan*. Morgan also printed the following letter to Daniel Macmillan.

Sir Walter Besant (1836–1901), a prolific novelist, founded the Authors' Society in 1884. The objects of the society included international copyright reform and the protection of 'sweated authors' against rapacious publishers.

4 Whitehall Court, London S.W.1, 11 September 1943

Dear Mr. Macmillan,

I have read the galley slips you sent me concerning myself in Mr. Morgan's history of Macmillans with interest and a very agreeable measure of astonishment.

I had no idea that the reports on novels I submitted were so appreciative. I consider them highly creditable to the firm's readers; for they make it clear that what was wrong was not, as I thought, any failure to spot me as a literary discovery, but the strangeness at that time of my valuations. In fact they thought more of my jejune prentice work than I did myself; for I really hated those five novels, having drudged through them like any other industrious apprentice because there was nothing else I could or would do. That in spite of their disagreeableness they somehow induced readers rash enough to begin them to go on to the end and resent that experience seems to me now a proof that I was a born master of the pen. But the novel was not my proper medium. I wrote novels because everybody did so then; and the theatre, my rightful kingdom, was outside literature. The coterie theatres in which I first reached the public as a playwright did not then exist.

But of course I did not understand all this at the time. My recollection, until your letter arrived, was far less encouraging. I began, not very wisely, by calling on all the publishers in person to see what they were like; and they did not like me. I did not like myself enough to blame them. I was young (23), raw, Irish from Dublin, and Bohemian without being in the least convivial or self-indulgent, deeply diffident inside and consequently brazen outside, and so utterly devoid of reverence that a phrenologist whom I asked what my bump of veneration was like replied 'Why, it's a hole!' Altogether a discordant personality in the eyes of the elderly great publishers of those days, a now extinct species. As I had a considerable aesthetic culture, and the English governing classes, of whom I knew only what I had picked up from Thackeray and Trollope, had none, they were barbarians to me; and I was to them a complete outsider. I was in fact outside the political world until I had written the first three of my novels; and when I came in I came in as a Marxist, a phenomenon then inconceivable even to Mill, Morley, Dilke, Auberon Herbert, the *Fortnightly* reviewers, the Positivists, the Darwinians, and the rest of the Agnostic Republicans who represented the extreme Left of the most advanced pioneers in the eighties of the last century. The Transvaluation of Values in which I was an obscure pioneer can hardly be imagined nowadays by people under seventy. I was a Nietzschean and an Ibsenist before I had ever heard of Nietzsche or Ibsen.

In view of all this you will see that Macmillans were very much ahead of the other publishers (I tried them all) in recognizing my talent. They corresponded with me a little;

and George Macmillan tried to soften my rejection by Alexander, who didn't like me personally, by sending me a long report by Morley, who turned me down as a victim of undigested Ruskin, of whom I had read little or nothing. Meredith turned me down for Chatto* without extenuating circumstances. Blackwood accepted my first novel; but afterwards renegued, to the distress of his oldest reader. Smith, Elder were polite and asked to see future efforts. None of the rest would have anything to say to me; and even those who gave some attention to my first attempt found its successors more and more impossible. When William Archer made Stevenson read *Cashel Byron's Profession*, and he and Henley applauded it, Bentley, who had refused it, sent for it urgently, and was furious because it was no longer at his disposal; but that was after I had given up novel writing, having designed a mighty work which I found myself too ignorant to finish; so I let its opening section go as *An Unsocial Socialist*. The novels, printed as padding in socialist magazines, got pirated in America; and when I, being ashamed of them, tried to suppress them, they broke out in spite of me as persistently as they had suppressed themselves before.

Macmillan's attention and George's kindly civility certainly made a difference to me. There are so many amateurs sending in crude MSS. to publishers and managers that no beginner can be sure that he is not one of the hopeless failures until his work is accepted, or he has had at least some response indicating that he is not quite out of the question. If Macmillan had simply declined with thanks like nearly all the rest, I should have had to set my teeth still closer.

I am now one of the few who personally remember the Grand Old Men of the publishing world of that day: Alexander Macmillan, Longmans and Bentley. They were so powerful that they held the booksellers in abject subjection, and were denounced by Walter Besant and his newly

* Actually Chapman & Hall.

organized Society of Authors as remorseless sharks. When
they died and were succeeded by their sons, the hereditary
system did not always work as well as it did in Bedford
Street; and the booksellers got the upper hand. John
Murray's Byronic prestige was so select that I did not dream
of trying him until years later, when I was an author of some
note and had already helped to bankrupt three publishers. I
offered him *Man and Superman*. He refused in a letter which
really touched me. He said he was old-fashioned and perhaps
a bit behind the times ; but he could not see any intention in
my book but to wound, irritate and upset all established
constitutional opinion, and therefore could not take the
responsibility of publishing it. By that time I could command sufficient capital to finance my books and enter into
direct friendly relations with the printers (this began my
very pleasant relations with Clarks of Edinburgh). I took
matters into my own hands and, like Herbert Spencer and
Ruskin, manufactured my books myself, and induced
Constables to take me 'on commission'.

Walter Besant never understood that publishing, like
insurance and turf bookmaking, is a gamble, with the
important difference that whereas an insurer can employ
an actuary who will tell him the odds at which chance
becomes mathematical certainty, and a bookmaker who bets
against every horse can lose on one only and is being
supplanted by the tote, the publisher has to take chances
which are incalculable, and must therefore play with all the
advantages he can get, leaving the author to take care of
himself. Besant assumed that a successful book ought to pay
for itself only, not knowing that it has to pay for several
others which, though they keep the shop open, barely repay
the overhead and the cost of their manufacture and sometimes lose even that. A loss of 100 per cent on the swings
makes a large hole in a profit of 300 per cent on the round-
abouts. If both authors and publishers understood this there
would be much less friction in their dealings. But the

G

publisher often knows everything about publishing practice and nothing about its economic theory, whilst the author as a rule knows nothing about either, and is constitutionally unfit to conduct his own business. I served for ten years on the Society's committee, and know the ropes pretty well.

Faithfully,   G. BERNARD SHAW

What extract from Shaw Macmillans wished to include in what schoolbook for India history does not record. But this postcard is characteristic.

Ayot St. Lawrence, Herts, 8 June 1931

Your TM/GJH/MFE dated 27 April, which arrived when I was on the continent, has only just come under my notice.

I have the strongest objection to the association in the infant mind of my name and work with school lessons. I have always refused to sanction the insertion of samples in school books. Why should I make my name loathed in India as Shakespear's is loathed in secondarily educated England?

Please don't.   G. BERNARD SHAW

JOSEPH HENRY SHORTHOUSE

1834–1903

A chemical manufacturer and a Quaker turned Anglican, Shorthouse took ten years to write *John Inglesant*. Having failed to find a publisher, he had the book privately printed in Birmingham in 1880. Macmillans accepted it somewhat unenthusiastically, on the recommendation of Mrs. Humphry Ward, and it was published anonymously in two volumes in the spring of 1881.

Lansdowne, Edgbaston, 20 January 1881

Dear Sir,

Mr. A. H. Johnson of All Souls College Oxford tells me that Mrs. T. H. Ward of Oxford has spoken to you about a philosophical romance of which I have printed one hundred copies for private distribution and that you have kindly expressed a wish to see the book. I have told Messrs. Cornish of Birmingham to send you the last copy they have (I have only two or three left myself), which I hope you will receive safely.

My chief desire is to get the book published *as it is*. I have not adopted the form and manner of the book without consideration and the book as it stands with all its peculiarities is just what I intended it to be : to alter it therefore and to turn it into something quite different (such as an ordinary romance) would be to render useless all the labour I have expended upon it : and would deprive it of its sole claim to public notice.

Of course there are several passages especially in the earlier part which might be altered to advantage, but even there the peculiarities are not without intention.

I am, sir, yours sincerely,   J. HENRY SHORTHOUSE

As a novel of ecclesiastical and political intrigue in the England of the Stuarts and the Italy of Popes Innocent X and XI, *John Inglesant* was apt to the controversies arising out of the Vatican decrees of 1870, controversies in which Gladstone, Cardinal Manning (1808–92) and Lord Acton (1834–1902) were prominently involved. It became an immediate best-seller. Acton's opinion of the book is expressed at length in *Letters of Lord Acton to Mary Gladstone* (1904). In August 1881 Macmillan wrote to John Morley:

Gladstone has just been in, full of force and brightness. He came to thank me for sending him *John Inglesant*, which he likes much, seeing its defects. He said laughing that it appealed to many of his weaknesses.

Some months later Manning wrote to Macmillan:

I am writing as a literary critic, not as a Catholic inquisitor. In the latter office I should, of course, burn the book and Mr. Shorthouse. Happily I have no need or duty to do so, and I wish him long life to give us many more books.

Dr. Alfred Barry (1826–1910) was a canon of Westminster, and later primate of Australia. The *Month* reviewed *John Inglesant*, together with Wilkie Collins's *The Black Robe*, under the title 'A Brace of Anti-Jesuit Novels' in April 1882. John Bigelow (1817–1911), American journalist, published in 1882 a study of Miguel de Molinos, the Spanish divine who was convicted of heresy by the Inquisition in Rome in 1687.

29 May 1882

My dear Mr. Macmillan,
 ... Mrs. Talbot told me of Lord Acton writing about *John Inglesant* and I am greatly obliged by a sight of his

letter. His admissions respecting the Jesuits and Romanists are very candid and valuable. He seems to misunderstand the character of the book and to have read it, as he says, hastily. His assertion as to confusion of dates is not denied : it was intentional. I return his letter, also Miss Gladstone's, as you may want to see the former before sending it back. I have written to Miss Gladstone to clear the book of some misunderstanding in *her* estimate of it. . . . I have *not* the least objection to Lord Acton or any one else printing anything about *J. I.* Indeed I had much rather they *did* print what they have to say, as in that case I am not bound to answer them. Most of Lord Acton's objections are in direct variance with Dr. Barry and the Jesuit in the *Month*.

The gentleman whose letter I showed you from New York is Mr. John Bigelow. I have received his monograph on *Molinos the Quietist*. It is very full and interesting, fully bears out the view I take, and is very curious as coming out almost at the same moment independently. He quotes three pages of *J.I.* (the last three) in entirety, beginning thus :

'Since the preceding pages were in type the author's attention has been directed to a recent English publication of rare interest and merit, entitled *John Inglesant, a Romance*, in which Molinos, doubtless for the first time, figures as a part of the machinery of a work of fiction. *John Inglesant* is a "philosophical romance" . . . of Molinos and his martyrdom. The author takes substantially the same view that is presented in these pages.'

. . . We have been talking about you and Mr. Macmillan and all your kindness. We lunched one day at Oxford with the daughters of the Archbishop of Dublin. They said their father always expressed the highest opinion of and regard for you. You may be well aware of this, but it is not unpleasant to hear such things incidentally through strangers.

Pray give our kindest regards to Mrs. Macmillan and to all your circle. *All* remain most pleasurably in our memory.

Yours very sincerely,   J. HENRY SHORTHOUSE

FRANCIS MARION CRAWFORD
1854–1909

Between 1882 and the time of his death Marion Crawford, an American living in Italy, entrusted all but three of his forty novels to Macmillans in London,* and all but five to Macmillans in New York. These included *Zoroaster* (1885), *A Tale of a Lonely Parish* (1886) and the two sequels to *Saracinesca* — *Sant'Ilario* (1889) and *Don Orsino* (1892). *Saracinesca* (spelt *Sarracinesca* when serialized in *Blackwood's Magazine*) was published as a three-decker by *Blackwood's* in 1887, and by Macmillans in New York and in the colonies in the same year.

Macmillan's Colonial Library was a new venture — the first of many such 'libraries' — resulting from Maurice Macmillan's discovery, on a visit to India and Australasia in 1884–5, that the colonies were starved of new books at cheap prices unless these were illegally imported from America. Authors were at first offered a lump sum, ranging from £10 to £40, for colonial rights. Later, under pressure from Crawford, Hardy and others, the publishers paid a royalty of 3*d* or 4*d* a copy on books priced at 2*s* 6*d* in wrappers or 3*s* 6*d* in cloth. Four of Crawford's novels appeared in the Colonial Library in its first year, 1886. No opera by Gounod based on *Zoroaster* is on record.

Villa de Renzis, Sant'Agnello di Sorrento,
8 January 1886

My dear Sir,

I received last night your note of the 4th inst. in which you speak of an experiment in publishing cheap editions for the colonies, and I hasten to answer that I am ready to do all I can to further the scheme so far as my own books are concerned.

---

* For their rejection of *To Leeward* see p. 276.

I think you will allow that, if the publications prove remunerative, it will be fair to pay a certain percentage on the copies sold. I do not mean in the first instance, but later, when the plan is working well. Therefore I think that this first arrangement ought not to be regarded as a precedent from which there is to be no deviation. From personal knowledge I am aware that a very large sale might be anticipated in India from a good book published at one rupee, and if you can publish at 12 annas (about 1s 6d) a volume like an English shilling edition, you would catch the whole Eurasian (half-caste) population, who read greedily. I once printed and published a small Annual in the office of my newspaper at Allahabad, containing a few Christmas stories. I sold it at 8 annas, about 1 shilling, and I disposed of 500 copies in Allahabad alone in about a fortnight. The cry in India is for cheap books, especially among the Eurasians.

As regards the *Lonely Parish*, I am quite willing to give you the publication of it in the colonies for £40, the price Tauchnitz has paid for each of my last books. You will soon know whether the sales are really important and whether you can afford, for another book, to pay a percentage. Dentu in Paris gives me £5 per the thousand for the French editions. I have not yet written to Tauchnitz about the *Lonely Parish*.

I may say here that I dispatched the last proofs on the 26th ult., registered. I trust they reached you safely. I made the alterations in the story told by Mr. Booley, as you suggested, and I think it now reads without inconsistencies....

I feel that I ought now to tell you the fate of the long novel of which I spoke some time ago, since the negotiations are practically concluded. The book is intended to be the first of three, giving the history of a Roman family from 1865 to the present day. This first novel is called *Sarracinesca*, and will shortly appear in *Blackwood's Magazine*. The arrangement includes also the English publication. I never thought of offering it to you for your magazine, as it seemed too long and was not planned originally for serial publication. Moreover, the *Lonely Parish* being intended for you, I could not offer you two books at once. There is no arrangement, however, for the two novels which are to form the sequel, as Mr. Blackwood did not wish to bind himself to publish what was not yet written. *Sarracinesca*, however, may form one of your colonial series, if you like it well enough. As it has to run about a year (290 pages of *Blackwood*) its appearance will not interfere with the sale of the *Lonely Parish*. I am still very anxious to write a serial for *Macmillan's Magazine*, and though I am bound to the *Atlantic Monthly* for a serial novel, I will send my next MS. to you first, on the understanding that if it does not answer for you, the *Atlantic* shall have it.

I am sure you will understand the position in which I stand to Mr. Blackwood, and that you will bear me no ill will on account of *Sarracinesca*. Perhaps I write too many short books, and it might be more advantageous to us both to produce the old-fashioned 1,000-page three-volume novel. But I do not feel equal to the task of sustaining the interest so long, in the way the interest should be sustained. It is a mystery to me that George Eliot's latest novels should have had so great a success, when I compare *Daniel Deronda* with *Adam Bede*.

It will interest you to hear that negotiations are being made with M. Ch. Gounod for writing an opera founded upon *Zoroaster*. I have sketched the libretto. What do you think of attempting an English version as a prose drama? In jotting down the *points* for the stage it struck me that the thing might be done.

I fear I have trespassed upon your time in this long letter. Let me wish you all manner of good and pleasant things for the New Year, and believe me, very truly yours,

F. MARION CRAWFORD

MALCOLM KINGSLEY MACMILLAN
1853–1889

This Malcolm Macmillan, eldest son of Alexander and godchild of Charles Kingsley, was trained in the firm but, owing to ill health, played little part in its activities. He disappeared (and was presumed to have died), at the age of thirty-six, walking on Mount Olympus.

The following letters* illustrate Malcolm's enthusiasm for historical fiction. (Sir) Julian Corbett (1854–1922), the naval historian, to whom the first extract is addressed, had been at school with Malcolm. His novel, *The Fall of Asgard*, which he had submitted without avowing the authorship, had recently been accepted by Macmillans.

Bedford Street, Covent Garden, 14 January 1886

I think that you are quite right not to let your pen grow rusty. But perhaps in the meantime it might be well to try your hand at some *short* story. I say this diffidently, because it is not always in the same writer's power to do long and short stories with equal ease. It struck me that perhaps, if you go out to the Rockies next summer, you might take that as the scene of your next large effort.

You could not do better than read Scott and Dickens. In Scott I would attend chiefly to the pictures of localities as they are determined by and determine the conditions of life in various classes, i.e. the Scotch and homely element, *Guy Mannering, Redgauntlet, Heart of Midlothian, Old Mortality* (the grandest of all in a way!) and the *Antiquary*. This is the truly *epic* quality of Scott, this living presentation of inhabited places. The dialogue in the mediaeval stories is not a good model. For gasconading dash and movement Dumas

* The text is taken from *Selected Letters of Malcolm Kingsley Macmillan*, London, privately printed, 1893.

is, I think, the great example. In Dickens the easy humour of the road scenes in *Pickwick*, the player-people in *Nickleby*, etc., is irreproachable and unmatched. Also the careful descriptive writing of some of his later essays (*Uncommercial*, *Reprinted Pieces*, especially 'A Plated Article') and Christmas or holiday tales is a specimen of the absolutely finished and masterly in literature.

You should, of course, re-read *Don Quixote* and *Gil Blas*.

Of early French romances I know little. I hope I shall some day. But I am sure you are right to read them for poetry of nature-feeling combined with adventurous and chivalrous spirit.

But as far as *modern fiction* is concerned (whose *earliest* origin is the *picaresque* or scamp novel), the rough outlines I indicate are a (badly-expressed) result of my specialized study so far. For the profound and moving Balzac (however unpleasant) cannot be neglected. *Eugénie Grandet*, *Père Goriot*, *Recherche de l'Absolu* and *Cousin Pons* are four which I suggest.

The next letter is to Louis Dyer, who married Malcolm's sister Margaret. Macmillans published Crawford's twelfth novel, *Greifenstein*, in 1889; Malcolm Macmillan's one book, *Dagonet the Jester*, a short medieval romance, had appeared anonymously three years earlier. *Ben Hur*, by the American Lew Wallace (1827–1905), had been a best-seller, not from Macmillans, in 1880.

Villa Crawford, Sant' Agnello di Sorrento,
19 February 1889

I am staying here with Marion Crawford and his wife. To think that he is only thirty-four, two years younger than I am, and has accomplished what he has! His last thing, *Greifenstein*, is a startling tragedy, and has excellent scenes of German student-life, more vivid and elaborate than

anything he has yet written. They are a very happy couple;
and he is building in tufa and basalt, contriving towers,
kitchens, laundries, terraces and loggias, like a feudal baron
— a Western settler. . . . He has two children and a huge
Danish bloodhound. We quite overhang the sea. This coast
is a perfect paradise. If one could combine the Langada Pass
with the orange-groves of Jaffa one could not even then quite
get it. The Crawfords are making me read *Ben Hur*, which,
by its faithful realism, has brought back Syria and Egypt,
and given me *la nostalgie de l'Orient*. Only Gautier was
literally born in India.

JOHN DUKE COLERIDGE
Lord Coleridge
1820–1894

Lord Coleridge, great-nephew of Samuel Taylor Coleridge, was Lord Chief Justice when Alexander Macmillan invited him in 1888 to contribute an introduction to a new complete edition of the poems of Wordsworth. Coleridge refers to the *Memoirs of William Wordsworth* (1851) by the poet's nephew Christopher (1807–85), bishop of Lincoln, and to F. W. H. Myers's volume on *Wordsworth* (1881) in English Men of Letters.

Judge's Lodgings, Stafford, 15 March 1888

My dear Sir,

I cannot but be gratified at the wish expressed in your letter which reached me here today. But to begin with I am a very slow writer and have scarcely any time at my disposal, and next, although few living men I suppose have read Wordsworth more constantly and thoroughly than I have, yet I will frankly own that I never *could* read Bishop Wordsworth's memoir ; and of the few facts of his uneventful life I have a most imperfect knowledge — of course no man's writing ever *quite* satisfies the independent judgment of another — but Mr. Myers's little book in John Morley's series seems to me quite admirable. May I suggest him to you? I am afraid really that I should make a hash of it and that my hash would be a long time cooking.

Faithfully yours,   COLERIDGE

Alexander Macmillan's anecdote, in his reply, concerns Julius Charles Hare (1795–1855), archdeacon of Lewes; William Whewell

(1794–1866), Master of Trinity College, Cambridge; and Louis Claude Baudry (1794–1852), a Paris publisher who, though Wordsworth called him a 'moral pirate', did much to popularize English literature on the Continent. Lord Coleridge resisted this further appeal, and Macmillans' edition of Wordsworth appeared with an introduction by John Morley.

16 March 1888

Dear Lord Coleridge,

I hope you will forgive my pertinacity, but I am very reluctant to abandon the hope of getting your name connected with our edition of Wordsworth. I am afraid that I gave you an idea of a more extensive essay than we really want. A dozen pages would be quite enough. An elaborate estimate of his works would be quite out of place in what we wish to put on the market as a cheap and popular edition. You must have known him personally. I saw him once and had an hour's talk with him, and he read some of his sonnets. His way of reading was so characteristic of his noble simplicity. Archdeacon Hare had written to Wordsworth who was staying at Trinity Lodge with Dr. Whewell suggesting his calling on my brother to whom Hare had been (I may say) paternally kind. We were two young Scotchmen just beginning a small bookselling business. Wordsworth at once began, on his first visit, on his early feeling for Scotland, and told us that the *Excursion* was meant to exhibit the *Spiritualities* of Scotland, the *Humanities* having already been most admirably done — its loves, its social joys, etc. But he thought the deep spiritual nature had never been given. I wonder if this could suggest anything to you !

He told us a story which if it does not — I hope it will — inspire you to write, will at least amuse you. He had recently had a letter from Baudry the French publisher asking him for a little sketch of his life to be prefixed to an edition of his works — pirated of course — which they were about to print and publish. Wordsworth was naturally indignant at laws that left men free to *steal* the money results of other men's brainwork. But he was also amused at the form Baudry's proposal took. 'You need not bother too much about detailed *accuracy*. *Piquancy* is our main object.' He seemed greatly to enjoy this idea.

I hope that you will see your way to a short sketch of Wordsworth, personal and poetical, for our edition. Pray say you will.

Most respectfully yours,   ALEXANDER MACMILLAN

SIR EDMUND WILLIAM GOSSE

1849–1928

Gosse was an editor in a wide field, and a Sunday newspaper critic. His edition of *The Works of Thomas Gray*, in four volumes, was prepared for publication in 1884. Armstrong & Son of New York asked that Gosse should add a brief biographical introduction. 'If the book appears without one', George Macmillan wrote to Gosse, 'Armstrong has reason to believe that it will be "slated" in the American press by certain critics who are worrying him now, apparently in the hope of being employed to write such an introduction.'

> 29, Delamere Terrace, Westbourne Square, W.,
> 16 October 1884

Dear Macmillan,

I am extremely unwilling to disoblige you in any way, but you are asking me to do a thing the nature of which you have not realized. To write the biographical sketch you speak of would necessitate the cancelling of the elaborate bibliographical preface which already exists, would necessitate the entire breaking up and reprinting of the first volume, which is complete, and revision of references throughout.

But in any case I should think the proposal to spoil a book which has been conscientiously made as good as possible, merely in order to save the book from being 'slated', an ignoble one. If the critics to whom Mr. Armstrong refers are capable of attacking a book for reasons so inconceivably mean as those he suggests, then their criticism can be of no slightest value, even for the moment, to any being.

I feel sure, when you reflect upon it, and especially when you glance at the first volume as it at present stands, that you will agree with me that the sacrifice Mr. Armstrong proposes is impossible, and would be as undignified for you as for me.

Believe me, yours truly,   EDMUND GOSSE

In 1885 Gosse sent Macmillans a short novel, ostensibly by an un-named friend. In his report Malcolm Kingsley Macmillan described it as a story 'about the jilting of a young Baptist minister's daughter by a young Government clerk aristocratically connected. . . . [The writer] is evidently penetrated through and through with the bitterness of non-conformity, and loses consequently his artistic self-control when he comes to represent the fashionable and prelatical side of things. His solecisms are frequent and extreme. . . .' The novel was, however, accepted for serialization.

13 August 1885

My dear Macmillan,

I have to acknowledge a very obliging letter from your cousin on the subject of a MS. entitled *An Unequal Yoke*. I have placed this letter before the author of the story, and he accepts with many thanks the offer you make of £30 now for its use on occasion in either of the magazines you publish. The money may be paid to my account.

The author of *An Unequal Yoke* is further very much indebted to you for sending him your reader's most flattering and encouraging opinion on the story. It will certainly, he thinks, persuade him to make a bolder attempt on a larger canvas. He retains the criticism, in order that, when the story is eventually submitted to him in proof, he may correct the expressions objected to.

Believe me to be very faithfully and mysteriously yours,

EDMUND GOSSE

The story was printed anonymously in the *English Illustrated Magazine*, April–June 1886. The authorship seems never to have been publicly avowed, nor was the story published in volume form. Gosse was to paint non-conformity more boldly on a larger canvas with *Father and Son* (Heinemann 1907), his one durable work.

Board of Trade, S.W., 3 June 1886

I want to ask you whether you will not publish my story *The Unequal Yoke* as a single-volume novel. I must tell you that I am very strongly urged to ask you by Andrew Lang, who guessed the authorship, and who is good enough to express a great deal of interest in the little story. He says I ought to press you to give it permanent form, and of course there are few men whose good word for a work is so well worth having just now as his. He told me to quote him to you as a reader who believed it would be a success.

Perhaps you may feel that you could venture without risk on such an adventure, as you have nothing to pay to the author, and as it would be no great expense to put the pages up in type. If you did do this, I should still be anonymous, and I should dedicate the book to Henry James, which would add a touch of mystification.

'ROLF BOLDREWOOD'
Thomas Alexander Browne
1826–1915

Browne was a police magistrate in New South Wales. His first novel, *Ups and Downs*, also called *The Squatter's Dream*, was serialized in the *Australian Town and Country Journal*. The magazine's editor, (Sir) John Henniker Heaton (1848–1914), later the architect of Imperial penny postage, sold the book rights to the London firm of S. W. Silver & Co., who had offices in Sydney, Melbourne and Adelaide, and who published a yellowback edition in 1878.

Robbery under Arms, an Australian classic, was serialized in the *Sydney Mail* in 1886, and published by Remington & Co. in three volumes in 1888: Gladstone found it 'of much interest and conspicuous talent' (see the postcard reproduced on p. 157). Next year Macmillans put it into their 3s 6d series and their Colonial Library. In 1890 Macmillans published *The Miner's Right* and *A Colonial Reformer* as three-deckers.

Captain Swift was a 'comedy-drama' by Charles Haddon Chambers (1860–1921). R. J. Jeffray acted as Browne's London agent.

Albury, New South Wales, 12 December 1889

Dear Sirs,

I am in receipt of your general statement of account of sales of *Robbery under Arms* which for the time stated (May 1889 to 30 June 1889) appears satisfactory. I trust, however, that sales will increase, particularly of the English 3s 6d edition.

The booksellers in the country complain very much that they cannot be supplied in sufficient quantities so that customers go away disappointed. One bookseller here has the names of nearly forty people on his list for copies, and has been unable up to this time to get a supply.

I am not aware of the name of your agents in Melbourne or Sydney. In the former city George Robertson & Co. would be the best firm; and in Sydney, Turner & Henderson, Hunter Street. The demand in Australia generally is large, and I should think would increase and remain steady. In Bathurst I was told that fifty copies were sold in two hours.

From New Zealand and Queensland, indeed from every part of Australia, from Lord Rosebery in England (a perfect stranger), I have received complimentary letters and newspaper notices. There has not been *one* uncomplimentary colonial review; and in England the *Saturday Review* was the *only one* which attempted a sneering and depreciatory tone. For this reason, if proper arrangements were made, I think at least three to five thousand copies might be sent to Melbourne and Sydney. It discourages readers, and hurts the sale of the book, when they are put off, as has been the case to a great extent.

I have given permission to Mr. Dampier, of the Melbourne Alexandra Theatre, to dramatize the book. It will serve as an advertisement, and should it have anything like the run which *Captain Swift* had will tend to increase the sale notably.

Inquiries are being made as to my first published work, *The Squatter's Dream, or Ups and Downs....* It went through a 4,000 edition and is now out of print. The copyright is now in my hands and I thought of having another edition printed when *The Miner's Rights* and *A Colonial Reformer* (two books which I sent to Mr. Jeffray) had come out.

I remain, dear sirs, yours faithfully,   T. A. BROWNE

With the expansion of the oversea book-trade that followed the reform of colonial copyright Silver & Co. sold their interest in *The*

Squatter's Dream to Edward Augustus Petherick (1847–1917), an Australian who ran an agency in London for the export of colonial editions. In 1890 Petherick negotiated the novel's inclusion in Macmillans' list: eventually Macmillans bought out Petherick's 'alleged rights'. Browne's *Nevermore*, after serialization in the Sydney *Centennial Review*, was published by Macmillan in 1892.

25 August 1890

I saw the announcement of *The Squatter's Dream* being ready for publication in the July number of the *Century*, I think, and intended to write or telegraph to you that Mr. Petherick had nothing to do with the copyright, and from something Mr. Jeffray wrote me I fancied he had been asserting some sort of claim. He has, as far as I know, *none whatever*, and I trust therefore that you will hold over any royalty or other profits accruing from the sale of it until the matter is definitely settled. I sent you an attested copy of Mr. Heaton's letter, in which, in 1887, he transferred *all the right, title and interest* to me. He was not empowered to do more than procure and arrange for its publication by a London publisher, and certainly was not empowered to sell or dispose of the copyright.

Now, as the book has been printed, the sale must go on, but I don't understand under what condition it has been printed.

There was another reason why I would rather not have had it published at present, which is that Silver & Co. rather mutilated the original work and altered the dénouement without my permission. Before it was republished I intended sending home a revised and corrected edition. . . .

The Miner's Right is selling very well in the colonies, many people preferring it to *Robbery under Arms*. The local bookstall keeper here told me that he had been informed by a leading bookseller in Sydney, from whom he purchases, that it was not now to be procured in Melbourne or Sydney.

Kipling paid a brief visit to Australia three months *after* the date of the next letter. He learned that his *Plain Tales from the Hills* had been banned from the Melbourne public library for its impropriety, and he was invited, satirically perhaps, to report the Melbourne Cup for a local newspaper. A 'waler' was a horse from New South Wales.

20 July 1891

I have just been reading your edition of *The Light that Failed*. In my humble opinion Mr. Rudyard Kipling is the strongest and most original writer in his own department since Dickens. That being so, he should not write about matters Australian, in which land he has (I take it) never set foot.

It's a pity when charming writers 'talk of things that they don't understand'. In *Plain Tales from the Hills* there is a short story about a 'waler' racehorse called Shackles and an impossible Melbourne jockey. In it he speaks of the 'Maribyrnong Plate' (a *two-year-old* race) as a *dangerous steeplechase* with *jarrah* logs for jumps — the which would have to be brought from Western Australia, 2,000 miles or so! He confuses the 'smash' which so affected the boy's nerves with that of the Caulfield Cup, *also a flat race*. However, this mistake apart, I have nothing but sincere admiration for him, prose and verse.

At the end of 1893 Browne dispatched to Macmillans another novel, *The Modern Buccaneer*, which they duly published.

3 January 1894

The scene is laid chiefly in the South Sea Islands, Norfolk Island and Sydney. With all deference to Mr. R. L. Stevenson, with whom in the matter of style I do not presume to compete, I think my tale will be found more generally interesting to all classes of readers. The incidents are strong and true to life, the characters numerous, varied and more or less original.

I have read *The Wrecker* as well as *Island Nights' Entertainments*, which has the advantage of *very* fine illustrations, and came out after I was nearly through my book. But I do not recede from my position. The public will, of course, deliver their verdict and by it I must abide.

GEORGE EDWARD BRETT

1827–1890

Brett, an Englishman with publishing experience in London, was manager of Macmillans' New York branch from its beginning in 1869 until the year of his death. His son and grandson, George Platt Brett senior and junior, both United States citizens, became successive presidents of The Macmillan Company, New York, founded in 1896.

Macmillans in London failed to buy the English rights in *Robert Elsmere* by Mrs. Humphry Ward (1851–1920), a novel which had a great but unforeseen success in the summer of 1888. They did, however, secure the American and colonial rights. Their tardiness in responding to Brett's orders for reprints of the $1.25 edition, and to his suggestion of a cheap paperback edition, allowed time for two piratical editions at 15 cents to flood the United States and Canadian markets.

Macmillan & Co., 112 Fourth Avenue, New York.
17 August 1888

Dear Mr. Frederick,

There is one general observation which this case of *Robert Elsmere* affords us the opportunity of making and it is well for us if the young men at Bedford Street would take it earnestly to heart, and that is that the Americans as a nation are extremely wide awake to their own interests and if you seek to compete with them you must be equally wide awake and must not allow a moment to be lost between the thought and the carrying it out in action. It is quite true that they did not dream of handling *Elsmere* until we pointed it out to them but having determined upon it the work has been carried through with a vim which we might equal but could not surpass. It should ever be before the eyes of the young men that we are in an enemy's country, and that that enemy is ever on the watch to discover and profit by our weaknesses no less than by our successes. Suppose for a moment for the sake of a possible illustration that the tables had been turned, that you in Bedford Street were in daily expectation of two editions of an important book being launched against you while you were not only powerless to take any step to prevent it but did not even know when the supply of your competing edition was coming along from this side. The opinion of all would be that I was unworthy of the confidence reposed in me. By putting ourselves in another's place sometimes we get a better insight into his feelings and it is with that thought that I have looked at the *Elsmere* matter from another point of view. . . .

I am cabling tonight for 10,000 in sheets at 7*d* or 8*d* in the hope that you will not only furnish them but get them (or some) off by the Cunarder on the twenty-fifth inst. . . .

Believe me, yours very truly,   GEORGE E. BRETT

JOHN NEVILLE KEYNES

1852–1949

J. N. Keynes, philosopher and social economist, was the father of John Maynard Keynes. In 1884 Macmillans published 'on commission' — that is, at the author's cost — his *Studies and Exercises in Formal Logic*, price 10s 6d. Two years later, with the first edition almost sold out, the publishers wrote that, if it was inconvenient for the author to put up more money, 'we shall be happy to publish a new edition at our own expense, dividing the profits with you'. The second edition appeared in 1887 at the same price; the fourth edition was in Macmillans' list until 1942.

6 Harvey Road, Cambridge, 1 October 1886

Dear Sirs,

I am glad to learn that the first edition of my *Logic* is so nearly exhausted. It was my intention to rewrite a considerable portion of it for a second edition, but I see the importance of getting out the new edition as soon as possible, and propose therefore to make comparatively few alterations. . . .

I shall be obliged if you will kindly give me a little further information with regard to the half-profits method. Is any commission charged in this case before profits are calculated? Is any interest charged on payments up to the time at which the sales of the book meet the expenses? What plan is adopted with regard to the few copies that I may wish to give away to friends? I presume that any arrangement come to will not apply to a third edition, should a third edition at any time be called for.

I anticipate that the printing will come to less this time as there will be fewer alterations after the book is once in type; also it may be safe to print a larger edition, say 1,000. In this case can the price be reduced? One or two teachers have told me that the present price has prevented them from recommending the book to their pupils so freely as they would otherwise have done. A lower price may therefore stimulate the sales. . . .

    Believe me, yours truly,   J. N. KEYNES

Frederick Macmillan replied:

Bedford Street, Covent Garden, 2 October 1886

We write to say that when we publish a book on the half-profit system we debit the account with the actual cost of printing, binding, etc. without any commission, and do not charge any interest on payments made up to the time at which the sales of the book meet the expenses.

    With regard to presentation copies we should allow you any reasonable number, say ten or a dozen, and any copies that were presented to teachers or other persons likely to promote the sale of the book would be regarded given away for the benefit of the book and charged to the common account.

    In case you determined to publish the second edition on half-profits we should stipulate that it should consist of not less than 1,250 copies, particularly if the price is to be reduced. We should however not advise the reduction of the price without careful consideration : a lower price may in some instances stimulate sales but it does not always do so to an extent that compensates for the loss of profit on each copy.

    We are willing to make an arrangement for the second edition only, though our agreements are usually made to last to the expiration of the copyright.

ALFRED MARSHALL

1842–1924

Marshall, professor of political economy at Cambridge, wrote to offer Macmillans the book he was engaged on, *Principles of Economics.*

Balliol Croft, Madingley Road, Cambridge, 12 April 1887

Gentlemen,

... This book will be the central work of my life; and I shall regard it differently from anything I have written or may write. Partly for this reason, and partly because I think I may want to publish a very cheap popular edition of it, or of some part of it, at no very distant date, I should like to retain control over the copyright. ...

I should like the price of the octavo edition to be not very high: partly because books on economics are read by many students whose means are small, and who are not taking the subject up for examination, so that they avoid high priced books on it. ...

Yours very faithfully,   ALFRED MARSHALL

The book was not ready until 1890 when Frederick Macmillan, at a crisis of his campaign for a 'net book system', was on the look out for a guinea-pig. Who more appropriate than an economist?

      Bedford Street, Covent Garden, 15 April 1890

Dear Sir,

... At present, as you are aware, it is usual for booksellers to allow their customers a discount of 2*d* and sometimes 3*d* in the 1*s* from advertised prices. This system is the cause of two evils : in the first place books have to be made (nominally) ridiculously expensive in order that there may be plenty of margin for taking off discounts, and in the second place the system of allowing discounts to retail purchasers has fostered a spirit of competition among booksellers so keen that there is not enough profit in the business to enable booksellers to carry good stocks or to give their attention to bookselling proper. They have to supplement their profits by selling 'fancy goods', Berlin wool, etc., and are in many cases, in the country especially, driven out of business altogether.

Our theory is that the proper thing to do is only to allow the retail bookseller such a discount from the published price as will give him a fair profit if he gets full price for a book. This, of course, would enable publishers to make books, nominally, cheaper. We have adopted the plan in isolated cases, but always with large books selling for several guineas — and it has met with approval of the better class of booksellers. We should like to try the same plan with a book of general interest intended for wide sale, and it has occurred to us that your *Principles of Economics* is well suited for the purpose. It is not a book that would in any case come in the way of the 'cheap-jack' booksellers, who are the only opponents of our scheme, and we think, therefore, that there is no fear that the experiment would have any ill effect on the sale of the book itself. It would, however, be an experiment, and we should not like to make it without your full approval. Our idea would be to make the price 12s 6d net instead of 16s and the trade price would be 10s 5d with a further discount at settlement averaging 5 per cent. We shall also abolish the 'odd copy' — i.e. 25 books will not be charged as 24, or 13 as 12½.

Perhaps you will kindly let us know your views.

We are, yours very truly,   MACMILLAN & CO., LTD

Marshall acquiesced, though with misgivings, and a long correspondence followed on the economic and moral principles behind
tradesmen's discounts. *Principles of Economics* was published at 12s 6d
net in July 1890. The Net Book Agreement was not established until
1899. Meanwhile Macmillan had invited Marshall's opinion, and they
resumed their correspondence on the subject nine years later again, at
the time of '*The Times* Book War'.

3 December 1897

Dear Mr. Macmillan,

You are good enough to wish to know my views on the
situation. So I will add a word on a point on which I do not
think I made my position quite clear.

I fell in with the notion that it is not reasonable to
publish a book nominally at 12s when practically no one will
pay more than 10s for it, and many people only 9s. But I did
not mean that it seemed to me unreasonable that those who
pay cash should get no gain by so doing. We academic
economists are a little divided as to some of the claims of the
co-operative movement. But I think we all — to whatever
country or shade of economic opinion we belong — are
agreed that the movement has done unmixed service to
economic and moral progress by compelling shopkeepers
generally to give some sort of discount for cash payments.
We are agreed that the trader may fitly borrow from the
private person (e.g., *via* a bank) : but that when the con-
sumer borrows from his shopkeeper it is economically a
forcing water to run uphill, and morally harmful in many
ways, direct and indirect. Publishers might therefore, in my
opinion, deserve well of the country if they undertook to
punish any bookseller who endeavoured to make cash buyers
pay for the indulgence allowed to credit buyers and for the
risks of the credit business. But to punish him for doing
what I think is right, would be a course with which I could
personally have no sympathy. . . .

I could declaim about the iniquity of capitalist tailors who avow that they will not send in accounts soon, for fear of letting in less wealthy rivals etc. etc. But you know the clack of the tongue of the economist with a fad which he calls a principle : and I spare you more.

Yours very truly,   ALFRED MARSHALL

17 September 1898

The attempt to class scientific books with art books, instead of with school books, seems to me to go against economic laws ; just as would an ordinance that the London cabman should receive 2s a mile. Such an ordinance would not make cabmen rich : for their work is simple. It would diminish the number of riders, increase the number of cabs a little, and the number of 'crawlers' very much.

I cordially approved the net system for my book when it was suggested to me. But that was because I misunderstood the proposal.

4 October 1907

I shall be glad when the Publishers have come to some arrangement with *The Times*. I dislike the methods and the tone of *The Times* manager. But, as you know, I think that the booksellers get too large a share of the price of those books which appeal to relatively small audiences. The net system as at present worked seems to me to put too great difficulties in the way of a man who must earn his living and yet wishes to think before he writes. Authors work : publishers exercise judgment and take risks. But I cannot discover what booksellers do for the extension of knowledge.

SIR JAMES GEORGE FRAZER

1854–1941

On 6 July 1884 Dr. James Gow (1854–1923), classical scholar and later headmaster of Westminster School, wrote to George Macmillan:

A particular friend of mine, J. G. Frazer (Fellow of Trin:, Second Classic in 1878), is very keen on translating Pausanias. . . . He is an excellent scholar, of prodigious learning and industry, and he wouldn't put his name to a book which wasn't as good as it could be made. He is also a reasonable person of methodical habits and would be inclined to meet any practical suggestions in a proper way.

Frazer was to become the most distinguished social anthropologist of his day. His letters to Macmillans, and those of his wife, number some thousands, ranging from 1884 to 1940.

Professor John Henry Middleton (1846–96) was director of the Fitzwilliam Museum at Cambridge.

Trinity College, Cambridge, 8 November 1889
Dear Sir,

I shall soon have completed a study in the history of primitive religion which I propose to offer to you for publication. The book is an explanation of the legend of the Golden Bough, as that legend is given by Servius in his commentary on Virgil. According to Servius the Golden Bough grew on a certain tree in the sacred grove of Diana at Aricia, and the priesthood of the grove was held by the man who succeeded in breaking off the Golden Bough and then slaying the priest in single combat. By an application of the comparative method I believe I can make it probable that the priest represented in his person the god of the grove, Virbius, and that his slaughter was regarded as the death of the god. This raises the question of the meaning of a widespread custom of killing men and animals regarded as divine. I have collected many examples of this custom and proposed a new explanation of it. The Golden Bough, I believe I can show, was the mistletoe, and the whole legend can, I think, be brought into connexion, on the one hand, with the Druidical reverence for the mistletoe and the human sacrifices which accompanied their worship, and, on the other hand, with the Norse legend of the death of Balder. Of the exact way in which I connect the Golden Bough with the priest of Aricia I shall only say that in explaining it I am led to propose a new explanation of the meaning of totemism.

This is a bare outline of the book which, whatever may be thought of its theories, will be found, I believe, to contain a large store of very curious customs, many of which may be new even to professed anthropologists. The resemblance of many of the savage customs and ideas to the fundamental doctrines of Christianity is striking. But I make no reference to the parallelism, leaving my readers to draw their own conclusions, one way or the other.

The MS. at present amounts to between 500 and 600 foolscap pages, and when completed will probably contain 700 pages or a little over. I hope to finish it either by the end of this month or early in December.

In offering you the book there are two conditions which I would propose for your consideration and, I should hope, acceptance. They relate to the 'get-up' of the book. One is that there should be a frontispiece consisting of an engraving or mechanical reproduction of Turner's picture of the Golden Bough. The other is that a drawing of the mistletoe or Golden Bough should be stamped in gold on the cover. A drawing of the mistletoe has been kindly made for this purpose by my friend Prof. J. H. Middleton.

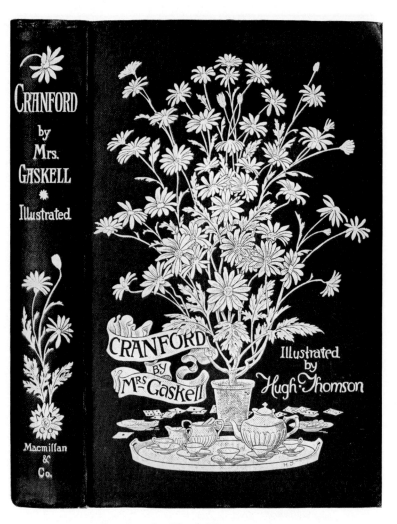

Binding by Hugh Thomson 1891

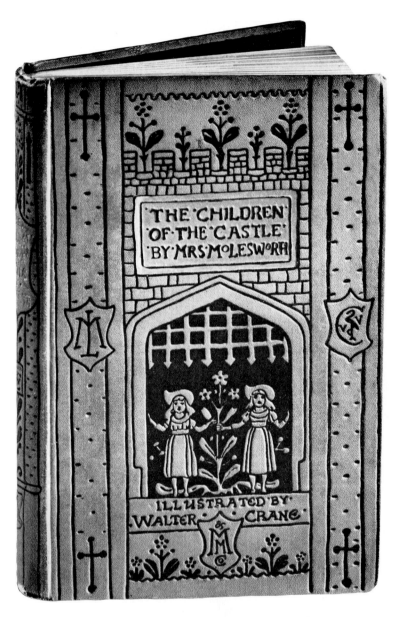

THE CHILDREN
OF THE CASTLE
BY MRS MOLESWORTH

ILLUSTRATED BY
WALTER CRANE

Binding by Walter Crane 1890

The title of the book will be *The Golden Bough; a study in the history of religion*, or perhaps instead of this *The Legend of the Golden Bough*.

With regard to terms, I have special reasons which make it convenient and desirable to receive a fixed sum in payment of the first edition, rather than accept a royalty or half-profits and I am advised by my friends that I should not accept, for the first edition, less than £100. The copyright I should certainly retain. I should be glad to hear whether you would be willing to accept the book on these terms.

I may here add that as soon as the book is off my hands I intend to go out to Greece and there finish the archaeological commentary on Pausanias, residing chiefly at the British School in Athens.

I remain, dear sir, yours faithfully, JAMES G. FRAZER

John Morley's highly favourable report on *The Golden Bough* is quoted at length in Morgan's *The House of Macmillan*. Further letters passed on terms and on 'the "get-up" of the book'. Frazer concerned himself with every detail of production. The page must not be crowded, nor yet the type too small. A variety of type-sizes and the provision of 'running heads' would assist the reader. He recommended not only particular types as legible and beautiful, but even a printer — fortunately R. & R. Clark, of Edinburgh, who did much of Macmillans' printing — and a Cambridge engraver for the frontispiece. In every detail, however, he wished to defer to his publisher's 'superior experience'. In almost every detail his proposals were adopted.

25 December 1889

I am anxious, and I am sure that you are equally so, that the book should look as well as possible. I wish to attract not only students but the general reader, and for this purpose I have aimed at giving the book a certain dramatic effect, especially at the opening and at the close. The ornamental

H

and appropriate binding and frontispiece are designed to contribute to the same effect, and I should wish that printing and paper should be in harmony.

The Golden Bough was published in 1890 (its final supplement in 1936) and the *Pausanias*, delayed by Frazer's preoccupation with the larger work, in 1898. In the latter year Frazer made a proposal which neither Macmillans nor any other publisher was prepared to adopt.

Herbert Allen Giles (1845–1935), who succeeded Sir Thomas Francis Wade (1818–95) as professor of Chinese at Cambridge, was a prolific writer: his *Chinese Biographical Dictionary* appeared in 1898. The other books mentioned in this letter are S. W. Williams's *The Middle Kingdom*, 1848; J. G. Wilkinson's *The Manners and Customs of the Ancient Egyptians*, 1837–41, and Mrs. Frazer's *Scenes of Familiar Life . . . for Students of Colloquial French*, illustrated by H. M. Brock, 1898. Frazer had married in 1896 Lilly (*née* Adelsdorfer), widow of Charles Baylee Groves. She had edited a number of French school-books for Macmillans.

14 July 1898

My dear Macmillan,

You see I have adopted your suggestion that we should drop the formal 'Mr.' in writing to each other. I am glad to do so and to think of the friendly relations established between us. I trust they will long continue, and that for many years to come we may work together each in his own way and to good purpose. I cannot but feel that I owe this happy result, like so much else that is good, in large measure to my wife, but for whom you and I would probably not have met to this day. Before my marriage I was growing almost morbidly averse to meeting strange faces, even when the faces were connected with hands whose writing was familiar to me.

Now to come to business. Do you think there is an opening for an authoritative work on China and the Chinese to be written by thoroughly competent Chinese scholars who have lived long in the country and to be well illustrated by photographs? The question has arisen from a talk I had the other day with our new professor of Chinese, Giles, who from long residence in China and study of the literature knows the Chinese intimately. He had been showing me the splendid Chinese library presented to the University Library by Sir Thomas Wade, his predecessor in the chair. After he had done so I asked him what was the best book in English or in one of the European languages on the Chinese. He said there was none really good. The book which used to be read, Williams's *Middle Kingdom*, was good in its time but has long been out of date, and the subject (he said) was too vast for one man to cover adequately.

I asked him whether he had any thoughts of undertaking a book on the subject. He said that he had entertained a plan of writing a book in conjunction with several other persons whom he knew to be competent and he had indeed applied to them. The arrangement he proposed was that each should write on a special aspect of Chinese life, he himself taking the social, another the political, and so on. I gathered that the men he applied to were quite willing to enter into the scheme, provided the funds necessary for carrying it out were provided. This he could not guarantee (he told me he had spent £2,000 in bringing out a Chinese biographical dictionary, which received a prize from the French Academy), and so nothing further has been done in the matter. I told him that I thought you might possibly see your way to taking up the plan, and he gave me leave to write to you about it. Hence this letter.

It seems to me that the subject is one of perennial interest to Europe and doubly interesting at the present time when the eyes of Europe are turned so much towards China. We are probably only at the beginning of the gradual absorption of China by the European powers and the consequent disappearance, little by little, of all the quaint old native civilization. Now if ever is the time to secure a faithful portrait of that old-world civilization by trained European observers who have witnessed it before it began to be saturated and transformed by Western ideas. Such a work, if well done, might remain the standard work on the subject for all time to come. It might be something like Wilkinson's *Ancient Egyptians*, with this enormous advantage over that book that it would be written by men who had seen the life they described, instead of only seeing pictures of it in tombs. What do you think of all this?

We have just seen Mr. Brock's drawings for my wife's *Scenes of Familiar Life*. They are charming, even better, we think, than the others.

Yours very truly,   J. G. FRAZER

HUGH THOMSON

1860–1920

Thomson was a frequent contributor of drawings to the *English Illustrated Magazine* almost from its start in 1883, and he illustrated many volumes in Macmillans' Highways and Byways series and Cranford series of English classics. Mrs. Gaskell's *Cranford*, with Thomson's illustrations, appeared in 1891; he did not illustrate Miss Edgeworth's *The Absentee*. His early connexion with the firm is recalled in this letter, written many years later.

Thomson served on the Commission Internationale de Ravitaillement at the Board of Trade from 1916 to 1919. Marion Harry Spielmann (1858–1948), art critic and editor, published a monograph on his work in 1931.

The verse quotation is from Wordsworth's 'Extempore Effusion on the Death of James Hogg'.

8 Patten Road, Wandsworth Common, S.W.18,

15 May 1918

Dear Sir Frederick Macmillan,

This morning I had an intimation from the Paymaster General's office that the Government have given me a pension of £75. I hasten to let you know of this, and of my gratitude for the generous letter which you sent to the Prime Minister. I need not say how proud I am, and always shall be, of that letter; and the very tangible benefit to me which has resulted from the exertions of my dear friend Spielmann is largely due to it. Thank you again and again, dear Sir Frederick, for it and for all your kindness. I don't write, nor do I call, but that is not to say that I ever for a moment forget. It is simply that I cannot face the risk of boring people.

Another piece of news which I know will interest you, as you are directly concerned in it, is that Sangorski and Sutcliffe the binders presented a copy of the first edition of *Cranford* (I mean the *Cranford* you commissioned me to illustrate) to the recent Red Cross Sale at Christie's. I had put a little sketch on the flyleaf, which, I suppose, gave rise to the misunderstanding that the gift was from me, for at the close of the sale an intimation was sent me by the committee that the copy had added £100 to the Red Cross funds. I hope this will gratify you as it gratified me.

I remember so well your giving me your copies of *Cranford* and *The Absentee* to choose which I should like to illustrate. Those happy days ! On Sunday I was dipping into one of the old volumes on my shelves and came on this stanza which sums up the dropping off of old friends and seems to me to express with intensity what has happened since 1914.

> Like clouds that rake the mountain summits,
> Or waves that own no curbing hand,
> How fast has brother followed brother,
> From sunshine to the sunless land !

Please give my kind regards and respects to Lady Macmillan and believe me ever, dear Sir Frederick Macmillan, your much indebted,   HUGH THOMSON

You will of course let Mr. George Macmillan, Mr. Maurice Macmillan and all my old friends at St. Martin's Street know of my bit of luck.

WALTER CRANE
1845–1915

In 1876 Macmillans published *Carrots, Just a Little Boy*, by 'Ennis Graham', illustrated by Walter Crane. The writer was Mary Louise Molesworth (1839–1921). In the next fifteen years Crane, one of the most popular illustrators of the period, designed both the bindings and the pictures for fifteen of Mrs. Molesworth's children's books published by the firm. *The Children of the Castle* appeared in 1890.

Beaumont Lodge, Shepherd's Bush, W., 6 August 1890
Dear Mr. Frederick Macmillan,

I cannot account for my deeply rooted impression that Mrs. Molesworth's book was entitled *The Children of the Castle*, when the other title appears at the head in larger type. As regards the story, as it is mostly about the Children of the Castle, it may just as well be called so — if Mrs. Molesworth has no objection — and I agree with you in thinking *The Princess with the Forget-me-not Eyes* is an awkward one. My cover design, too, is emphatically 'The Children of the Castle' though the 'Forget-me-nots' are not absent, and I fear, now, I should have no time to alter anything : so that if you could explain matters to Mrs. Molesworth, and she would consent to alter the title it would be greatly to everybody's advantage.

Very truly yours,   WALTER CRANE

CHARLES EDWARD BROCK
1870–1938
and
HENRY MATTHEW BROCK
1875–1960

The Brock brothers illustrated innumerable books for Macmillan between the 1890s and the 1930s. Their fame rests largely on the Cranford series — they at one time named their house Cranford — and the Illustrated Standard Novels. It was for the latter series that they undertook the novels by John Galt, Captain Marryat, Jane Austen, Samuel Lover, James Fenimore Cooper and Charles Kingsley mentioned in this letter.

3 North Terrace, Cambridge, 3 January 1895

Dear Sir,

I am just sending off to you twenty-five drawings for *The Annals of the Parish* and twenty-one of my brother's drawings for *Jacob Faithful*. These two books will be finished before the end of the month but I cannot give you the exact day. The remaining fifteen illustrations to John Galt's book I am of course going to devote to the *Ayrshire Legatees* and I have them well on the way. When they are finished I shall proceed immediately with *Pride and Prejudice*. I cannot of course say exactly how long this will take me but will let you know as soon as I can. My brother proposes going on with Lover's *Handy Andy*.

The remaining five books are of course Fenimore Cooper's Leatherstocking Series, and as I shall have to start as soon as possible on the *Westward Ho!*, I don't quite know

what is to be done about them as I am sure it will take all my
time this year, and I fear will make them much later than
you wish. If you would like us to relinquish them please
don't hesitate to let us know, but if you think we could be in
time for you, we will do our very best. It would most
certainly be a good way into 1896, I am afraid, before we
could finish them off.

I trust you will find the drawings we forward today
satisfactory and, with many thanks for your kind wishes for
the new year which I heartily reciprocate, I remain, dear sir,
faithfully yours,   CHAS. E. BROCK

In spite of the warning in the foregoing letter Macmillans became
restive when the Fenimore Cooper drawings were delayed, and decided
not to proceed with the Leatherstocking novels. Later the decision was
reversed, but the number of illustrations in each volume except the first
was reduced from forty to twenty-five. S. Hutt was Macmillans'
production manager.

14 Brunswick Walk, Cambridge, 18 November 1896
Dear Sir,
Thank you for the cheque which I received this morning ;
I enclose receipt.
With regard to the Fenimore Cooper novels of course I
am very sorry, especially as my brother has the first book
half done. The drawings are all started and he has spent
nearly a fortnight in the country doing sketches for the
trees, etc. : he has also gone to a good bit of expense in
having a studio and a model for the Indians in London for
the past fortnight. In addition to this we have had some
dresses made purposely for the books with which we intended to take special pains. His drawings for the first book
would be done by Xmas. I intended to do the next one and
my drawings would follow his very closely as I didn't mean

to undertake anything further till they were done. We have in fact been gathering materials for the whole five books.

If your decision is irrevocable, as I sincerely hope it is not, will you kindly telegraph to that effect to me and I will then summon my brother home as of course it will be no use for him to spend more time on the model. . . .

Believe me to remain, faithfully yours,

CHAS E. BROCK

15 May 1898

Dear Mr. Hutt,

Thank you for your letter received last night. I am glad to hear that the Fenimore Cooper drawings are to be published but I am extremely sorry to hear of your intentions with regard to them ; not that I do not like coloured illustrations to a book, but these particular drawings, not having been done with any idea of colouring, contain — it seems to me — far too much shading to look at all well when printed with colour.

In my opinion a coloured drawing to look well should have for a key-block a drawing in almost pure outline, with perhaps a few pieces of solid black ; but certainly not a lot of shading and cross-hatch. However as you have decided to do them in this way I would certainly much rather do them myself than let any one else do them, as I should probably spoil them less.

As to the price, I do not know quite what you would be willing to pay, but I should think about five or six guineas for the set, an average of about five shillings each. If you will kindly let me have a set of proofs (or it would be better to have one or two of each drawing to allow of trials of colour) I will colour them for you and let you have them as soon as I can.

Believe me, dear Mr. Hutt, very truly yours,

H. M. BROCK

JOSEPH PENNELL

1857–1926

Pennell was an American artist who spent more than thirty years of his middle life in Europe as an illustrator of, for the most part, topographical works. In 1894 he was commissioned to illustrate *The Makers of Modern Rome* by the novelist and historical writer Margaret Oliphant (1828–97); the book appeared in 1905 with more than fifty of his drawings.

Rome, 2 June 1894

Dear Mr. Macmillan,

Although I hesitate in writing this letter I think it had better be done. I fear I must give up the *Rome* — for this reason, Rome has ceased to exist. The Rome that even I saw years ago is gone. The shores of the Tiber are a waste of mud, sand, stones, filth — and unfinished embankment; the Castle of St. Angelo is hidden by apartment houses, the bridge is down, the Ponte Rotto has vanished, the Island is a sandbank — even the steps of St. Peter's are up; the Pincian trees are *now* being cut down. The Borghese palace is a bric-à-brac shop, all old Rome is labelled and tagged like a museum, and the friends, I'm told, of those who are buried in the English cemetery are about to be told, or have been, that it is wanted. The Ghetto has gone, and the only thing I've found is the theatre of Marcellus. Rome only remains in the photograph shops, and it's too sickening for life.

As it is only the first of June I don't think you will be delayed by me, and I'll go on till I hear from you. I'll do some of the villas — the few that are left — and gardens, and Keats's tomb and the gates. But the City itself I cannot do — *because it isn't here*. Now shall I go on and do these few interesting things that still exist, or give it all up? To try to do the scraped vulgar town would really finish me, and I do want to make something fine of the Alhambra. So please let me know at your earliest convenience if you care to have me do the few things that remain or whether I shall give it up.

Yours truly sorrowfully,   JOSEPH PENNELL

2 June 1894 — evening

I'm afraid I wrote you a rather blue letter, but really I couldn't help it. For instance, this afternoon I went to do my favourite pine grove in the Borghese and found it made into a bicycle track with a rough wooden fence around it, while the fact that the electric light wires from some charging station to the City run right across the terrace of the villa does not improve that place.

Still, I have found out that I must give up old Rome, and there are some really good new things here, and if you will give me a week or so more I may be able to get something out of the place; and if Mrs. Pennell comes to you in a very pathetic mood, say you have had another letter from me. Really there are some very fine night effects and I will do them. And the old things, if Mrs. Oliphant wants them, can be done from photographs. I really don't want to give the work up, but really new Italy is a little too much.

In 1905 Pennell was commissioned to illustrate the book on London which Henry James failed to write. He made about 160 drawings and etchings,* from which, in 1924, Macmillan proposed to make a selection for publication. This selection appeared as *A London Reverie* two years after Pennell's death.

Nicholas Murray Butler (1862–1947), American philosopher and educationist, was a Republican politician of great international repute.

* These were presented by Macmillans to the Library of Congress in 1928.

Brooklyn, N.Y., 19 May 1924

Your letter certainly was a surprise and I am glad the drawings are to be used, though I wish they were more up-to-date. I would like if you could have some statement of that sort made in the book — the long-ago days in which they were done. Another matter. I thought the drawings were destroyed in the war, when many of my other things went. But if you have them in your safe will you send them over here, as I could make a show of them in New York when the book comes out. . . .

Yes, I am well enough physically, but mentally and morally sick unto death, for the country is rotten, the people putrid, it stinks. Look yesterday — Congress re-votes the bonus bill, brought in by degenerate cowards who, worthless oafs, sell the country they have grabbed to keep their grafting seats (they are mostly the descendants of mongrel degenerates, the U.S. Congress) to 'patriots' who fought for this very bonus, not for anything else, and above all because they were made to. But 'patriotism is the last resort of scoundrels'.

I see English papers still and I know not how much you believe of the twaddle supplied by paid Jews and fanatic cranks as to the state of this country and its dryness. I can only tell you I had a glass of whiskey, three cocktails and a bottle of wine yesterday in this stone and bone dry city — and, with the exception of the glass of whiskey in a hotel room, perfectly openly in a restaurant. The only man in a public position who has any courage left and any brains left is Nicholas Miraculous Butler, but he can do nothing for no one will back him — we are a race of cowards. We are worse governed — or dictated to (there is no government) — than Russia ; by old maids in petticoats and pants, even by bootleggers, bandits, and fools.

LAURENCE HOUSMAN
1865–1959

Laurence Housman, younger brother of the author of *A Shropshire Lad*, began his career as an illustrator of books and designer of bindings. In 1893 he offered to illustrate Christina Rossetti's *Goblin Market* (originally illustrated by D. G. Rossetti in 1862). The 'mediaeval' confrontation of illustrations proposed in this letter to George Macmillan was adopted in the book, published later that year.

61 Marloes Road, Kensington, W., 20 March 1893

Dear Sir,

Enclosed I submit to you one specimen drawing and some rough sketches to show my proposed treatment of *Goblin Market*, the poem in reference to which you have previously heard from me.

The sketches I have mounted, to indicate the size of page I would like to suggest, and also the arrangement, in certain cases, of illustrations facing each other and forming two halves as it were of one picture — a revival of a mediaeval usage which I think might be made effective and pleasant.

As you will probably be referring these drawings to Miss Rossetti I should be glad to be allowed to say a word here in explanation of the masks which I have introduced as a pictorial allegory. I have imagined the goblins wearing animal masks in order to hide the wickedness that their own faces would reveal; this will give me the opportunity of a dramatic climax when in the poem they are finally defeated by Lizzie. I propose then to show them throwing aside their masks as they make their escape. I hope Miss Rossetti will not think this idea is in any disagreement with the spirit of her poem.

It will perhaps be premature for me to make any further suggestions as to the form and amount of illustration until I hear whether what is here submitted to you meets with approval.

I trust you will be able by comparison with the finished drawing to make a proper allowance for the crudeness of the other sketches.

I am yours faithfully,   LAURENCE HOUSMAN

Bedford Street, Covent Garden, 18 April 1893

Dear Sir,

I had hoped to write to you before this in regard to your proposed illustrated edition of Miss Rossetti's *Goblin Market*. The matter has been under the author's consideration and as you know we could come to no decision until we knew her views. They are not on the whole unfavourable to the idea, but she cannot bring herself to sanction the 'masks' which you introduce in your treatment of the goblins. 'They might', Miss Rossetti writes, 'illustrate some better poem, but mine they falsify. Would not a study of my goblins as they stand supply an adequate variety and versatility of expression, a roguishness easily transformable into atrocity?' She then refers to her brother's original frontispiece.

The first question then is whether you are willing to give up this part of your scheme, and to treat the goblins in some other way. If so we should be very glad to submit another specimen or two to Miss Rossetti and if she approved there would be no difficulty, I think, in arranging with you for the publication.

Yours truly,   GEORGE A. MACMILLAN

Housman eliminated the objectionable masks, and Christina Rossetti wrote to George Craik:

16 May 1893

I am fully satisfied. . . . I am obliged to Mr. Housman for his compliance with my wish, and assure him that my goblins will keep peace with all his.

Title-page by Laurence Housman

THE TOWER   BY W. B. YEATS

MACMILLAN·AND·CO

Binding by T. Sturge Moore 1928

ALFRED EDWARD HOUSMAN

1859–1936

Housman, poet and classical scholar, planned to edit Propertius when still an undergraduate at Oxford. In spite of contributions on the subject to learned journals, he never published his text, which, in accordance with his wish, was destroyed after his death.

39 Northumberland Place, Bayswater, W.,

11 December 1885

Gentlemen,

I propose that you should, if you think fit, publish my recension of the text of Propertius, a specimen of which, consisting of the first book with its *apparatus criticus*, I send by the same post with this letter. There are few authors for whose emendation and explanation so much remains to be done. The collation by Baehrens, in his edition of the text in 1880, of four important MSS. previously overlooked has in a measure rendered obsolete all texts preceding or simultaneous with his own ; while he himself was prevented, partly by haste and partly by a very natural bias of judgment, from making a really scientific use of his materials.

No commentary possessing original value, with the exception of Mr. Postgate's *Selections*, has been published since Hertzberg's of 1845. Six years ago I formed the design of producing an edition and commentary which should meet the requirements of modern critical science, and have now completed the first of these two tasks : the emended text accompanied by a register of such among the MS. readings as are of import for constituting the words of the author or for classifying the MSS. themselves. The collection and arrangement of materials for the commentary will naturally demand further time and labour; and I therefore judge it best that the text with its *apparatus criticus* should be issued separately, especially as I annually find not a few of my corrections anticipated by German scholars in philological periodicals.

I am, gentlemen, yours faithfully,   A. E. HOUSMAN

Macmillans rejected not only the *Propertius* in 1885, but *A Shropshire Lad* ten years later and Housman's edition of *Lucan* in 1924. The *Lucan* was published 'Oxonii apud Basilium Blackwell' in 1926: Housman's other Latin texts — *Manilius* and *Juvenal* — had been published 'Londinii apud Grant Richards'. Charles Whibley (1859–1930) was one of Macmillans' chief readers.

Trinity College, Cambridge, 16 November 1924

Dear Sirs,

In the last twenty years I have produced several editions of Latin classics, which are printed at my expense, offered to the public at less than cost price, and sold for me on commission.

I am just completing an edition of *Lucan*, which I wish to produce in the same way. The printers of my last three books, Messrs. Robert MacLehose & Co. of the Glasgow University Press, are prepared to undertake the work; and Mr. Charles Whibley has suggested to me that you may be willing to act as publishers for me on the usual terms, and to be the channel of my communications with the printers. As in 1895 you refused to publish another book of mine, *A Shropshire Lad*, under similar conditions, I did not think this likely; but he assures me that you are now less haughty.

If so, I will send you the text and notes, which are already complete and constitute the bulk of the work, that you may transmit them to Messrs. MacLehose and obtain an estimate of the cost.

I am yours faithfully,   A. E. HOUSMAN

The *finale* came at Christmas-time two years later.

                    St. Martin's Street, W.C., 22 December 1926
Dear Professor Housman,

My meeting with you at Jesus College on Monday last reminded me of a correspondence which took place between you and my firm just two years ago, and when I got back to London I had the letters looked up to see exactly what happened.

I find that in November 1924 you were good enough to suggest that we should undertake the publication on commission of your edition of *Lucan* and that we declined to do so on the ground that commission publishing was not in our line of business. I remember thinking at the time that this was possibly a case in which it would be wise to relax our rule, but I expect that what decided us not to do so was a phrase in your letter describing us as 'haughty' — an adjective that seemed then, as it still does, singularly inappropriate.

I am now writing to say that if you have not already made other arrangements, and are still willing to entrust the publication of your *Lucan* to us, we shall be proud to undertake it and to do our best for you.

It may be that it is too late, but this letter will at all events convince you that the quality of humility has not been omitted from our composition.

Believe me, yours sincerely, FREDERICK MACMILLAN

                                    27 December 1926
Dear Sir Frederick Macmillan,

I am much obliged by your amiable letter. The *Lucan* however was published last January, and is now nearly sold out, which testifies to such efficiency in the publisher as even you could hardly surpass.

I am yours sincerely,   A. E. HOUSMAN

'MARIE CORELLI'
Mary Mackay
1854–1924

Marie Corelli was a best-selling novelist of the late Victorian and Edwardian period. Several of her books were taken over by Macmillans when they bought the firm of Richard Bentley & Son a few years after the date of this letter.

With the letter she enclosed two press cuttings. The first read, 'The Queen, it is said, is reading Marie Corelli's book, *A Romance of Two Worlds*, with the deepest interest'. The second was an account of a trade dinner at which Frederick Macmillan had assured young aspirants to authorship that the publishers' need for successful books was only equalled by their assiduity in looking for rising genius: in 1891 Macmillans' readers had reported on 315 manuscripts, of which 293 had proved unsuitable for publication.

47 Longridge Road, Earl's Court, S.W., 22 March 1892
Dear Sir,

I have read the enclosed account of your speech with *great* interest, as I am writing on that subject just now; but as an author who is now entirely successful, you will perhaps allow me to say that I am very reluctantly compelled to declare that I *know* positively of cases where authors' MSS. have not even been unfastened, much less read by the 'readers' to whom they have been entrusted! In my own case, I once wrote to your firm (just at the time my name was rapidly rising) to offer you one of my productions; I had a very formal note, saying that if I sent it, it would be 'considered'. Naturally I proceeded no further, as all my books find acceptance both here and in America, and command large sums *without being even glanced at*; but on the behalf of struggling authors I am bound to say that the reception accorded to 'aspiring' authors, by publishers generally, is not encouraging ! The book that made my name and has brought large sums of money into the hands of both Mr. Bentley and myself — viz., *The Romance of Two Worlds* — *was refused by all Bentley's readers !* He himself revoked their verdict, and published it, with extraordinary success. Publishers are frequently misled in the reports they receive and often lose a very excellent bargain.

You must excuse me for troubling you with this note, but I am writing for America a book touching on these subjects ; and I feel a deep interest in the matter. A very dear old friend of mine Dr. Edward Lane, very much wished to introduce me to you — but his lamented death prevented him from fulfilling his intention — so you must not mind my introducing myself ! I have long ceased to be the slave of the publisher's 'reader' — and I feel a true sympathy with all those who are not yet fortunate enough to escape the judgment of that often narrow and prejudiced 'oracle' ! I much wished to write a book for you at one time — but was literally frightened away ! — so the 'assiduity in looking' for successful books seemed to be lacking *that* time !

With best wishes and compliments, I am, faithfully yours,

MARIE CORELLI

MAURICE HENRY HEWLETT
1861–1923

Soon after the acceptance of his novel *The Forest Lovers* (1898) Hewlett wrote to Frederick Macmillan; 'My wish has always been to publish everything with the same firm, but this a beginner cannot always do.' The same firm published his *Richard Yea-and-Nay* in 1900, but for his volume of magazine stories, *The New Canterbury Tales* (1901), he was tempted away by William Maxse Meredith, the son of George Meredith and a partner in Archibald Constable & Co.

At the time of these letters Hewlett's next novel, *The Queen's Quair*, had been accepted by George P. Brett of The Macmillan Company, New York, and was on offer as a serial to George Roland Halkett, editor of the *Pall Mall Magazine*.

Bowerhope, St. Mary's Loch, Selkirk, 20 July 1901

Dear Macmillan,

The New Canterbury Tales was done to oblige Will Meredith who is a friend of mine. I have reserved the right of including the volume in a collected edition.

If it had been a book done on my own initiative I should have offered it to you, because I think the old-fashioned system the best — or rather I should have told you that I had it to dispose of and waited till you asked me for it — so that I could have been sure that you really wanted it, as I am now sure that you want to have *The Queen's Quair*.

To speak frankly, I have had a suspicion for some time that you did *not* particularly care for novels : I don't mean mine in particular, but novels as such. It has seemed to me that I never heard from you about them — how they were going, what was being said, what your clients thought, etc.,

etc. I did not see that you advertised them — except at first and as one of 'Six popular novels' or 'Twelve new novels' — in fact, I felt that I wasn't particularly wanted by your people. Now as it appears I am very particularly wanted by many of your brethren, this ruffled me a little. It would be foolish of me to pretend that I don't know what is said and written about me, or that my stuff isn't good. I know it is, devilish good ; therefore I like it to go where it is appreciated.

I don't stand out for extravagant terms. I'm neither greedy nor poor ; but I think the relation between author and publisher ought to be a human as well as a business one, and that is what I should like ours to be.

With regard to *The Queen's Quair* (as to which I have already agreed with Brett), it is to be serialized in August 1902, and will be ready for publication in August 1903. I have arranged for American serial publication, and have spoken to Halkett of the *P. M. Mag.* about it. If he can't manage it, it might suit your own editor. I want £600 for the serial rights. Publication as a book shall be on the same terms as the last, if you please. But I must ask you now to raise the royalty on *The Forest Lovers* to 25 per cent, as Brett has raised his to 20.

You see by this, my dear Macmillan, that all I ask is your interest in my stuff, and reasonable terms. In return you will get from me the loyalty which in my opinion an author owes to a good publisher, and you will always get it. I have refused half a score of offers from firms of your own standing in the trade and from others of second rank. My answer has always been that I have no mind to desert the Macmillans unless I am sure that they wish it.

I think my books would pay for being advertised — as M. Crawford (e.g.) is advertised, I suppose you don't do it, because you think I may carry my goods elsewhere. You will see by this letter that, if I do, it won't be of my own accord.

On hearing from you your sentiments as to what I have

proposed here, I will sign an agreement for *The Queen's Quair* as soon as you please.

Very truly yours,   MAURICE HEWLETT

St. Martin's Street, W.C., 23 July 1901
My dear Hewlett,

I am much obliged to you for your full and friendly letter received this morning. It clears the air, which in some unaccountable manner seems to have become to some extent befogged.

As to *The New Canterbury Tales*, I must confess to having been a little bit hurt (even publishers have feelings), not because Constable & Co. are to publish them, for the explanation is a simple one, but because simple as it is, it was never brought to my notice. . . . I am glad to know that the reason for this is that the book was suggested by the firm that is to bring it out, and not because you have lost confidence in Macmillan & Co. As a sincere admirer of *The Forest Lovers* since the day when I read it at one sitting from the typewritten copy, and as a friend keenly interested in your literary career, I should have felt very sorry if you had deserted us.

I cannot imagine how you came to think that we did not care about publishing novels. We do not care very much about novels that don't sell, and we do not care at all about novels, whether they sell or not, that have not (or do not seem to have) a distinct literary quality. But when we are fortunate enough to come across novels like yours which not only have high literary merit, but also sell very well indeed, we are very keen to see them in our lists, and it is our ambition to do all that can be done for them and for their author.

I had no idea until last week that you were at work on *The Queen's Quair* or I should have written to you about it sooner. However, all's well that ends well, and I am very glad that the book is to come to us. I enclose a memorandum of agreement which I think embodies the terms suggested by you, and if you will sign and return it to me I will send you a duplicate signed by ourselves. . . .

Believe me, yours sincerely, FREDERICK MACMILLAN

Hewlett wrote again about the comparative prominence of the advertising of *Richard Yea-and-Nay* and Marion Crawford's *In the Palace of the King*, and Macmillan replied:

29 July 1901

I notice that in both your letters you have referred to the question of advertising as though we had been somewhat amiss in that direction, and indeed in your first letter you said that you wished your books could be advertised as widely as Crawford's. It is notorious that authors never see any advertisements of their own books. I can assure you they have appeared and have been paid for. I have had the curiosity to inquire of our advertising department into the actual amount of money spent on *Richard Yea-and-Nay* and Crawford's last book, and I find that though we did spend more on Crawford's than on you, the difference between you was only forty shillings ! !

That refers to advertisements in newspapers. We also do a great deal in the way of distributing catalogues and leaflets which you probably don't ever see but which the public does see. I enclose a selection of some of the recent ones which have literally been distributed by the hundred thousand.

SIR WALTER ALEXANDER RALEIGH
1861–1922

Professor of English literature at Glasgow (and from 1904 at Oxford), Raleigh had published studies of Milton and Wordsworth, and a book on *Style*, before George Macmillan invited him to contribute a volume on Shakespeare to the English Men of Letters series. The series had started in 1878, but, as Macmillan remarked, 'Shakespeare, the greatest of all, is still vacant'.

Uffington, Faringdon, Berks, 30 August 1903

Dear Sirs,

I am highly honoured by your proposal. Two days ago I should have said, with emphasis, that I would never write for a series. But I could not guess that I should be given the opportunity of designing a monument for the poet I love best, in the national cathedral church. The English Men of Letters is not as other series are.

I need not tell you how much I should like to do this thing. I want to write on Shakespeare, have always meant to, and have always felt that no harm would come of delay. But the tide has come to the flood before I looked for it, and perhaps I ought to take it.

I should have to defer some existing engagements, and to postpone a work on Chaucer (purely my own affair) which has begun to engage me this summer. In any case I am pledged to do work on an edition of Hakluyt which must make large inroads into the summer of 1904. So that my answer to you must depend on the question of time. I hoped to write on Shakespeare at ease, and at large. In any case I must have time to do my best. The winter (October–May) is of no more use to me, for writing, than if I were in prison. If you must have the work under two years I shall be compelled, with great regret, to refuse. And I should feel easier if you gave me three. You need not fear making me lazy; if I undertake it I shall begin at once, and when it is ready you shall have it.

I will not trouble you with *my* misgivings. Shakespeare is no man's several; it is impossible to please all his lovers. I had meant (if I were fortunate) to please myself; and if you think that in so doing I shall probably please you — it is not for me to contradict you. The scale of the work makes it quite certain that it will be censured for omissions.

I have often wished (partly for the uses of an academy) that the Men of Letters included more names from the sixteenth and seventeenth centuries. With some, biography would be difficult — Marlowe, Herrick, and others who, on their work, deserve a place. But there is a fair scantling of biographical facts in the case of Jeremy Taylor, or Hooker, or Wiclif, or Jonson, or Cowley. Pope and Johnson are still permitted to dictate the current opinion on Cowley. He will regain esteem some day. But I do not deny that by opening your doors to him you would be raising the whole question of the Minor Poets.

Believe me, yours very truly,   W. A. RALEIGH

Macmillan replied that Raleigh could take two, or even three, years before delivering his manuscript. 'After all, we have waited more than twenty years for a competent writer to undertake the task, so that a year or two more or less now matters little. . . . We are confident that if you succeed in pleasing yourself you will please both us and the public.' He also suggested that Raleigh's *Chaucer* should be submitted to Macmillans.

The Shakespeare finally appeared in 1907.

2 September 1903

I thank you for your kind letter.

> 'I am settled, and bend up
> Each corporal agent to this terrible feat';

and I have no objection to the announcement that *Shakespeare* is in preparation.

I take it that the right length will be about 60,000 words. I shall endeavour to avoid duplicating or vying with existing authoritative works. Mr. Lee's *Life* and Professor Dowden's *Primer* cannot be better in their own kinds. I must attempt to include Life, Times, Works, Criticism, in a condensed whole, freely treated after my own fashion.

The difficulty of the attempt will be much increased by the veneration (and the superstition) that hedges Shakespeare's person. Very few private persons succeed in assassinating Kings. The magnificence of the attempt unnerves their arms, and all their practice with fire-arms goes for nothing. I must try to remember that the King is but a man.

I am glad that the plan of your series excludes apparatus and notes, which are good to bury Shakespeare, but not to praise him.

My *Chaucer*, now set aside to cool, was designed to complete a kind of trilogy with *Milton* and *Wordsworth*. I meant to ask Mr. Edward Arnold to publish it, and if he will, I think it must go along with the other two. And it would be talking insolently for me to discuss what I shall do when I have 'finished' Shakespeare and Chaucer. I have always longed to escape from this parasitical kind of literature, and to speak for myself; but my profession makes this kind natural to me, so I suppose I shall die a mere critic.

So far as thinking goes, I will get to work at once.

In 1906 Macmillan sought Raleigh's opinion on a manuscript submitted by Frank Harris (1856–1931), novelist and journalist.* Replying to the next letter Macmillan wrote that Harris's book was 'hardly one upon which we should care to have our imprint. There are, in our judgment, limits to the extent to which a publisher who values his reputation should play the part of Chaucer's genial host.'

Oxford, 27 October 1906

Dear Mr. Macmillan,

I have read through *Shakespeare the Man*, and will say what I think of it.

The faults of the book — to begin with them — are written broad and large upon it. It is arrogant, rude, and vain in manner. Words like 'slush', 'balderdash', 'gibberish', applied sometimes to Shakespeare's weaker work and sometimes to work of his that other critics have admired, are too frequent ; and phrases like 'poor Coleridge', 'an unintelligent actor like Salvini', and so on, will not conciliate the general reader. The book is certain to annoy ; I can hardly conceive of a reverent and sensitive critic like my friend Professor Bradley having the patience to read it through.

The author, in his contempt for others, overestimates his own originality. Most of what he says has been said before, more delicately. What has not been said before, and is all his own, seems to me wrong. His view of Shakespeare is partial and one-sided, and strangely touched with a kind of contempt.

---

* In the course of a friendly letter to Harris, rejecting his book, Frederick Macmillan wrote that, although it would interest many people, 'We do not believe that it will be accepted by scholars as an important contribution to Shakespearean criticism. I must say that to me personally a great deal of it seems fanciful....' Harris replied on 1 November:

Thanks for your letter. Professor Freeman, I believe, regarded Carlyle's book on the French Revolution as 'the worst attempt at history writing he had ever come across'. This is only to say that the so-called scholar's opinion, as a rule, is worthless, or worse than worthless, on any question of art.

You yourself however regard the book as 'fanciful', and 'fanciful' in England is surely sufficient by way of condemnation.

The identification of Shakespeare with (among others) Posthumus in *Cymbeline* is an example of how far theory may carry a critic. When he speaks, by way of summary, of Shakespeare's 'imperial intellect and small snobberies; his giant vices and paltry self-deceptions; his sweet gentleness and long martyrdom', I find the patronage intolerable. It makes Shakespeare the hero of a bad melodrama. The subtlest and most many-sided of minds cannot be judged in this off-hand fashion by a writer who is simple, loud, vigorous and brusque.

All this is merely to say what I think of the book if it is to be considered among the important contributions to Shakespeare criticism. The question whether you should publish it is quite another thing. My lack of sympathy with the writer, which I have not concealed, is hardly relevant to this. So I must begin again.

In the first place, the faults of the book are mainly faults of manner. The same things, or something like them, might easily be said in a courteous and suggestive fashion. The writing is good, clear and incisive, commanding attention. There is no question in my mind that the book will find readers. Further it is a real book, and if the author had not explained its genesis, one could easily have guessed it. He read Shakespeare, with deep interest, from boyhood upwards. By degrees a theory, a portrait of the man, began to take shape in his mind. Then he hunted through the plays for confirmation, and last of all he turned to the critics, and found that he was the first to understand Shakespeare. The consequence of all this is that he gives the frank and sincere impressions of an untrained mind — and gives them in very telling language. Some of these impressions are worth recording, and, in reading the book, one is arrested, fairly often, by a just thought or a new parallelism. There is enough virtue in these pages to justify a book. The chapter on 'Hamlet-Macbeth' I think good, for all its extravagance.

The book, I should say, will easily find a publisher, and,

in my opinion, deserves to be published — certainly deserves it better than most treatises by Shakespeare adventurers. What you have to consider is whether you would dislike the handling that it would be pretty sure to get from those critics and scholars whom it is quite sure to enrage. I don't see why you should mind this. I picture you as the genial Host in charge of the Canterbury Pilgrims. Some of them, by their tales, annoy others ; and there are squabbles by the way. But the Host gives to each of them his turn, and when the Wife of Bath is interrupted, he protests — 'Let the woman have her say'. The only stories that he himself interrupts are those that are tedious and dull. But this book is not dull ; it is brisk, and will very possibly make some stir.

Yours sincerely,   W. A. RALEIGH

SIR WINSTON SPENCER CHURCHILL

1874–1964

In the autumn of 1905 Frank Harris, acting on behalf of the author, offered Churchill's life of his father, Lord Randolph, successively to Murrays, Cassells, Hutchinsons, Longmans, Heinemanns and Methuens. Eventually Macmillans accepted the book for a fee of £8000 on publication (plus a royalty on American sales) with a provision for shared profit later.

TELEGRAPHIC ADDRESS:
"PUBLISH" LONDON.
TELEPHONE NUMBER, 2688 GERRARD.

MACMILLAN & CO. Ltd.
St MARTIN'S STREET.
LONDON. W.C 30 oct 19 05

Dear Mr Macmillan,

The terms contained in your letter of this day are perfectly satisfactory to me & I hereby accept them as the conditions under which my Life of Lord Randolph Churchill will be published by you.

Yours truly,

Winston S. Churchill .

St. Martin's Street, W.C., 2 November 1905

Dear Mr. Churchill,

... I happened to see Mr. Longman only yesterday afternoon, and he congratulated me on getting your book, but I am afraid he thinks we are going to pay too much for it ; I hope that he may be wrong. By the way, we do not propose to tell the world at large what our arrangement with you is ; it always seems to me that gossip of this kind serves no good end and is a little bit undignified....

I am, yours sincerely,   FREDERICK MACMILLAN

Macmillan arranged that the proofs should be read by F. Moy Thomas, 'an experienced journalist, and quite competent', and Churchill replied:

105 Mount Street, W., 8 November 1905

Dear Mr. Macmillan,

I send you herewith the preliminary matter and the first five chapters of the first volume. These can be put up at once into page-proofs numbered consecutively from the beginning to the end. Only a word here or there may be altered in the future and there will be perhaps a few alterations in punctuation....

I hope the discretion of Mr. Moy Thomas is to be implicitly relied upon. I gather from him that he proposes to correct the proofs at the National Liberal Club. If you know him well of course it will be all right, but I have rather hesitated sending the chapters to the National Liberal Club as I think great care should be taken in handling matter of such journalistic value, and I have asked Mr. Thomas to call for them here ; I only mention this as I know nothing of the gentleman in question....

Please let me have the last revises back from Spottiswoode as soon as they are printed. I will return them forthwith.

WINSTON SPENCER CHURCHILL

I

13 November 1905

Dear Mr. Macmillan,

I have been considering the punctuation of Mr. Moy Thomas rather more carefully than I did hitherto and I am seriously disquieted by a growing feeling that it is permeated throughout by an absolute lack of system. I enclose the second chapter in which I draw your attention to two or three discrepancies in green pencil. I am very much concerned about this, as I am above all things anxious that the grammar and punctuation should be strictly correct. In these circumstances I suggest to you that the book should be read for punctuation solely once again before it goes to press. I am incompetent to do this, for I know the book nearly by heart and cannot concentrate my attention by reading.

I should have most confidence in my friend Mr. Frank Harris, of whose scholarship and precision in such matters I entertain the highest opinion. I am sorry to cause a delay at the last minute and to add to the expense of the publication, but I hope you will meet my views on this point.

Feeling sure that you would oblige me in this matter and realizing that time is pressing, I have already seen Mr. Frank Harris and I regret to say that he tells me that his time is fully occupied until Saturday, but that he would undertake to complete the entire revision by Monday morning.

I do not desire by this to reflect at all upon Mr. Moy Thomas and I should especially regret if it ever came to his ears that I was not satisfied with his work. It has been painstaking and thorough, but as I say there has been a certain lack of any definite system. May I suggest therefore that Mr. Moy Thomas should know nothing of any extra revision that we may make?

Will you send me word in the morning. Yours sincerely,

WINSTON S. CHURCHILL

27 November 1905

Mr. Frank Harris has now completed fully his revise of the proofs of my book. He has taken a great deal of trouble over them, and I now feel some confidence in submitting it to the public so far as grammar, construction and punctuation are concerned.

Lord Randolph Churchill was published in two volumes at 36*s* on 2 January 1906. A few months later the 'book war' broke out between *The Times* and the publishing trade. *The Times* Book Club, treating Churchill's book as a 'loss-leader', advertised it at 7*s* at the head of a list of 'remainders'.

Blenheim Palace, 6 June 1906

Dear Mr. Macmillan,

I am very sorry to see by a cutting which has reached me from *The Publisher and Bookseller* that *The Times* have played you a shabby trick. I do hope you will find it will not cause any serious injury to the sale of the book. It certainly cannot in any way reflect upon your credit as a publisher.

I do not see how you can stop people selling things they have bought below the cost price, but I can quite understand the annoyance and derangement which it causes. . . .

With good wishes, yours very sincerely,

WINSTON S. CHURCHILL

Churchill took his later books elsewhere, and did not return to Macmillans until 1941. His publishers, Messrs. Thornton, Butterworth, having gone into liquidation, he entrusted a number of his works* to Macmillans for five years. In 1945, after prolonged negotiations, the contract was not renewed, and Macmillans also felt

* *The World Crisis, 1911–18; The Aftermath; The Unknown War, 1914–17; My Early Life; Thoughts and Adventures; Great Contemporaries; Step by Step, 1936–39.*

unable to pay the price — £200,000 — which Churchill was asking for an option on his projected history of the second world war.

28 Hyde Park Gate, S.W.7, 21 November 1945

My dear Harold,

Thank you so much for your two letters of November 20. I take this opportunity of saying how grateful I am for the constant consideration and goodwill with which the great firm of Macmillan have always treated me.

Yours very sincerely,   WINSTON S. CHURCHILL

HENRI BERGSON
1859–1941

L'évolution créatrice, the *magnum opus* of a great French philosopher, appeared in Paris in 1907. In March of the following year Frederick Rothwell, one of Macmillans' regular readers, submitted to the firm a specimen of a translation which he wished them to publish. Macmillans ultimately published *Creative Evolution* in 1911 in the translation by Dr. Arthur Mitchell, of Harvard, who had been recommended by the American philosopher William James (1842–1910).

Villa Montmorency, 18 Avenue des Tilleuls, Auteuil,
Paris, 3 mai 1908

Messieurs,

En réponse à la lettre par laquelle vous m'informez que vous êtes disposés à publier une traduction anglaise de mon volume *L'évolution créatrice,* j'ai l'honneur de vous faire savoir que j'accepte les conditions que vous me proposez (une royalty de quinze pour cent sur le prix publié de chaque exemplaire vendu). Mais une grosse difficulté vient de surgir. Mr. Rothwell m'a envoyé, ces jours-ci, le commencement de sa traduction, et quoique ce soit un homme de talent, quoiqu'il ait remarquablement traduit des ouvrages d'un autre genre, je trouve que sa traduction ne pénètre pas assez dans l'esprit du texte et n'en rend pas non plus les nuances. Je dois d'ailleurs dire que la traduction de mon livre présente des difficultés exceptionnelles. Il faudrait un traducteur très compétent en matière de philosophie, et capable en même temps de donner une forme un peu artistique à son travail. Connaissez-vous quelqu'un qui réunisse ces qualités ? Si ce traducteur vraîment exceptionnel se rencontrait, je lui ferais des conditions aussi avantageuses qu'il le désirerait. Je lui abandonnerais ma royalty de 15 pour cent tout entière jusqu'au jour où une certaine somme (que nous fixerions ensemble) aurait été atteinte : à partir de ce moment, la royalty serait partagée également entre lui et moi.

Si vous ne connaissez personne, en ce moment, qui offre des garanties suffisantes, et si vous n'êtes pas pressé d'avoir cette traduction, nous attendrons qu'une occasion se présente. Parmi les professionnels de la philosophie qui étudieront mon livre en Angleterre et en Amérique, il se trouvera peut-être quelqu'un auquel l'idée viendra d'entreprendre cette traduction. Et c'est dans ces conditions, peut-être, que la traduction sera le mieux faite.

Recevez, je vous prie, Messieurs, l'assurance de mes sentiments distingués.   H. BERGSON

24 février 1910

Par ce même courrier je vous adresse la plus grande partie de la traduction de mon *Évolution créatrice*, juste les trois quarts (300 pages, sur les 400 que contient le livre). Les cent dernières pages sont entre les mains de Miss [Millicent] Murby, qui les soumet à une dernière révision et qui aura terminé ce travail dans une ou deux semaines. Si vous pouviez commencer à faire imprimer dès maintenant ce que je vous envoie, je crois que ce serait une très bonne chose, car la traduction doit être très attendue et demandée : j'en juge par les nombreuses offres de traduction qui m'ont été faites, depuis quelques mois, par des traducteurs ou éditeurs anglais. De plus, on s'occupe du livre dans les universités — notamment à Oxford, où un 'lecturer' consacre à ce sujet son cours de cette année — et aussi dans les revues anglaises et américaines, même dans des revues qui ne sont pas spécialement philosophiques, comme *The Nation* de Londres, *The*

Nation de New York, *The Times* (literary supplement), *The English Review*, *The New Age*, etc. Tout cela m'a fait penser que le moment de publier la traduction serait bien choisi, et qu'il serait à désirer que cela se fît le plus rapidement possible.

Voici quelques détails au sujet du manuscrit. Vous vous rappelez que je vous avais soumis, il y a quelques mois, la traduction de Mr. Mitchell complète, et que vous m'avez dit que vous l'accepteriez telle quelle si je pouvais vous la garantir. Après l'avoir relue de plus près, je m'aperçus qu'elle avait besoin d'être remaniée, et je fis part de mes observations à Mr. Mitchell. Mr. Mitchell ne s'est pas borné a remanier sa traduction ; il l'a refaite d'un bout à l'autre et l'a dactylographiée (typewritten) pour la seconde fois. J'ai soumis cette seconde traduction à une révision très attentive, qui m'a pris à peu près deux mois de travail ; et j'ai prié Miss Murby, de Londres, de la revoir une seconde fois après moi. Toutes les corrections à l'*encre rouge* sont de moi ; celles à l'*encre violette* sont de Miss Murby. Ma révision est entièrement terminée ; mais à celle de Miss Murby il manque, comme je vous le disais, les cent dernières pages, qui seront bientôt revues. Ce que je vous envoie aujourd 'hui est ce qui a été définitivement révisé par Miss Murby et par moi-même.

Il résulte de ce travail considérable de révision et de perfectionnement que le manuscrit est surchargé de ratures, qu'il est quelquefois difficile à lire et qu'il faudra le recommander tout spécialement à l'attention de l'imprimeur. Mais aussi, je crois que nous avons obtenu une traduction réellement adéquate au texte français, et qui pourra avoir le même succès que l'ouvrage original. Vous savez que l'ouvrage français a eu six éditions en moins de trois ans — succès dont il n'existe peut-être pas d'autre exemple pour un gros livre de philosophie pure.

Une traduction en russe a paru il y a déjà quelque mois, sans mon autorisation. On annonce pour bientôt une traduction polonaise, que je n'ai pas autorisée non plus. La traduction allemande, que doit publier la maison Diederichs, de Jena, ne pourra paraître que dans un certain temps, parce que j'ai demandé qu'elle fût remaniée complètement. On m'a proposé de traduire le livre en italien, mais je n'ai pas cru devoir accepter pour le moment.

11 mars 1910

En réponse à la lettre que je lui avais adressée il y a déjà un certain temps, Mr. Mitchell vient de m'écrire qu'il s'en remet entièrement à moi (et à Miss Murby) pour la correction des épreuves de sa traduction de *L'évolution créatrice*. Il désire seulement qu'on lui envoie les épreuves au fur et à mesure qu'elles seront prêtes ; mais il ne les corrigera pas et ne les renverra pas. Auriez-vous donc l'obligeance de dire à l'imprimeur de tirer *trois* exemplaires de chaque épreuve, l'un pour moi, l'autre pour Miss Murby, le troisième pour Mr. Mitchell, et d'envoyer simultanément l'épreuve à chacune de ces trois adresses ? Un seul de ces trois exemplaires lui sera retourné, car je demanderai à Miss Murby de m'envoyer ses corrections et je les combinerai avec les miennes, de sorte que c'est mon épreuve à moi, et elle seule, qui reviendra à l'imprimeur.

Avant de mettre en train la composition typographique, auriez-vous l'obligeance de faire imprimer une 'page-specimen' du livre et de me la communiquer? Peut-être pourrai-je vous suggérer quelque changement. Le choix du caractère et du papier auront, je crois, une certaine importance pour ce livre. Il a été lu en France par le public cultivé en général, et non pas seulement par ceux qui s'intéressent spécialement à la philosophie et à la science. Plus l'aspect extérieur en sera agréable, plus nous aurons de chances d'obtenir le même succès avec la traduction.

Villa Bois-Gentil, Saint-Cergue (canton de Vaud),
Switzerland, 15 août 1910

J'envoie aujourd'hui même à Messrs. R. & R. Clark les sept premières 'page-proofs' corrigées de *Creative Evolution*. Quoique aucune des corrections ne soit assez grave pour nécessiter un remaniement de la mise en pages, il y a un si grand nombre de petites corrections de détail qu'une seconde série d'épreuves me paraît absolument indispensable.

La raison de ces corrections assez nombreuses se trouve dans le fait suivant. La traduction de Mr. Mitchell n'était pas tout à fait, malheureusement, ce qu'elle aurait dû être ; il faut dire, d'ailleurs, que sa tâche était extraordinairement difficile. J'avais dû consacrer deux mois entiers, cet hiver, à réviser le manuscrit et presque à en refaire certaines parties, interrompant pour cela toutes mes autres occupations ; puis Miss Murby l'avait révisé à son tour. Dans ces conditions, j'ai tenu à soumettre les 'page-proofs' (je regrette seulement de ne pas l'avoir déjà fait pour les 'slip-proofs') à celui des philosophes anglais qui a le plus étudié mon livre, Mr. Wildon Carr (hon. sec. of the Aristotelian Society) qui a consacré trois belles et profondes études à *L'évolution créatrice* dans les 'Proceedings' de sa Société et dans le *Hibbert Journal*. Mr. Wildon Carr a consenti à cette révision, et c'est une véritable bonne fortune pour la traduction. Pour ne pas avoir à faire des changements trop considérables sur les épreuves en pages, Mr. Wildon Carr s'est abstenu de tout ce qui n'aurait été qu'un simple perfectionnement et s'est borné aux corrections qui lui ont paru indispensables au point de vue de la *clarté*. Mais, même ainsi, les corrections de détail se trouvent être assez nombreuses. Depuis que mon attention a été appelée par Mr. Wildon Carr sur ces détails — qui échappent naturellement à l'oeil d'un étranger — je me dis que nous aurions gravement compromis le succès du livre en ne le soumettant pas à cette dernière révision.

Je ne puis demander à Mr. Wildon Carr de se presser encore davantage, car je sais qu'il ne perd pas de temps pour

cette révision et qu'il fait tout son possible. Dans ces conditions, malgré le vif désir que j'ai moi-même de voir la traduction paraître sans retard, je ne suis pas d'avis que l'éditeur
américain commence la composition avant le milieu ou la fin
de septembre *au plus tôt* (et mieux voudrait *la fin* que le
milieu). S'il commençait plus tôt, il serait obligé de s'inter-
rompre, la révision de Mr. W. Carr ne pouvant naturellement pas aller aussi vite que la composition typographique,
surtout pour la seconde moitié du livre, qui est la plus
difficile.

Je vous serais reconnaissant d'appeler l'attention de
l'éditeur américain sur l'impossibilité où nous sommes de
publier hâtivement, et sous une forme incorrecte ou in-
suffisamment claire, un livre que nous désirons sans doute voir
paraître le plus tôt possible, mais qui n'est pas un livre
d'actualité et qui peut bien attendre quelques semaines de
plus, après avoir attendu trois ans pour être traduit. Le
succès croissant de l'ouvrage français est dû, en grande partie,
à la précision des détails et à la clarté de la forme. Si la
traduction ne présente pas des qualités analogues, on pré-
férera lire l'original, à moins d'ignorer absolument le français.

A year after W. B. Yeats had failed to persuade Macmillans to
publish a translation of Charles Péguy,* Bergson wrote the following
letter. Bergson's proposal was turned down because 'it is next to impossible to understand Péguy in selections, he having been a distinctly
prolix writer', and because, it being war-time, 'in view of the great
difficulty we are experiencing in getting books printed at all, we do not
feel that this is a time for making any experiments'.

31 Rue d'Erlanger, Paris, 9 novembre 1917
Cher Sir Frederic Macmillan,
Vous connaissez probablement de réputation Charles
Péguy, un des écrivains qui ont eu l'influence la plus
profonde sur la jeunesse française avant la guerre et qui ont

See page 292.

grandement contribué à revivifier l'âme du pays. Officier au début de la guerre, bravant tous les dangers, il fut tué à la veille de la bataille de la Marne. Pendant bien des années il a édité une revue intitulée *Cahiers de la Quinzaine*, où il a fait paraître tout ce qu'il a écrit — les études les plus variées sur des sujets de philosophie politique et sociale, de littérature, de philosophie pure, etc., ainsi que de fort beaux poèmes. C'était un esprit profondément original et un véritable écrivain. Il est naturellement peu connu en Angleterre, aucune traduction anglaise n'ayant encore paru. Cependant divers journaux anglais ont parlé de lui, et votre grand critique Edmund Gosse lui a consacré quelques pages très pénétrantes dans son récent volume *Inter arma*. En même temps que la présente lettre je vous adresse ce livre d'Edmund Gosse. Vous trouverez, aux pages 59–65 et aussi à la page 69, ce qui concerne Péguy.

Un jeune professeur d'anglais, M. Emile Saillens, actuellement mobilisé comme interprète, et qui figure parmi les admirateurs enthousiastes de Péguy, a traduit en anglais un certain nombre de pages de prose et de vers, choisies parmi celles qui pourraient le plus plaire au public anglais et américain. Il a fait précéder sa traduction d'une notice sur Péguy, qui me paraît fort bien faite. Le livre ne serait pas très gros (27,700 mots pour la partie de prose, et 2,429 lignes pour la section poésie). Seriez-vous disposé à prendre en considération la publication de ce livre, et voulez-vous que M. Saillens vous envoie son manuscrit?

Au cas où vous vous décideriez à le publier, j'écrirais volontiers quelques mots de préface pour présenter Péguy au public anglais et américain. Entre Péguy et moi la sympathie intellectuelle était grande. Il m'a d'ailleurs fait l'honneur de me consacrer un assez grand nombre de pages dans ses écrits.

Croyez, je vous prie, cher Sir Frederic Macmillan, à mes sentiments bien dévoués. H. BERGSON

COUNTESS VON ARNIM

1866–1941

Mary Annette Beauchamp married first Count Henning August von
Arnim (died 1910). In 1898 she offered Macmillans an anonymous
novel, *Elizabeth and her German Garden*, 'by Elizabeth Careless'. At
the publishers' suggestion the pseudonym was dropped, and no author's
name appeared on the title-page. Her anonymity was to be jealously
guarded. However, on 1 April 1899 the *Athenaeum* wrote, 'The
author of *Elizabeth and her German Garden*, who promises a new
volume shortly, is said to be Miss May Beauchamp, now Countess von
Arnim'.

Schloss Nassenheide, Boeck, Pommern, 4 April 1899

Dear Sir,

. . . I wish to ask you whether it would be possible for you
to contradict what they say. They have got my maiden name
wrong, as it is Mary and not May, so that it could be
contradicted truthfully, as 'Miss May Beauchamp' never
existed. Could you not say that 'the statement that the book
was written by the lady who before her marriage was Miss
May Beauchamp is incorrect'? I assure you this is giving me
very great annoyance, as after this in every review of the new
book it will probably be mentioned.

I should be greatly obliged if you could take advantage of
the mistake in the name to contradict it, and let me beg you
to advertise the new book *only* as by the author of *Elizabeth
and her German Garden*.

I remain, yours truly,   M. V. ARNIM

A disclaimer from Macmillans was printed in the next week's
Athenaeum, and *The Solitary Summer* 'by the author of *Elizabeth and
her German Garden*' appeared later that year.

19 August 1900

Would you kindly, if opportunity arises, contradict the report that Princess Henry of Pless wrote my books?

In 1916 'Elizabeth' married Francis, Earl Russell (1865–1931), of Telegraph House, Chichester. They proved incompatible, and separated after three years. In 1921 Macmillans published her novel *Vera*.

23 Bush Lane, Cannon Street, London E.C.4,
5 October 1921

Gentlemen,

Our client, Earl Russell, has had his attention called by several people to a book entitled *Vera*, in which, under the name of Wemyss, his person and character are insultingly caricatured and brought into contempt. This book is stated to have been written by the author of *Elizabeth and her German Garden*, who is well known to be our client's wife, and it is published by your house.

It is probable that you, as publishers for Lady Russell, were unaware of her intention to make this covert and scurrilous attack upon her husband, and we feel sure that directly this is pointed out to you a house of your reputation will not hesitate to take immediate and effective steps to prevent any further circulation of a libel of so serious and damaging a kind. To show how serious and how damaging is the libel, we need only refer you to the terms used by the reviewers in dealing with the character of Wemyss.

Our client is extremely anxious to avoid the public scandal which an action at law would involve, and if your response to this letter is prompt and satisfactory he is disposed to allow the matter to rest so far as you are concerned, although the injury and annoyance he has suffered are already of a very grave and aggravated nature. . . .

We are, gentlemen, yours obediently,

VANDERCOM & CO.

On Macmillans' assurance, confirmed to them by telephone by Lady Russell, that the character of Wemyss was 'purely fictitious' the solicitors replied that their client did not propose to pursue the matter further, adding:

18 October 1921

He regrets that Lady Russell's usual acumen failed her on this occasion, and did not warn her that descriptions of his appearance, and of portions of his residence, Telegraph House, and its furniture, would be likely to lead to regrettable misunderstandings on the part of the public, who had been prepared to believe from former examples that she makes a practice of lampooning her husbands.

Meanwhile 'Elizabeth' had not enjoyed the reception of her book.

Chalet Soleil, Randogne sur Sierre, Switzerland,
26 September 1921

Dear Sir Frederick,
... My battered body goes on getting one whack after another from reviewers, but I don't mind so long as it doesn't interfere with the sales, in which case I should be involving you, which would distress me — and I don't mind because I know [*Vera*] is the best thing I've done. *The Times Lit. Sup*. review wasn't a review at all, it was just bludgeoning, and did seem to have a trace of *personal* flavour. But perhaps crushed authors always suspect this. Meanwhile I'm well on in the next book, which I thought of calling *The Enchanted April*. Do you like that title? ...
    Yours very sincerely,   ELIZABETH RUSSELL

17 September 1922

Would you mind publishing [*The Enchanted April*] either a day sooner or later, because I am full of distrust of Fridays, and 27 October *is* one? I was married to Lord Russell on a Friday.

HERBERT GEORGE WELLS
1866–1946

Wells's early books were divided among half a dozen publishers, but with *The Food of the Gods* (1904) and *Kipps* (1905) he established what he hoped would be a permanent relationship with Macmillans. Sales, however, were disappointing, and Macmillans, who had taken over some of his earlier books, offered to let him take them back for cheap reissue elsewhere.

Spade House, Sandgate, 3 October 1907

Dear Mr. Macmillan,

... I note your offer to relinquish my books. Well, that's not a matter to go into in a hurry. I like your firm in very many ways. I don't think you advertise well, and I think you're out of touch with the contemporary movement in literature. I don't think you have any idea of what could be done for me (but that you will of course ascribe to the Vanity of Authors). But on the other hand you are solid and sound and sane. . . .

Yours ever,   H. G. WELLS

Of the 'three good novels' which he was planning in the autumn of 1908, Macmillans published *Tono-Bungay* in February 1909, but not, as will be seen, either *Ann Veronica* or the 'modern political novel', *The New Machiavelli*.

The new 'half-crown monthly review' was Ford Madox Hueffer's *English Review*, in which *Tono-Bungay* was serialized in 1908–9.

15 September 1908

My dear Mr. Macmillan,

Mrs. Wells tells me she has already written you about the date of publication of *Tono-Bungay*. It must I think be this spring of 1909. I want it to be the first of a succession of three good novels and I want them to follow each other up, one in the spring of 1909, one in the autumn of that year and one in 1910.

I am clearing up the autumn with two books. One is a small one that Constable will publish, *First and Last Things*, and which will really and finally end up the series of metaphysical, sociological and political 'spring-cleanings' that began in 1901 with *Anticipations* ; and the other is that *War in the Air* book which you released from our agreement. That will come late in October and ought to sell well.

With 1909 I want to make a fair bid for standing as a novelist and, if I possibly can, to specialize with novels of the type of *Tono-Bungay*. But only book-sales will render that possible. *Tono-Bungay* is too long for the popular magazine and too free-spoken. With that sort of book it is book success or nothing.

There is talk of a half-crown monthly review to begin this autumn which may serialize *Tono-Bungay* in five or six big instalments, but I do not think that anything of that sort is worth while delaying publication for. When do you think is the best month, February, March or April? I should be glad of your suggestion. Do you think February is too early?

I have now under revision a second novel, *Ann Veronica*, which I propose you should publish in the autumn of 1909. It is shorter than *Tono-Bungay*, about 80,000 words, but it is, I think, the best love story I have ever done. I will send you the MS. in a few weeks' time. Behind the cover of these two books I want now to get on with a third one which I have planned out in the last few weeks and which is to be a modern political novel. I want it to be big and various in the same way that *Tono-Bungay* is, and to give Westminster, a big north-country election, a country-house party, and at the same time a lot of the subordinate life, socialist meetings and fried-fish shops, political photographers, and so on and so on. I would like to give what is left of this year and all of

1909 to that, and if the book sales of the other two novels justify it, to put it out as a book right away in 1910.

There are my plans. Have you looked through *Tono-Bungay*? I hope you have, and I hope still more you like it and believe in it. As I told you long ago I want to specialize as a novelist. I think now my opportunity is ripe, and that if now novel follows novel without anything to distract people's attention — any other sort of work by me I mean — it will be possible to consolidate the large confused reputation I have at the present time. Are you game to back up the idea?

Yours very sincerely, H. G. WELLS

Anxious though the publishers were that novel should follow novel from St. Martin's Street, *Ann Veronica* proved too much for them. Wells, however, agreed that their rejection of it need not disturb harmonious relations.

St. Martin's Street, W.C., 19 October 1908

Dear Mr. Wells,

...I regret that we cannot publish *Ann Veronica* for it seems to me a very well written book and there is a great deal in it that is attractive, but the plot develops on lines that would be exceedingly distasteful to the public which buys books published by our firm. The early part of the book with the picture of middle class suburban life is very entertaining; indeed up to and including the episode of the Suffragette riot there is nothing to object to. When, however, Ann Veronica begins her pursuit of the professor at the International College, offers herself to him as a mistress and almost forces herself into his arms, the story ceases to be amusing and is certainly not edifying.

I can't help thinking that all this part of the story is a mistake: the moral of the book, if there be one, is not such as to commend itself to the majority of people.

I am, yours very sincerely, FREDERICK MACMILLAN

Early in 1910 Macmillans accepted *The New Machiavelli*, unread, and sent the manuscript piecemeal to the printer. Frederick Macmillan wrote on 21 June:

As the manuscript of the final chapters of *The New Machiavelli* only reached the printers last week, we have not until now had the opportunity of reading the complete book. I much regret to say that in spite of the fact that it contains a great deal that is brilliant — parts of it seem to me to be better than anything you have done hitherto — the whole book is a great disappointment to us.

You will remember that at the interview which took place here when the terms of the agreement were discussed, I said that it would have to be distinctly understood that the novel (which was then unwritten) should not contain any of the elements which led us to refuse *Ann Veronica*, and that you agreed to this, saying that the novel was to be a political one. Now this it cannot be called. It is true that it deals incidentally with politics, that the hero goes into the House of Commons, and that some of the most amusing parts of the book are the sketches of political life and persons, but in its essence *The New Machiavelli* is a novel dealing with social questions, and particularly with the question of sex.

It is unnecessary for me to particularize, but I feel sure you will agree that the kind of thing we objected to in *Ann Veronica* is here intensified, and that if we had good reason for rejecting *Ann Veronica*, there is twice as much reason why we should not publish *The New Machiavelli*.

My partners and I have discussed the matter very carefully, and have decided that the step which we now take with much regret is one that must be taken at any cost. We regret it because we are sorry not to be associated with a writer whom we regard as one of the ablest of the day; also, as I am sure you will believe, because we are sorry to do what may put you to some inconvenience.

I say nothing about breaking a contract, because in view of the proviso as to its contents which we made before the book was written I do not consider that the breach of contract is on our side. Fortunately the book has never been announced in any of our lists.

17 Church Row, Hampstead, 22 June 1910
Dear Sir Frederick,

I cannot of course allow you to break our contract in this fashion. I have a very clear recollection of our conversation about the subject of *The New Machiavelli* and I am quite sure there was no such exclusion of sexual interest as you now suggest. Every novel *must* have a sexual interest. I quite perceive, however, that there are strong practical objections to forcing a publisher who has changed his mind about a book to go on with its publication, and if you are prepared with any proposals for the transfer of the book to some other firm or for any arrangement that will not inflict grave pecuniary injury upon me, I shall be ready to consider it. I rejected an offer of Methuen (of £1,000 down and 25 per cent) in order to accept yours, but I cannot of course go to him now, and indeed the whole position becomes impossible for me and leaves me no alternative but litigation unless you are prepared for a much more careful consideration of any difficulties in the matter than you appear to have given them so far.

I don't want litigation if it can possibly be helped; our relations have hitherto been fair and frank and satisfactory, and I suggest therefore we have a conference before carrying the matter to our solicitors.

Very sincerely yours,   H. G. WELLS

After a conference Wells set about revising the proofs of *The New Machiavelli* with a view to making it 'more in accordance with your views', but to no avail. Macmillans set about finding another publisher but the book was rejected by Heinemann, Chapman & Hall, Duckworth and Hutchinson before acceptance by John Lane. It appeared in 1911. Wells wrote to Sir Frederick:

> I close the incident with my liking for and confidence in Messrs. Macmillan very considerably enhanced.

The publishers also, perhaps, had learnt a lesson, to judge by the following passage in a letter from Frederick to Maurice Macmillan. The book is *The Passionate Friends*, which the firm published in 1913. John St. Loe Strachey (1860–1927) was owner-editor of the *Spectator*, in which *Ann Veronica* had been reviewed under the heading 'A Poisonous Book', and in which, in the stirring correspondence that ensued, the Rev. Herbert Arthur Bull (1854–1928), a prep-school headmaster, had appealed for funds to facilitate the prosecution of authors and publishers of 'moral poison'. Of more than forty novels by Marion Crawford only three, including *To Leeward* (1884), were not published by Macmillans.

Le Grand Hôtel, Cannes, 8 February 1912

I should certainly like to see the MS. of Wells's novel, and I hope we may not be obliged to refuse it. I don't want to publish indecent books, but if we are to deal in literature at all it will not do for us to be bound by the prejudices of the Rev. Mr. Bull and St. Loe Strachey. We made a mistake of this kind years ago when we refused Crawford's *To Leeward*. It fortunately had no bad result because it suited Crawford to stick to us, but I felt it rather ridiculous when we took the book over from Chapman & Hall some years afterwards. . . . Don't refuse the book till I have seen it.

RUDYARD KIPLING
1865–1936

Macmillans were the principal publishers of Kipling's prose writings from the 1890s until his death. He corresponded with them almost entirely through the literary agents A. P. Watt & Son, and only a dozen brief notes written by him to Macmillans between 1890 and 1928 survive. One of these is reproduced overleaf. It refers to a collection of Kipling's stories published on the continent and in America as *Mine Own People*: before Macmillans' London edition was ready he learnt of a novel of that title by Louisa M. Gray, and changed his to *Life's Handicap*.

Kipling's *If* was printed in phenomenal quantities, either as a leaflet or as a display card, in the first world war. He normally charged a copyright fee. In 1916 the honorary superintendent of Waterloo Station Free Buffet for Soldiers and Sailors ('buffet, offices and stores in subway from no. 12 platform') sent Macmillans a copy of a letter she had written to Kipling:

12 November 1916

Dear Sir,

As hon. Superintendent of this buffet which serves hundreds of men going to the Front each day, I am writing to ask you if you would be good enough to grant me permission to have 30,000 copies of your poem 'If' struck off in leaflet form, for presentation to every man going out, as a Xmas and New Year card.

Working amongst the men as we have done, I realize what a tremendous influence for good the poem would have on them and how it would help them to endure the hardships of the trenches during the coming winter.

Hoping to receive a favourable reply, yours sincerely,

BERYL C. M. WILSON

101. 26 Lr Rd.

May 8th 91.

Gentlemen.

I have just made the unpleasant discovery that a female writer has written & published a book called "Mine own people".

Under these circumstances I imagine that I am compelled to alter the title of the book now with you. It must now be called "Life's Handicap" with sub title "being stories of mine own people". I believe there is no objection to keeping the sub-title as it is.

Sincerely
Rudyard Kipling

Macmillans replied that the cost of the leaflets would be £55, but when Kipling decided to forgo his royalty the charge was reduced to £30.

In 1919 the post-war drop in Kipling's sales led to the following characteristic exchange of letters.

Hastings House, 3 November 1919

Dear Sir Frederick,

The following is a copy of that part of Mr. Kipling's letter which I read to you this morning :

'Macmillan's letter to you regarding the falling off in my sales has annoyed me more than a little. He takes the pre-war scale of sales as his standard of average and seems to accept the last six months' drop in them as not only beyond his control but as almost beneath his notice.

'During the war my sales increased. Surely then was the time for Macmillan to take advantage of the larger public which my books had attracted and to hold and increase this connection. But when you get down to the facts, my books were allowed to sell themselves and when any effort was needed to sell them neither the will nor the machinery to do so was put into motion.

'Given a business even one third the extent of mine this would be unwise, but, as things stand, it is worse than unwise. For the last quarter of a century Macmillan has been in charge of an extraordinarily valuable property of mine which was developed, I do not say in spite of his exertions, but certainly with the minimum of attention and expenditure on his part. The same applies exactly to Methuens. In both cases the profit of the business was taken for granted and any lapse in a long established proposition was considered as a dispensation of Providence. If nothing is done now by these firms we shall have the sales steadily running downhill, while we shall continue to be put off with figures which can be made to prove anything.

'I have no doubt that, to keep up the sales, effort, expenditure and attention are required, but I wish it to be distinctly understood that I expect that effort to be made by the firms who have my property in charge.'

Yours sincerely,   A. S. WATT

St. Martin's Street, W.C., 4 November 1919

Dear Mr. Watt,

I am very sorry that the expression I used in my letter — viz., that there was no reason to be unhappy about the position of affairs — should have led Mr. Kipling to think that I was indifferent to the sale of his books, and I shall be grateful if you will assure him that this is very far from being the case.

I should indeed be unhappy if I had reason to think that the drop in the sales — I hope only a temporary one — was due to any inattention or want of activity on the part of Mr. Kipling's publishers, but I have no reason to attribute it to such a cause. We are fully conscious of the advantage to ourselves both in honour and profit of having Mr. Kipling's books in our Catalogue and we are most anxious to be worthy of the confidence he has been good enough to place in us for many years. I can assure Mr. Kipling that there is no one in this house, from the Chairman to the smallest office boy, who does not consider it his duty to advance Mr. Kipling's interest in every way in his power. There are standing orders to the effect that whatever the difficulties of production may be, the stock of 'Kipling' is always to be ample, and however great the demand the portion of the warehouse assigned to his books is always to be kept full. We have a full staff of travellers constantly on the Road whose business it is to see that the retail booksellers replenish their stock frequently, and we make a point of keeping the various editions in the eye of the public by direct advertisement.

Since your visit of yesterday I have been considering

whether anything could be done that was left undone, or any existing method improved, and I have only been able to make one suggestion — that is, to try the effect of increased newspaper advertising. I have therefore arranged that between now and Christmas the standing advertisement of Mr. Kipling's editions should appear not at intervals as at present but in *every* list of general publications that we insert in the newspapers.

Finally I hope that Mr. Kipling will believe that my reading of the Horatian precept about keeping an equable mind in adversity does not, and never has prevented me from taking the most active steps to improve the adverse circumstances.

I am, yours very truly,   FREDERICK MACMILLAN

JOHN MAYNARD KEYNES
Lord Keynes
1883–1946

Macmillans published several books by Maynard Keynes, including his *Indian Policy and Finance* (1913) and *The Economic Consequences of the Peace* (1919). His letters to the firm, for the most part disappointingly dull, are enlivened with occasional light touches. When told by Daniel Macmillan that the *Shoe and Leather Record* wanted a portrait of himself to accompany a review of his *Tract on Monetary Reform* (1923) he was provoked into replying: 'No such thing available. I could let them have a pattern of my shoes.' He edited the *Economic Journal* from 1912 to 1945.

Keynes acted as Macmillans' reader of economic books. In 1913 they sent him *Work and Wealth, a Human Valuation*, by John Atkinson Hobson (1858–1940), which they published in the following year.

King's College, Cambridge, 25 October 1913

My dear Dan,

Before opening the parcel which contains Hobson's book, I ought to say that I am doubtful if I am the right person to report on it for you. Hobson has his public and his admirers. But personally I take, on the whole, a very unfavourable view of his books. See, for example, my review of his latest work in the *Economic Journal* for September.

If you want to know whether the book is likely to pay I can say, without looking at it, that a work by Hobson entitled *Work and Wealth*, is certain to have a respectable circulation. But I have so much prejudice against what I regard as his sophistries that it is scarcely fair that I should report on his work for a publisher. Shall I return you the package unopened?

Many thanks for the figures you sent about the circulation of [*Indian Policy and Finance*]. The English circulation is, to me, very satisfactory. But I am surprised that more copies have not been sold in India. Perhaps the book has not been available there for very long. I got a letter a week or two ago, which must have been written in September, from the Financial Secretary to the Government of India, who said incidentally that they had had difficulty in getting hold of the book, and as a matter of fact that the only person at headquarters who had been successful in getting one was the Viceroy. But I suppose that I may assume that these delays were only temporary.

Yours ever,   J. M. KEYNES

To Frederick Macmillan:

29 October 1913

I have sent back unopened the manuscript of Hobson's, in regard to which I have corresponded with Dan. I do not think Hobson is a man who ought to be prevented from publishing his work, and I do not wish, therefore, to discourage you from giving it full consideration. I only feel that I am too hostile a critic of his work to be a satisfactory reporter on it.

Keynes was elevated to the peerage in 1942. In 1945 he went to America to negotiate Lend-Lease aid to Britain. He died less than three months after the last of these letters was written.

Keynes's *Treatise on Money* had appeared in two volumes in 1930, and his *General Theory of Employment, Interest and Money* in 1936. Sir Stafford Cripps (1889–1952), whose unhelpful letter concludes the series, was president of the Board of Trade in 1945–7 and Chancellor of the Exchequer in 1947–50.

Tilton, Firle, Lewes, 1 January 1946

Dear Sirs,

Returning from America, I have been looking through the records you sent me of the sales of my books last year and what is in print and what is not. The following points seem to arise :

(1) Since there were only 263 copies of the *General Theory* in stock on 30 June last, it is presumably out of print by now or will be very shortly. I would plead very strongly that, whatever happens to my other books, this should be kept in print. I regard it as highly essential that copies should be available to the students now returning to the universities. This book has rather a special position amongst my writings, and I cannot readily contemplate its being out of print. I should be much obliged if you could let me know what you can do about it, and do about it urgently. A fairly large edition would, I think, be in place. As regards the price, I would leave this to your discretion, though, as you know, I like it to be kept as low as possible.

(2) *The Economic Consequences of the Peace* is now out of print. I feel the question of reprinting this is quite another thing from the *General Theory* and of nothing like the same importance, though I see that as many as 300 copies were sold last year. Here I should be grateful for your opinion whether you think this is a book which should go permanently out of print, or what your ideas about it are.

(3) What about the *Treatise on Money*? Judging from the copies in stock at the end of last June, it is likely that this is already out of print, or soon will be. Am I right in thinking that the standing type is available? Here I should suppose that the book ought to be reprinted as soon as possible, but I do not regard it as of anything like the same urgency as the *General Theory*.

I am, of course, well aware of the difficulties of paper supply, though the President of the Board of Trade has alleged, I do not know with what accuracy, that enough paper has now been available for all text-books. One would, however, appreciate being at any rate informed and consulted before all one's most important books are allowed to go out of print.

Yours faithfully,   KEYNES

46, Gordon Square, Bloomsbury, 5 January 1946
My dear Dan,

Thanks for your letter of 4 January. I think that the *Economic Consequences* and the *Treatise on Money* can be left on one side, at any rate for the time being. But I am very unhappy about the suggestion that the *General Theory* will not be available before May. It does seem to me really essential to have that in print for students at the very earliest moment. If I had not been away in America I would, of course, have discovered sooner that it was about to get out of print.

It seems to me quite unnecessary to wait for 'suitable paper'. Any paper whatever would do. Nor is it essential that the book should be bound, though I think you said on a previous occasion that the shortage of labour for paper-bound books was just about as bad as for cloth-bound. Do please see if you cannot get it out with the booksellers, in however shabby a form, at the earliest possible moment.

If the book is not available, the students read all kinds of books about it instead of the original. I have enough pride of authorship in the book not to relish that. I am content that the price of the new edition should be 10s 6d; though, if you can agree to a temporary, *ersatz*, shabby edition, perhaps that should be cheaper until it can be printed properly.

I return your cutting about paper for text-books. I rather think my quotation from the President of the Board of Trade was something he said behind the scenes, where he was not in a position to be contradicted. Perhaps, if I get a good opportunity, I will tackle him about it.

Yours ever,　　　　　　　　MAYNARD KEYNES

9 February 1946

You may remember that in a recent letter I quoted Cripps as having said there was plenty of paper for text-books. You replied that he was talking through his hat. So I thought I would take the opportunity to write to him to do a little propaganda.

After some delay he has replied as below. I send this for your private eye — not wanted back.

Board of Trade, Millbank, S.W.1, 29 January 1946

My dear Keynes,

Thank you for your letter of the 5th January about paper for text-books.

As you point out, there is still a shortage of text-books. In some cases this may be due primarily to shortage of paper and in others to shortage of labour in the printing industry. So far as paper is concerned, we have been able to increase publishers' quotas very considerably over the last six months (they now stand at 65 per cent of pre-war) and I hope that a further increase will be possible at the end of February. Apart from these quotas, however, a special reserve of paper, on the distribution of which I am advised by a committee under the chairmanship of Sir Walter Moberly, has been set aside since fairly early in the war for books of special importance for which publishers cannot provide paper from their quotas. It is open to any publisher who can show that he is unable to produce an important text-book from his regular quota to apply for a special allocation from this reserve ; but, as I have said, there are labour as well as paper problems in book publishing, and it has not always been possible for a firm to use for book publishing as much paper as could have been made available to it had it made full use of this reserve.

Yours very sincerely,   R. STAFFORD CRIPPS

JAMES JOYCE

1882–1941

Joyce's *Dubliners* was accepted, but not published, by Grant Richards in 1906, rejected by Elkin Mathews (who had meanwhile published Joyce's poems, *Chamber Music*) in 1907, and accepted, but again not published, by Maunsel of Dublin in 1910. Eventually Richards published the book in 1914. Macmillans' reason for rejecting it can only, but easily, be surmised: no reader's report survives.

Via Donato Bramante 4, II, Trieste, 13 July 1913

Dear Sirs,

Will you kindly let me know whether you are disposed to consider for publication a volume of stories, *Dubliners*, dealing with life in Dublin today?

The book which is printed in proof was accepted and set up by Maunsel of Dublin who then withdrew from their engagement. The entire first edition in fact (save one copy which I have) was burned by the printer. I have written for the book a preface in which I narrate its strange and, I hope, unique history extending over eight years. The disaster in which the history closes is explicable only on the assumption that it was brought about by what in these latitudes is called a *camorra* as there is nothing in the book itself to warrant or excuse such conduct. Needless to say both the publisher and printer had had the MS. in their possession for a long time — over two years — and had set up and pulled first proof and revise before they decided to act in such a manner.

Mr. W. B. Yeats or Mr. Arthur Symons, if he be still in London, or Mr. Elkin Mathews, publisher (who brought out five years ago a book of verses by me), will be able to give you any further information you may need about me.

Should you publish I can engage myself to take 110 copies at trade rates for sale in Trieste, these orders having been booked for some time, and can also arrange for the publication of translations of two of the stories in the *Nuova Antologia*.

Awaiting your courteous reply, I am, dear sirs, sincerely yours,   JAMES JOYCE

K

WILLIAM BUTLER YEATS

1865–1939

Yeats's abundant correspondence with Macmillans between 1913 and 1938 is for the greater part concerned with proof-corrections, presentation copies, permissions for others to reprint his poems, and the like. The following letters have been selected to illustrate his interest in promoting the fortunes of other writers.

Yeats was the most indefatigable of several Irish and English friends who revised the English texts of the prose and poetry of Sir Rabindranath Tagore (1861–1941), the Indian philosopher. Another was Thomas Sturge Moore, the minor Irish poet. For Tagore's *Fruit-Gathering* (1916) Yeats suggested to Frederick Macmillan that someone should write an introduction; failing 'some Hindu competent to comment', Ezra Pound, 'who made a study of Tagore's prosody when Tagore was in London, is the best available man'. Yeats is writing, soon after the Easter Rising, from the house of his Irish nationalist friend Maud Gonne (Mrs. MacBride, 1866–1953).

c/o Mme. Gonne, Colleville, Calvados, France,
9 July 1916

Dear Sir,

... I suggested an essay on Tagore's poetry because I thought it would remind reviewers that Tagore is not a writer of facile English for English religious readers, but a master of very arduous measures whom they read in a tongue that is not his. I feel that there is a reaction against his reputation, and that it is important that we should feel once more that he belongs to a different civilization and does not speak directly to us at all. However, I may be over-anxious on the subject, and in any case this reaction may not go very far....

Yours sincerely,   W. B. YEATS

Tagore's works mentioned in the next letter were all published by Macmillans between 1913 and 1918 (*A Lover's Knot* as *Lover's Gift and Crossing*, and the autobiography as *My Reminiscences*).

18, Woburn Buildings, W.C., 28 January 1917

I send *A Lover's Knot*. It is rather an embarrassment. I hope you will not mind if I write to Tagore that you have asked me to make as few alterations as possible as American publication hurries us. I can add from myself that his English is now much more perfect. You probably do not know how great my revisions have been in the past. William Rothenstein will tell you how much I did for *Gitanjali* and even his MS. of *The Gardener*. Of course all one wanted to do 'was to bring out the author's meaning', but that meant a continual revision of vocabulary and even more of cadence. Tagore's English was a foreigner's English and, as he wrote to me, he 'could never tell the words that had lost their souls or the words that had not yet got their souls' from the rest. I left out sentence after sentence, and probably putting one day with another spent some weeks on the task. It was a delight and I did not grudge the time, and at my request Tagore has made no acknowledgment. I knew that if he did so his Indian enemies would exaggerate what I did beyond all justice and use it to attack him. Now I had no great heart in my version of his last work *Fruit-Gathering*. The work is a mere shadow. After *Gitanjali* and *The Gardener* and *The Crescent Moon* (exhaustively revised by Sturge Moore), and a couple of plays and perhaps *Sādhanā*, nothing more should have been published except the long autobiography which has been printed in the *Modern Review*, a most valuable and rich work. He is an old man now and these later poems are drowning his reputation. I told this to Rothenstein and he said 'we must not tell him so for it would put him into the deepest depression'.

I am relieved at your letter though I would not like to tell

Tagore so. I merely make ordinary press revisions for there is nothing between that and exhaustive revising of all phrases and rhythms that 'have lost their soul' or have never had souls. Tagore's English has grown better, that is to say more simple and more correct, but it is still often very flat.

Excuse my writing so much unasked criticism, but I have been deeply moved by Tagore's best work and that must be my excuse.

I am still prepared to make the old exhaustive revision if you wish it, but it would take time and I shall hope that you do not wish it.

Charles Péguy (b. 1873, killed before the Battle of the Marne, 1914), Catholic apologist and poet, had a profound influence on French thought. The project outlined in the following letter did not materialize, and no English translation of the dramatic poems on Joan of Arc was published until 1950. The proposed translator of 1916 was Iseult, daughter of Maud Gonne.

The books about which Yeats, writing from the Savile Club, inquires in his postscript were *Reveries over Childhood and Youth* and *Responsibilities and Other Poems*, both published in October 1916.

63 St. James Street, W., 14 September 1916

... A young friend of mine has begun a translation of the first volume of Péguy's Joan of Arc trilogy. The first volume is Péguy's masterwork, and this translation is, I think, entirely admirable. Would you be inclined to publish this book if she obtains permission from Madame Péguy? I will, if need be, write a preface or introduction.

For various reasons I am very anxious to introduce the French school of Catholic writers to Ireland, and look upon this book as a start. I should think that a book of Péguy's would sell well, as his death in the war has made his name well known. The Joan of Arc trilogy is devoted to Faith,

Hope and Charity. The first volume is on Charity, and is a dialogue between Joan and a Nun. It is a devotional work of great beauty, which stands by itself.

My friend is half English and half French and has, I believe, a remarkable sense of style, a remarkable feeling for the music and colour of words.

I am going to Ireland, but I think you had best for the present write to me at the above address, which is that of my club. The hall porter is more prompt at sending on letters than my house-keeper. . . .

When do you propose to publish my two books?

Esmé Stuart Lennox Robinson (1886–1958) was associated with the Abbey Theatre, Dublin, as manager, director and playwright, for nearly fifty years. As a result of Yeats's recommendation Macmillans published *Six Plays* by Robinson in 1928 — the five named in the second paragraph of the next letter, together with *Give a Dog* . . . *The Round Table* had been published by Putnam in 1924.

Hôtel St. Georges, Route de Fréjus, Cannes,
12 January 1928

Dear Sir Frederick,

I write to you upon a matter which has been in my mind for some time. Lennox Robinson is at present the most accomplished dramatist of the Abbey Theatre. Casey has more startling material, but he has nothing like Lennox Robinson's mastery of his art. His talent has in the last couple of years reached maturity.

I think a volume containing a just finished play to which he has not yet given a name, *The Big House*, *The White Blackbird*, *The Portrait*, and the revised version of *The Round Table* if it can be got out of Putnam's hands who has the first version, might have a very considerable success. *The Big*

House, which always draws large audiences in Dublin, is exceedingly topical, as it deals with the effect of the Irish Civil War on the Protestant landowner and his family.

There are other plays which could be added : *The White-headed Boy*, for instance, which had a considerable run in London and toured America and Australia. These other plays, however, are more objective, more national in the narrow sense of the word, and might perhaps come later, especially as he will, I know, revise some of them.

His work has been scattered here and there ; of some of the plays there are only paper-covered editions published in Dublin for the use of players. My feeling is that the time has come when critics would be glad to give a serious consideration to his talent if they had before them a sufficient mass of his entirely mature work. I feel myself confident that he is a man of very great power and very great subtlety. May I ask him to write to you and propose a volume?

Yours sincerely,　　　　　　　　　　　　　W. B. YEATS

SIR MAX BEERBOHM

1872–1956

In 1915 Macmillans invited Max Beerbohm to contribute an introductory note to *Six Portraits of Sir Rabindranath Tagore* by (Sir) William Rothenstein (1872–1945). They offered a fee of two guineas.

26 Oxford Terrace, W., 27 August 1915

Gentlemen,

I enclose the corrected proof of my 'note' for Mr. Rothenstein's drawings. I shall be much obliged if you will send me a 'revise' of it.

Really I do not wish to receive any fee for it. I undertook it with the greatest possible pleasure in the opportunity of expressing a part of my admiration for Mr. Rothenstein's work ; and this pleasure is a quite sufficient reward.

But, since a fee has been offered by you, you might perhaps send the amount to the Red Cross Fund.

I am yours faithfully,　　　　　　MAX BEERBOHM

'A.E.'
George William Russell
1867–1935

'A.E.', a leading figure in the Irish literary renaissance, was indefatigable in support of his younger compatriots. The outcome of his recommendation of James Stephens is related on pages 302ff. below.

Macmillans published Stephens's *Mary*, as *The Charwoman's Daughter*, in 1912. Shan F. Bullock (1865–1935) was a novelist of Ulster rural life; Richard Whiteing (1840–1928) was a minor Victorian novelist whose one success was *No. 5 John Street* (1899), a 'realistic' story of London slum life.

17 Rathgar Avenue, Rathgar, Dublin, 27 October 1911

Dear Sir,

You may remember perhaps that I sent you seven or eight months ago the MS. of a volume of verse by James Stephens. Your reader did not think it showed more than promise, but you were willing to publish them. On considering the matter I thought it best to let the verses wait, as his work was getting better every month. But I mentioned, I think, in my letter to you that I thought he was a born story-teller and his best work would be in prose.

You said you would be glad to see more of his work, and I am sending herewith his story *Mary*, which has been running through the *Irish Review* for some months and which will be concluded next January. I think it is a story any publisher should be glad to publish, and my own opinion of its merits is confirmed by novelists like Shan Bullock; and I believe Mr. Whiteing, author of *No. 5 John St.* is one of Mr. Stephens's most enthusiastic admirers. I would be greatly pleased if James Stephens's story met with your approval as a publisher. A copy has been sent to the Macmillan Co. of America who are publishing a volume of Mr. Stephens's poems and who have asked for the MS. of the story.

Stephens is young and I believe has a great future before him, and his power as a writer and his invention grow continually. He has already a very considerable reputation, and I do not think a publisher could lose anything by so delightful a tale as *Mary*, which is the best picture of Dublin life I ever read. I believe he will come yet to write a masterpiece and I want recognition for him to encourage him. He has had all the adventures in his youth to fit him up for the next twenty years, has starved, fought for bread with a man, slept in the open, tramped the roads and is now working as a typist about ten hours a day, and it cannot be good for him to have to write his stories at night after a long day's work often with overtime. He is as proud as he could well be and won't take any help but will sell his literary wares. I hope your reader will think more favourably of this story than of the verses.

Yours sincerely,   GEO. W. RUSSELL

'A.E.' was not related to George William Erskine Russell (1853–1919), journalist, politician, privy councillor and author of the English Men of Letters volume on *Sydney Smith*.

14 January 1917

Dear Sirs,

I came to an understanding with my namesake Rt. Hon. Geo. W. E. Russell some years ago that he was to accept the credit of my verses when the young ladies in poetry clubs wrote to him congratulating him on his poetic genius, and that I, living in a poor neighbourhood, was to accept without protest the glory attaching to the title of 'Right Honourable' by which I am frequently addressed. But I distinctly made no agreement with him to pay his bills when by chance they came to me. I doubt if he has paid any of mine. I am shocked to find that he has not paid for books bought before the war and has stretched the moratorium to cover two trifles of $7d$ each. He got the books, and I the bill and the obloquy of not paying. Please send this letter to my namesake and tell him I am open to a deal about paying his Dublin bills if he will engage to pay my London bills for books.

    Yours sincerely,   GEO. W. RUSSELL, 'A.E.'

    P.S. Please note that in my case the 'E' is not sandwiched between the 'W' and 'R', but comes after my name — 'A.E.' This is the minute difference between my namesake and myself. It is like the pink and blue ribbons nurses put on twins to distinguish them.

    The next letter, to Frederick Macmillan, refers to *The Candle of Vision*, published by Macmillans in 1918.

                                        8 July 1918

Dear Sir,

    I wrote to you I think a little over a year ago that I hoped to send you shortly the MS. of a book I was writing. I was unable to complete the book when I hoped as I was engaged for six months as a member of the Irish Convention. I have now finished the book, or rather have written enough for a volume, for if it excites interest I could continue the speculations through another volume.

    The book may be described as the efforts of one who is both artist and poet to discover what element of truth lay in his own imaginations. I think it will interest the people who read my poems and perhaps others who will read prose but not poetry. I have tried, unlike the ordinary psychologist, to write with as much beauty as if I were writing verse, and it may be read for its prose if not for its subject matter. I think it will have, like my verses, not a very large sale, but the demand would I believe justify publication and the sale would be fairly steady. . . .

I do not think anything quite of the same kind as this book has been attempted before, and its originality may attract attention to it even in such an epoch as we are living in. I would be glad to hear your opinion about publication.

Yours sincerely,   GEO. W. RUSSELL, 'A.E.'

A.E. edited the *Irish Homestead* from 1906 until its amalgamation with the *Irish Statesman* in 1923. Early in 1925 Macmillans published *Two Plays* ('Juno and the Paycock' and 'The Shadow of a Gunman') by Sean O'Casey, and *History of the Irish State to 1914* by Alice Stopford Green (1847–1929), widow of J. R. Green.

The Irish Statesman, 84 Merrion Square, Dublin, 24 February 1925

Dear Sir Frederick,

A copy of the Spring Circular of your company was sent to the *Irish Statesman* which I edit, with a note saying that books would be sent for review if asked for. I wrote for some books which would be of interest to Irish readers, among them Sean O'Casey's plays. I see they have been sent to other journals but I did not receive a copy. The paper I edit is practically the only weekly review in Ireland which tries to interest its readers in literature and the arts. Among those who write for it are W. B. Yeats, James Stephens, Mrs. J. R. Green, Lady Gregory, Lennox Robinson, Sean O'Casey, Sir Horace Plunkett, Dr. Douglas Hyde, Dr. Bergin, Professor Curtis, Dr. George O'Brien, Liam O'Flaherty, Padraic Colum, Stephen Gwynn, Walter Starkie F.T.C.D.,* W. Fearon F.T.C.D., in fact all who

* Fellow of Trinity College, Dublin.

have won any distinction in literature or science or economics. I believe that the readers of the paper include the vast majority of those in Ireland who are interested in literature, and I have many readers in Northern Ireland.

I write hoping you will give instructions that when books are asked for review they will be sent to the *Irish Statesman*. I do not wish books to be sent which I could not find space to deal with, but only those for which I am certain of finding a competent reviewer who will take an interest in his subject. I have secured a promise from John MacNeill, the Minister for Education and the greatest living authority on ancient Irish history, to review Mrs. Green's forthcoming volume for which I have also asked. I am sorry for troubling you but my letter seems to have been neglected. I know the number of review copies sent out is a considerable expense, but it would in my opinion be better to cut off any other Irish paper than this because there is no other which could be called literary at all. I enclose a couple of copies for your confirmation.

Yours sincerely,   GEO. W. RUSSELL, 'A.E.', ed. *I.S.*

'Frank O'Connor' was the pseudonym of Michael O'Donovan (1903–66), librarian, novelist and playwright. A.E. had published a number of his short stories in the *Irish Statesman* before writing the next letter, which resulted in Macmillans publishing O'Connor's first book, *Guests of the Nation* (1931), and the greater number of his later books.

17 Rathgar Avenue, Dublin, 30 October 1930

My friend 'Frank O'Connor' tells me that he has finished a book of short stories which he desires to submit to you for publication. May I supplicate attention for his MS.? He is a young man of very great talent, an admirable poet and something of a scholar. His translations from Gaelic are the best I

know. His stories are, I believe, about the civil war in Ireland
and he had exceptional opportunities for gathering intimate
knowledge of this dark period in our history. But his interest
in writing these stories is not political but human. That is,
his interest is in the characters, not in the political situation. I
recommended James Stephens to your attention a good
many years ago. I have come across no young Irish writer
since in whose future I have more confidence.

JAMES STEPHENS
1880–1950

Stephens's first book of verse, *Insurrections*, dedicated to 'A.E.', was published in Dublin in 1909. In the autumn of 1910 'A.E.' (George Russell) sent a new manuscript of Stephens's poems to Frederick Macmillan, who replied that, though the firm's reader was not enthusiastic, nevertheless, 'in the hope that your prophecy as to his future success in the line of prose fiction may be fulfilled', he would publish the book. Russell's next letter on the subject, nearly a year later, is printed on page 296 above.

Two of Stephens's novels, *The Charwoman's Daughter* and *The Crock of Gold*, were published by Macmillans in 1912, and a third, *The Demi-Gods*, was contracted for. Meanwhile the book of poems hung fire. On Christmas Day 1913 Frederick Macmillan wrote to his cousin George from Paris:

I had a very satisfactory interview with James Stephens, who is a funny little creature exactly like a Leprechaun. I find that he does not mean to give up Pinker for the sake of another agent, but to give up agents altogether, and he has come to the sensible conclusion that he can do as well or even better for himself and save 10 per cent. We must see that we treat him liberally so that he may realize that he is losing nothing by dealing with us direct.

He tells me that his novel (already arranged for) will not be ready for publication before the autumn, but he will have a volume of poems (probably under the title of *Songs from the Clay*) ready for the spring. I agreed that we would publish the volume on a 20 per cent royalty, with a moderate sum (say £20) on account. . . .

Of course the poems are not very attractive, but it won't

do to let Stephens go elsewhere as he is one of the most promising of the young men. I am glad to say that although he has a wife and children he is not greedy, and does not sacrifice his art for the sake of making money. This is all the more reason for encouraging him.

11 rue Campagne-Première, Paris, 16 February 1914
Dear Sir Frederick Macmillan,

I write to ask if it would be possible to delay the publication of my poems *Songs from the Clay* for a little time. I sent them to A.E. and he is strongly of opinion that it would be unwise to publish them until certain other poems had been added so as to give a greater variety to the collection, and, as a matter of fact, I am now engaged in writing these additional poems. I am quite sure that with a little delay I can make the book, not alone much bigger, but very much better. I wish this first book of verse which I am publishing with you to be as good as ever I can make it, and I can promise that it will be good. If you can agree to this delay you will very much oblige me.

As to the advance royalty — I can return this to you to be held until I send you the completed MS.

Please pardon me for the trouble I am giving in this matter. Very truly yours,   JAMES STEPHENS

In August 1914 Stephens, returning proofs of *The Demi-Gods*, wrote that 'A.E.' 'considers that this is the best book that I have yet written, and very much superior to *The Crock of Gold*. I agree with him. . . .' He suggested submitting a volume of 'children's poems, or rather poems about children, with which I am very pleased': the title would be *The Adventures of Seumas Beg*. *The Demi-Gods* was published in October 1914, *Songs from the Clay* in March 1915, and *Seumas Beg* in October 1915.

George P. Brett was the head of The Macmillan Company, New York.

Paris, 16 December 1914

I have your letter and the 'copy' for *The Adventures of Seumas Beg*. When you require this MS. I shall return it. I note you have postponed the publication of *Songs from the Clay* until 12 March 1915.

As to Mr. Brett's remarks re *The Demi-Gods*, I believe myself that his confidence will be justified. At the first, and perhaps for a couple of years, my work will be a little difficult to handle and the critics may be puzzled, as he suggests. My work is in several respects different from current American fiction, but the critics will discover a standard of some kind whereby to measure it. I continually receive letters from American writers and others congratulating me very warmly on my books. These ideas will become more audible as time goes on.

As to an agreement for another novel, I shall be very glad to enter into one with your firm. The only suggestion I make is that the American royalties should begin with 15 per cent, and 20 per cent after 5,000 have been sold.

There is another matter as to which I should be glad of your advice. I believe that in a very short time my books will begin to move more freely. I also believe that the most popular of them all will ultimately be *The Charwoman's Daughter*. I have not yet written anything better than this book ; I do not think I ever will. However, that is all for the future to show.

I think that the format of the book is wrong, it looks too skimpy, and that the price (3*s* 6*d*) is a mistake also. I think that this price is always a mistake. Bookbuyers often consider that a second-hand price means second-hand matter. In America this book is sold at 5*s*, and by the use of a somewhat larger type, etc., the volume is quite large enough for that price. I consider it would be quite worthwhile to re-issue this book (there are 270 pages in the American issue) and list it at 5*s*. If this suggestion meets your approval I will be glad to revise the book for such re-issue and make it as perfect as I can. I believe *The Charwoman's Daughter* will be the most successful of my books and that is why I make this suggestion.

Having made the suggestion, however, I will be quite willingly governed by your experience, but I beg you will consider the point. The 3*s* 6*d* price not alone depreciates the profits of both publisher and author : it also, by implication, depreciates the literature on which it is marked.

In his reply Macmillan rejected the proposal to alter the price of *The Charwoman's Daughter*, but offered to increase the author's royalty from ten to twenty-five per cent, an increase which was to find an echo in the somewhat Galsworthian letter that follows.

In 1918 Sir Frederick Macmillan, the head of the family and the firm, was sixty-six years of age, his brother Maurice sixty-five, and their cousin George sixty-three.

Overstrand, Norfolk, 14 July 1918

My dear Maurice,

George has sent me the enclosed letter* addressed to me by A.E. and tells me that he has answered it — I presume after consultation with you. I wish it could have been sent down to me here for I very much prefer to answer my own letters when it is possible to do so. There are no doubt occasions when circumstances require a reply by return of post, but they are not frequent and this was not one of them : in fact Russell's letter must have reached St. Martin's Street on the 9th and was not answered until two days had elapsed.

I do not like to feel that I cannot go away for a holiday without losing touch with the business and particularly with my own correspondence. As you know I am not one of those men who drops all thoughts of business when he leaves his office chair. Ever since I have been in a responsible position

* Printed on page 298 above.

it has been my practice to think things over when I am in my study, or on horseback or in bed, and the letters which I dictate at St. Martin's Street have generally been composed in my head before I got there.

When I had my little breakdown in the spring of this year, you were good enough to say that you would not consider I was neglecting my work if I became somewhat irregular in my office hours, and took no part in reading and answering the unimportant correspondence; but in making this proposal I had no idea of suggesting that I should take a less active part than formerly in the serious management of our business. I think it is desirable that any important step such as the publishing of a new book should be the result of consultation between us, and if this sometimes means a little delay, no harm will be done as a hurried decision is very often not the most satisfactory one. I know of course that I am only one of a committee and that if you and George decide on a particular course of action I must give way. There is however a difference between being over-ruled and not being consulted at all. If one is consulted one has the opportunity of putting forward views that might otherwise be overlooked and that may seriously affect the decision.

In the particular case under consideration I cannot help feeling that an error of judgment has been made; at all events there is a point on which I should like to have said a word, and that is as to the terms on which we have offered to publish A.E.'s new book.

I know of course that he has a Royalty of only 15 per cent on his *Poems*: the conditions, however, were peculiar. We did not publish the *Poems* originally, but took them over from John Lane who transferred the agreement made some years previously and a certain amount of unsold stock. When we brought out the volume of *Collected Poems* it was under the old agreement.

This is the first book we have ever had offered to us by A.E., and I certainly think that we should have proposed a

20 per cent royalty considering that we give 20 per cent to W. B. Yeats and 25 per cent to James Stephens. I cannot help thinking that if, as is probable, Russell tells Stephens what we have offered and hears what terms the latter gets from us, he will think that we are not treating him fairly, and will either take his book elsewhere (which I should much deplore) or will ask for more, which of course we shall have to give.

So strongly do I feel about this that I should be inclined, even if A.E. accepts the offer made in George's letter, to amend it when we send him the agreement.

I am, your affectionate brother,

FREDERICK MACMILLAN

ROBERT LAURENCE BINYON

1869–1943

Laurence Binyon published several volumes of verse with various publishers from 1894 onwards. The last lines of his 'For the Fallen', written at the beginning of the first world war —

> *At the going down of the sun and in the morning*
> *We will remember them —*

were inscribed on many memorials after the war, including one in the British Museum, where he worked for nearly forty years in the department of prints and drawings. He was one of Macmillans' principal advisers on art books.

Frederick Macmillan was a member of the Royal Commission set up in the war to control the import and distribution of paper.

118 Belgrave Road, S.W.1, 4 April 1917

Dear Sir Frederick,

I called today at the Paper Commission but learnt that you only go there for meetings ; and at your office they tell me that you are away. I hope you will forgive my worrying you on your holiday, but I want to ask you about something rather urgent. Last autumn I arranged for the publication of my poems on the war, in America with Houghton, Mifflin and here with Elkin Mathews. Owing to the shortage of labour here, I arranged for the MS. to be printed in Boston, and it was all printed before the Order about imports of paper came into force ; but as the book was not to come out till the spring the sheets were not sent over.

Mathews applied to the Paper Commission for a licence on 9 March, and wrote again last week ; but has had no answer. Meanwhile Houghton, Mifflin has announced the book as to be published in U.S.A. on March 17: and I suppose it has come out.

I want to ask if the matter has come before your notice. Naturally I am very anxious to get the licence; and I think if any books in sheets are allowed to be imported mine deserves some special consideration. The poems were written from a national point of view. The Foreign Office has asked to use some of them for propaganda in neutral countries (I was asked to treat this as confidential so give you the information as such) and they have been used in speeches, and in memorials to the fallen, both here and in the Dominions.

The book is a small one and the edition we want to import is only 500. Without wishing to magnify the importance of the little book, I think the poems have done something as 'war-work', and I have had many requests for a collected volume. Some of the poems have also been translated into French, and recited at meetings in Paris and other French cities. If the matter has not come to your notice on the Commission (as is very likely) could you tell me of anyone at Central House whom I could go and see. As I do not know of anyone but yourself who is on the Commission I am bothering you — unwillingly.

Yours very truly,   LAURENCE BINYON

Thomas Sturge Moore (1870–1944), Irish poet, had worked for Macmillans for some years as a designer of bindings, and had corresponded with the firm about his editorial assistance to Rabindranath Tagore. (His binding for Yeats's *The Tower* is reproduced facing page 241). In 1926 he asked Binyon to recommend to Frederick Macmillan his aesthetic treatise *Why Beautiful?*

24 May 1926

My dear Macmillan,

My old friend Sturge Moore is sending you the MS. of a new prose book of his, which I gather is on the nature of art. He asked me to give him an introduction to you, but I told him I thought this was quite unnecessary, though I said I would write you a line to notify you of the MS. coming along.

Personally I think Moore is one of the great neglected writers of the day. I haven't read this new work but feel sure it will be full of originality and power, and hope you may be able to see your way to publishing it. He will never be a popular writer, but I believe his books will wear well and sell in the long run.

Sincerely yours,   LAURENCE BINYON

Moore's book was published three years later by Grant Richards with the title *Armour for Aphrodite*. On the strength of Binyon's next letter Macmillans undertook Moore's *Collected Poems* (four volumes, 1931–3). They also published Binyon's *Collected Poems* in two volumes in 1931.

The Athenaeum, Pall Mall, S.W.1, 27 May 1930

I have a decided opinion on Sturge Moore's poetry. I think he has written some of the very finest poems of our time. At one time I thought he would surpass everybody living : he hasn't quite fulfilled his promise, but the body of his work is considerable, and among it are some longer poems — such as 'The Rout of the Amazons', 'The Gazelles', 'The Centaur's Booty' — which are splendid. He is not a lyrist (to my mind) : his verse carries too much thought and imagery ever to be light and melodious : and I think this is why, with all his outstanding power and originality, he has never received anything like his due of recognition. He is often difficult, sometimes a little *naïf* and clumsy : but he has a weight, vigour and abundance that make many more popular poets seem thin.

I have no doubt, then, that his collected poems ought to

be published. The other question, whether they would repay publication, is more difficult to answer. I am convinced that much of Moore's work will last, but I think it will take time to be accepted, and the sale might be slow. I am not at all sure however that the time hasn't come when he might be recognized at his proper value. For instance I know that Desmond MacCarthy (now, I imagine, an influential critic) feels very strongly on the anomaly of Sturge Moore's lack of recognition hitherto. He has a very high opinion of his poetry. So has Yeats. I can't pretend to forecast what the sale would be likely to be : but I should say that Moore is a poet whom in the future you would be glad to have published.

SIR JOHN WILLIAM FORTESCUE

1859–1933

In 1896 Macmillans invited Fortescue to write a popular one-volume *History of the British Army*. Instead he wrote a classic extending to thirteen volumes (1899–1930). His *Story of a Red Deer* (1897) attained a success never approached by his other children's books, *The Drummer's Coat* (1899) and *The Three Pearls* (1916). His threepenny pamphlets *The Foot Guards* and *Welsh Regiments* were published in 1915.

Admiral's House, Hampstead Heath, N.W.3,
1 October 1917

My dear Mr. Macmillan,

I have today received the annual statement of my account with you. I confess that the sale of *The Three Pearls* has disappointed me ; though I cannot say that I am altogether surprised at the smallness of the figure. The book was well reviewed ; but not the slightest effort was made to push it, and I can say from actual experience that many leading booksellers had hardly heard of it. Half a dozen other firms were eager to have it ; and I do not think that it would have fared so ill in their hands.

The little regimental history of the Guards (the pamphlet) was also (I hope this is not a hard word) mismanaged. Numbers of people were anxious to get it, but literally could not find it at the booksellers'. A relation of mine asked for it at six different shops in vain. Only a month ago I got down a couple of dozen copies for a charity bazaar at Windsor. They were snapped up in a few minutes. But I do not suppose that any attempt has been made to push it at Windsor (the Coldstream depot), or at Caterham (the Guards' recruiting depot) or anywhere else. I know that in your enormous business these pamphlets, and *The Three Pearls* for that matter, are a trifle ; but it is not a trifle to me to get nothing for my work. I expected no profit from the pamphlet ; but when I see some 10,000 copies unsold, whereas I know that there are some 20,000 Guardsmen who would be glad to have them, I cannot help regretting that no greater effort is made to dispose of them.

Always yours,   J. W. FORTESCUE

Frederick Macmillan's reply, besides the paragraphs given below, explained at length the steps taken to promote the sale of *The Three Pearls* and the two pamphlets.

St. Martin's Street, W.C., 4 October 1917

Dear Fortescue,

I have received your letter of 1 October with much regret because it is in effect a serious reflection on one of the things nearest to my heart, the honour and probity of my Firm. If I admitted for a moment the justice of your charge that 'not the slightest effort was made to push' your book I should feel ashamed of myself and of the business with which I have been connected for fifty years. As it is I content myself with being not a little indignant. . . .

The fact is that it is impossible for an author or anybody else to say beforehand with certainty whether a book will take the fancy of readers, and if it does not do so all the advertising and drumming in the world will not make it sell. You will remember that when you were almost unknown as a writer we published *The Red Deer*, which was at once accepted as a book that made an appeal to young people and has almost become a classic. Some years later you wrote *The Drummer's Coat*, which for some reason failed to make the necessary appeal and has never had anything like a sale. Yet I don't suppose you consciously put better work into your first book than into the second — nor that it occurred to you to attribute the success of *The Red Deer* to the ability of your publishers, nor the failure of *The Drummer's Coat* to their incapacity....

I hope you will pardon me if I have expressed myself strongly in the course of this letter, but it is a matter on which I feel strongly. I am proud of my Firm and jealous of its good name, and the suggestion that the sale of a book has been injured by our carelessness when I am conscious of having given it unremitting attention — or that it would have done better in the hands of some other publisher — fills me with a burning sense of having been unfairly treated.

I am, yours ever,   FREDERICK MACMILLAN

Fortescue's reply ran to some 1,400 words of which fewer than half are given here.

6 October 1917

Dear Macmillan,

I have often heard complaints of the sensitiveness of authors to criticism; but after reading your letter I feel inclined to think that the reproach should not be confined to them. I am at a loss to divine how my letter can be construed as 'a serious reflection upon the honour and probity of your firm'. It certainly was not intended to be so; and I cannot see how it can bear any such construction....

I may add that, in my experience, I have, from without, always heard the same account of your firm, that it is solid, straight and upright as a firm can be; but that, with its enormous educational business, all other books are, relatively speaking, secondary and do not — can not — receive the attention which they would receive from a firm which would regard them as primary. I may say that, knowing this,

I never expected that you would even look at *The Red Deer* ; and naturally should not have felt aggrieved if you had not.

For more than twenty years now our relations have been pleasant and friendly ; and I am sorry that this state of things should be threatened with interruption ; but, after reading your letter, I begin to think that its long continuance has been due chiefly to my own moderation. You took my first writings on trust when I was unknown ; and I do not think that I have abused that trust. I have troubled you with but two branches of literature ; and in each, I may say without vanity, I have written a classic. I do not know that a client can do much more. . . .

The Red Deer is my one real success, financially speaking ; and I remember that you took it originally upon the agreement that I was to have half-profits. Immediately that the book made its hit you proposed to cancel that agreement, and to substitute for it a new one under which I was to receive a royalty of one-sixth on the retail price. Acting upon the advice of Mowbray Morris, I accepted the change. Whether he advised me as my friend or as yours ; and whether the change was to the advantage of me, then a struggling author, or of you, the wealthy publisher, you know better than I, and I am content to be ignorant. To inquire would be, I apprehend, an insult to the honour and probity of your firm ; and, even if it were not, I am far too proud to do so. Meanwhile, for a book which is a classic in its kind, less than 30,000 copies in twenty-two years does not strike me as a remarkable sale.

Upon the whole, if a fair balance were struck of the advantages which each of us has received from our connexion, I do not think that the scale would incline in my favour. I have worked for you and the country now for nearly twenty-three years at starvation wages. You have never offered to raise them ; and I am the last man to ask it of you. I have lively recollection of the difficulty with which I obtained last year slightly better terms from you for *The*

Three Pearls ; and when, after nearly a quarter of a century's honest work for you, I complain — as I think with justice — that you have not pushed my little book as steadily as you might have, you turn upon me as though I were an unknown scribbler troubling you with his first manuscript. I shall not forget the experience.

Yours very truly,

J. W. FORTESCUE

9 October 1917

Dear Fortescue,

I am sorry if my letter gave you the impression that I am thin-skinned and unable to accept criticism. But I am proud of the work to which I have devoted my life and it hurt me not a little to be accused by an author for whom I have a great respect and for whom I have always tried to do my very best of having injured the sale of his book by carelessness or inattention. I went into considerable detail in describing what we had done for *The Three Pearls* because I hoped to be able to make it clear to you that we had spared neither trouble nor expense to put the book on the market in the best possible way.

There was another suggestion in your letter which I resented as being without foundation, viz., that because we are in a largish way of business we are unable to give proper attention to any one book. The fact that we have a large business and therefore an extensive machinery for selling books enables us to do better and not worse for our authors than a smaller firm whose operations are less extensive. Our relations with the trade all over the world, our numerous travellers and salesmen, and our very complete organization make it easier for us to give the books we publish a chance of sale than would be the case if our business were on a smaller scale. We undoubtedly have a large number of books in our catalogue, but we only deal in those which we believe to be good in their various ways, and we consistently refuse to have anything to do with books which we do not think good but which authors ask us to publish for them without risk to ourselves.

The number of books for young people that we have published is perhaps not very great, but when I remind you that among them are *Tom Brown's Schooldays*, *The Water-Babies*, *Alice's Adventures in Wonderland* and *The Jungle Book* you must admit that we have not been unsuccessful in that line of literature.

I do not think that anything will be gained by prolonging this correspondence, but I do want you to believe that we have done and shall continue to do all that is in our power to promote the sale of *The Three Pearls*, and that if, as I hope may be the case, its fortune improves in the future nobody will be better pleased than

Yours very truly,   FREDERICK MACMILLAN

10 October 1917

My dear Macmillan,

Many thanks for your letter. Let me too express regret for having hurt your feelings ; and let this correspondence end, as I believe it does on your side and I know it does on mine, with our old relations of the past twenty-five years unbroken and unimpaired.

Always yours,   J. W. FORTESCUE

SIR HUGH WALPOLE
1884–1941

Hugh Walpole was a rising young novelist before the first world war. In 1916 Macmillans accepted *The Green Mirror*. Two years later, through the agency of J. B. Pinker, agreements were signed for Walpole's next three novels and for the purchase of his earlier books from other publishers — agreements which led to an association which was to last to the end of the novelist's life.

Frederick Macmillan had written what Walpole described as 'a delightful letter, saying that they hope I'll always be with them, and wishing to make any agreement I like'. By 1923 Walpole was writing to Sir Frederick, 'Let me say, quite between ourselves and for no other eye, that I love you as a son loves his father'.

The novels which he is now offering are *The Secret City* and *The Captives*.

Foreign Office, 4 March 1918

Dear Sir Frederick,

Your letter is the nicest thing that any publisher has ever done to me. It makes me more than before proud to be connected with you.

It *was* my wish that I should be fixed down to three books with you. I am very anxious to settle and I have always from the first wanted ultimately to be with you. I am the more convinced that this is the best moment to go to you because I have real hopes of my next two books. The first, dealing with the beginning of the Revolution in Petrograd, cannot fail, I think, to do decently because of its subject, and the second, of which I have written about a quarter, is my best work so far.

However my other great desire is that you should take

over two or three of my first books and re-issue them in your two-and-sixpenny or three-and-sixpenny libraries. I would revise them and I fancied they might be published like Mason's early books, for instance. I don't know whether this is too ambitious of me, but I think that they would have a sale and you need not print a large edition. It would give me great happiness and encourage me to go on.

Anyway I leave the details of this to Pinker, but it *is* my wish to be connected with you as closely and permanently as Fate, circulation and my ability will allow. . . .

Yours very sincerely,   HUGH WALPOLE

Judith Paris, the fourteenth new Walpole novel to come from Macmillans in fourteen years and the second of the *Herries* series, was published in August 1931. Twenty thousand copies were sold within a fortnight, after which sales began to fall off.

Brackenburn, Manesty Park, Keswick,
30 September 1931

Dear Dan,

Harold said I was to appeal to you if I was in a difficulty and so I do. Now it simply is that I have had in the last four days an epidemic of letters from friends, authors, book-sellers asking why *Judith* is not being advertised. I'm an old aged author and know what these letters from friends mean. Moreover I think that *Judith* has been *very well advertised*. All the same every one is asking — why do you not adver-tise in the *Observer*? I think *Judith* has been once in the *Observer* but not since, and beyond question that paper is ten thousand times the advertising medium that the *Sunday Times* is. I fancy that a great many people are watching *Judith's* career for many different reasons. The drop in sales last week was very sad and that plus these letters from friends makes me ask whether for one or two weeks *Judith* might not appear in the *Observer*.

Don't let me be a querulous author. I am aware of the bad times and the egotism of novelists ! But these four books are the chief work of my life and *Judith* had so good a press and is so much liked that it is disappointing to watch her sinking so rapidly.

Yours ever,   HUGH WALPOLE

Daniel Macmillan was able to reply that *Judith Paris* was selling well, and to send cuttings of advertisements of the book that had in fact appeared in the *Observer* on two Sundays in September. Others in both the *Observer* and the *Sunday Times* were booked at fortnightly intervals, but, as Walpole showed a preference for the former, the advertisements would appear there weekly.

Nevertheless, Daniel wrote:

I think your friend is wrong about the *Observer* being so much better than the *Sunday Times*. We have almost conclusive evidence that the *Sunday Times* and the *Observer* have just about the same value for advertising, so I do not propose to discontinue putting your book in the *Sunday Times*.

Walpole replied:

6 October 1931

Thank you so much for your letter. It is delightful to be on such excellent terms with one's publisher ! Once an election is over and Christmas approaches books, I think, should do well again. One little favour — would they kindly use, in advertising *Judith*, one sentence used by your young friend McNair Scott in his review in the *English Review* : 'Mr. Hugh Walpole is the chief romantic writer living.' That sounds conceited ! But it emphasizes my romanticism which just now I want emphasized.

In 1934 Messrs. Dent planned to add living writers to their Everyman series for the first time, and asked Walpole's permission to include
Mr. Perrin and Mr. Traill. Macmillans, who had a cheap edition on
the market, sought to dissuade Walpole from agreeing: they had
already, they wrote, refused permission on Thomas Hardy's behalf.

90 Piccadilly, W.1, 24 January 1935

My dear Harold,

Your letter came half an hour ago and I am replying to it
at once. It has really distressed me because here I see for the
first time that we are really at an issue. This, as I will try and
show you, is a thing which I feel very seriously.

In the first place I think you have read the Dent suggestion quite wrongly. It is not a question of giving them a book
for their ordinary list. They are starting a development of
their world-famous Everyman series. They have already
published some 2,000 volumes in that, all of classical works
by dead authors. They are adding to this now a series of
books by modern authors, books that may reasonably be
considered to have some surviving quality. Their first six
volumes contained works by Galsworthy, Wells, Chesterton
and D. H. Lawrence.

The books for the series are being most carefully selected
and I find from talking with other writers that everyone
regards it as a great honour to be chosen. Every famous
author in England practically is accepting and I hear that
you are the only publisher who has refused permission. Of
course you know your own business much the best, but here
I am arguing for something which I regard as extremely
important. It is a kind of selection by a very serious committee of the living authors who are considered to have some
permanent value and it will be very invidious if I am omitted
from the list.

More than that. The Everyman public is a very special
public of its own and I regard this as a most excellent

L

advertisement. It is nothing to do with my having a name under some other publisher's list, as I have said every famous living author in England is to be included in this list.

I am very sorry to be tiresome about this, but I regard it as really serious and if you continue to oppose it, I would feel that for the first time in our relations together, you are treating me with real unfairness. I can only repeat that I would never dream of fighting for this point if a book of mine were simply going on to Dent's list. I can see all your objections to that, but this is another matter and I do hope that you will see my point of view about it. . . .

Yours, as always,   HUGH

Harold Macmillan replied next day:

St. Martin's Street, W.C.2, 25 January 1935
My dear Hugh,
. . . I have read very carefully what you say, and I can only reply that I still think I am right. I think you very much overestimate the importance of Everyman. I hope your niche in the Temple of Fame is secured without that; if it is not, I don't believe Messrs. Dent can underpin it. Moreover, I still think it is rather cool of Dent to build up a profitable library merely by trying to get other people's authors.

Nevertheless you know our other guiding principle, which is that publishers exist to satisfy their authors and not to impose their own views upon them. So — after discussing it with the others — I agree, not, my dear Hugh, with your views, but with your wishes. So go ahead and let *Mr. Perrin and Mr. Traill* appear in the new library, where I wish them all success ! . . .

I hate quarrelling with you ; but I feel we must state our views and you would prefer me always to be frank. But I quite understand your anxiety about an important matter, and we much prefer to meet your views, rather than you should feel we have not treated you with that generosity and friendship which we should like always to be the governing factor of our relations with you. . . .

Yours ever,   HAROLD

Mr. Perrin and Mr. Traill duly appeared in Everyman, and the fact that it is still in print in that series in 1967 suggests that Walpole's judgment was not at fault.

26 January 1935

My dear Harold,

Your letter this morning is surely the very kindest and nicest any author has ever had from a publisher. I shall keep it to show the kind of relations authors and publishers *can* have if things go well. . . .

Yours affectionately,   HUGH

John Cornelius was published on 4 July 1937. On 17 November Walpole wrote to Harold Macmillan from Edinburgh. 'The Pilgrim novel' was *So Great a Man* by 'David Pilgrim' (Hilary Saunders and John Palmer). Ratcliffe was Macmillans' advertising manager.

Here is a little yelp of distress! Yesterday in Glasgow I was the guest of the booksellers at lunch, opened the Book Exhibition in the afternoon and was the guest of Sir Walter Scott at dinner in the evening! This morning the *Glasgow Herald* had pages about the Book Fair with a book supplement — photographs of me all over the place. Wouldn't you have said my publishers might have collaborated? Not a thing did they do for me. It's true that there was a list of Macmillan novels with *Cornelius* among them, but actually on this day of all days the special advertisement was given to the Pilgrim novel!

Wasn't it a real chance for pushing the *Herries* books and the 3s 6d edition? I wanted to say something about this at lunch the other day but you were so nice I couldn't! Ratcliffe seems in the last year to have dropped entirely all advertising of myself as a whole. People always said to me: 'Why I like Macmillans so is that they keep your whole work before the public, not only one book'. Now only last week someone said to me 'Why don't Macmillans advertise your older books any more?' Is it because the fiction list is now much bigger? But after all, now Kipling is gone, I am your best novelist for this. It does you good as well as me — and it isn't as though the 3s 6d edition doesn't sell still!

Anyway, dear Harold, after the Glasgow affair yesterday I feel awfully depressed. I think when you're away no one in Macmillans cares a damn about me.

Drafting a conciliatory reply Harold Macmillan had before him a statement from Ratcliffe of the amount spent on advertising *John Cornelius* (£320 on sixty advertisements) and on the Herries novels (£66 in ten newspapers) in the past five months. Thomas Mark was the editor, and more than editor, who dealt with Walpole's manuscripts.

The Joyful Delaneys was in the press. Naomi Royde-Smith's 'melodramatically tragic' novel was *For Us in the Dark*.

Brackenburn, 23 November 1937

My dear Harold,

Thank you so much for your splendid letter. I bet no other publisher would take so much trouble. When I make a plea for myself I always tell myself of the egotism of authors; their idea that they are the *only* authors and so on. On the other hand I am nearly as proud of Macmillans as you are and when, as happened in Glasgow, two or three people suggest that my old books and the *Herries* have been dropped by you, I react to it. About Mark I can't say enough — he is my guiding star, my Socrates, my suckling mother, but I value more than anything in my writing life your treatment of me as a *whole*. . . .

Let us lunch together every time I come to town. I love being with you apart from all business. Mark has just written me a rapturous letter about *The Delaneys*. I believe we may have a big success there.

How good the Royde-Smith novel is ! I've only just *really* read it. It should have been the novel of the year — it's too melodramatically tragic I suppose.

Affectionately,

HUGH

P.S. Don't ever think I don't appreciate your generosity to me. You should hear the stories I tell of it !

CHARLES TUNNACLIFF DIMONT

1872–1953

Theological College, Salisbury, 5 March 1929

Dear Sirs,

A short time ago I found in a bookshop a copy of Mr. Walpole's book *The Cathedral* and I was surprised to see that it still has a wrapper with a picture of Salisbury Cathedral upon it. May I convey to you the fact that considerable surprise is felt that a great publishing house such as yours is should descend to a device of this kind. If Mr. Walpole chooses to make cathedral life the topic of his somewhat crude melodrama, that cannot be helped. In his latest effort he gives us an elegant picture of canons with running noses which they are too palsied to blow. Whether this refined portrait is drawn from Salisbury or from some particular cathedral I do not know. But as I say if the public choose to buy these libels upon us no doubt Mr. Walpole is well advised to continue to write them. But we do feel that to identify his writing with a particular cathedral in the way in which your wrapper does it is unnecessary and offensive. More than that, it might have the effect of misrepresenting us altogether in a distant country, for example, America. If an American felt inclined to respond to an appeal for restoration such as we have sometimes to make he would certainly think twice about carrying out his intention if he picked up a picture of the cathedral attached to Mr. Walpole's novel.

I hope that if you are reissuing that book you will see your way to discontinuing the use of that particular wrapper.

I am, yours faithfully,

C. T. DIMONT
Canon of Salisbury

SIR GEORGE OTTO TREVELYAN

1838–1928

Trevelyan was eighty-five when he wrote this letter. His biography of Lord Macaulay had appeared in 1876, five years before the death of Thomas Carlyle. Carlyle's letter to which he refers was printed in a new edition in 1923, and reprinted in G. M. Trevelyan's memoir of his father (1932). Charles Eliot Norton (1827–1908), American scholar and a close friend of Carlyle's, edited several volumes of Carlyle's letters which Macmillans published.

Wallington, Cambo, Morpeth, 1 July 1923

Dear Sirs,

I venture to trouble you about a matter on which I am extremely desirous to succeed, and in which perhaps you can help me. My *Life and Letters of Macaulay* was published in April 1876, and about ten days afterwards Mr. Carlyle wrote me a letter of great interest, and even beauty, with a sort of appreciation of Macaulay, singularly his own, which gave me great pleasure, and (I am quite sure) would keenly interest others. The letter is one which honoured the writer, and the subject of it. It is of course in the hand of an amanuensis, for Carlyle had then ceased to write letters himself; but the signature is in his own hand. I may say that at that happy period of my life I enjoyed Carlyle's intimacy and kindness, and (I think I may say) his friendship. Next year, amidst an awe-struck crowd of members, he came in person to vote for me at a critical ballot at the Athenaeum Club.

I am now bringing out what will be the final shape and form of the *Life and Letters of Macaulay*; and I am exceedingly desirous of putting this interesting letter in a conspicuous part of the volume. The letter, (omitting some too partial compliments to myself) would about cover a page of print. But I am told that it would be necessary for me to obtain the leave of Mr. Carlyle's representative, or representatives. Can you help me in this matter by telling me to whom I should apply; or even, if you were very kind, in putting my case to them by showing this letter. I know that your house published Charles Norton's deeply interesting collection of the *Early Letters*. If it was desired, I would copy out the part of the letter which I propose to insert. Earnestly hoping that you can assist me on a point which I have so much at heart,

    I remain, yours very truly,

GEORGE OTTO TREVELYAN

FREDERICK EDWARD GREY PONSONBY
Lord Sysonby
1867–1935

Sir Frederick Ponsonby had been assistant keeper of the privy purse to Queen Victoria and King Edward VII, and in 1924 was keeper of the privy purse to King George V.

Sir Sidney Lee (1859–1926), editor of *The Dictionary of National Biography* and author of a life of Victoria, was invited by George V to write an official *Life of King Edward VII*. The first volume was published by Macmillans in 1925 and the second, completed by F. S. Markham after Lee's death, in 1927.

Privy Purse Office, Buckingham Palace, S.W.,
31 January 1924

Dear Macmillan,

Sir Sidney Lee asks whether he may publish the first volume of his biography of King Edward and postpone the publication of the second volume till later, when he has had time to complete it.

The difficulty I see about this is that the whole object of his writing the biography was that he should in some degree dissipate the unfortunate and erroneous impression of King Edward which he gave in *The Dictionary of National Biography*. The first volume will of course be useless for this purpose as it deals mainly with social questions with which Sir Sidney Lee is singularly unfitted to deal. There is also the consideration that as he is getting on in years he may never finish the second volume. It is undoubtedly the part as King that will excite the interest of everyone in this country and probably in Europe.

Before I talk this over with the King, I should like to hear how you view the request.

Yours very truly,   F. E. PONSONBY

Frederick Macmillan's reply was, in effect, that if the later period of King Edward's life had been the less interesting, postponement of the second volume might have proved 'a hazardous experiment', but that in fact the publication of the first volume by itself should whet the public appetite for the second.

19 February 1924

The King has agreed to Sir Sidney Lee's request to be allowed to publish Volume I of his biography of King Edward and to defer the publication of Volume II until later, but I have asked him whether he can give me any idea of when Volume II will be ready.

Sir Sidney Lee has been told that he can publish nothing without obtaining the consent of myself and, secondly, of some politician who would be capable of reading through the proofs and seeing that nothing harmful from the Government point of view is inserted in the text. Lord Morley originally undertook to do this, but I am proposing to the King that possibly Lord Crewe would now be the best person to read through the proofs.

In 1927 Harry Levy-Lawson, second Viscount Burnham (1862-1933), managing proprietor of the *Daily Telegraph*, offered £2,000 for the first British serial rights in the second volume of Lee's life of Edward VII. Ponsonby wrote:

21 June 1927

I spoke to the King about the offer which Lord Burnham had made for the second volume of King Edward's biography to appear in abbreviated form in the *Daily Telegraph* and His Majesty said that while he did not altogether like the idea, he thought it was impossible to refuse, because the money would go to Sir Sidney Lee's family. I am therefore to tell you that the King approves of Lord Burnham's offer being accepted.

JAMES MATTHEW BARRIE
1860–1937

Thomas Hardy died on 11 January 1928 and was buried in West-minster Abbey a week later. Macmillans made the arrangements for the funeral, as they had done for Tennyson's funeral thirty-six years before.

Adelphi Terrace House, Strand, W.C.2, 19 January 1928
Dear Messrs. Macmillan,
   Please let me say that I think you carried through splendidly your arduous duties connected with Mr. Hardy's funeral at the Abbey. So little time to do it, and so efficiently done. We should have been in great straits without you. The pious work of a famous house for its great author.
   Yours sincerely,   J. M. BARRIE

SIR EDWARD MARSH

1872–1953

In 1922 Marsh had recently given up editing *Georgian Poetry*, (Sir) John Squire (1884–1958) was editor of the *London Mercury*, and Archibald Young Campbell (1885–1958) had just become Gladstone professor of Greek at Liverpool. Campbell's Trojan tragedy was never published, except for a brief extract in his *Poems* (Longmans, 1926).

A. S. M. Hutchinson's novel, *If Winter Comes* (Hodder & Stoughton, 1921), was the best-seller of the year. For Mr. Boffin's struggles with Gibbon, see Dickens's *Our Mutual Friend*.

5 Raymond Buildings, Gray's Inn, W.C.1

My dear Macmillan,

I hope you won't mind my writing to you about something that is no business of mine. Jack Squire of the *Mercury* lent me a typewritten MS. to read at Easter ; it is by a man called A. Y. Campbell, who is professor of Greek, I think at Liverpool — I met him once or twice years ago at Cambridge, and have since much admired a few poems of his that I have seen ; but I don't really know him at all, and there is nothing personal in my interest in his work.

The MS. is a tragedy about the Trojan War ! in prose and verse. It is immensely long — in a prologue and five acts — but I have hardly been able to put it down. It seems to me equally admirable in the general conduct of the drama, in the strength and imagination of the character-drawing, in the magnificence of the verse passages in the grand style, and in the humour and life of the prose-scenes. It certainly has a few faults. One side of Campbell's equipment is a great ingenuity and verbal dexterity, and occasionally I feel he has been led astray by this into a certain artificiality which contrasts with the extraordinary directness and vigour of the rest; but this is only a sunspot, I mention it to show that I am not completely dazzled.

Now for the object of this letter. Squire tells me to my horror that this masterpiece, as I think it, has been touted all round the publishers, and that no one will take it. Among others it has gone to your firm, but while you were away; and what I want you to tell me is whether it would be any use my sending it to you to read? or do you think the rejection was final and irrevisable? I believe Macmillans are almost the only firm nowadays who ever publish for glory without profit, and I am sure this book would do them nothing but honour. But I also think there is 'money in it', and that if the reading public were properly led it might easily become a best-seller in the long run. I judge by myself. I find myself getting more and more low-brow with advancing years, and I devoured *If Winter Comes*, yet as I said to start with, I could hardly put this MS. down till I had finished it.

I think I can undertake that you would not be bored if you read it slap through (as Mr. Boffin did not read Gibbon) — but if you liked I could indicate three or four of the most striking scenes, by which you might sample the whole.

With renewed apologies, yours sincerely,

EDDIE MARSH

Another of Marsh's recommendations of a poet — Christopher Hassall (1912–63) — was more successful. Hassall later wrote *Edward Marsh, Patron of the Arts, a Biography* (Longmans, 1959).

21 January 1935

Dear Harold Macmillan,

I want to consult you about a young friend of mine who I *think* may have the makings of a considerable poet in him — so will you lend me your ear? He is Christopher Hassall, son of the well-known poster-artist John H., and he is on the stage, having been the Romeo in a very successful production of *R. and J.* at the O.U.D.S. a few years ago.

As a poet, he is of the traditional school, quite out of the 'modern' movement, and writing sense in metre. (I don't think you will look on this as a fatal drawback!) He has got together quite a considerable volume of poems of various lengths (some fairly long) and on various subjects : and what I want you to tell me is, whether it would be any use his sending them to Macmillans for consideration. (I know you *do* publish new poets.)

When he was at Oxford both Edmund Blunden and David Cecil formed a very high opinion of his promise, and I have seen a letter of Blunden's to his father in which he says 'I don't know his equal here (*i.e.* at Oxford) as a born poet, wealthy in that gift' — that was in May 1933, and in the time since then he has in my opinion made very great strides towards achievement.

The poems are now typing out, and no doubt I shall have them back in the course of this week — so do please tell me if it would be any use trying Macmillans, and if so whether I should send them to you or to someone else.

Yours ever,   EDDIE MARSH

Macmillan replied that if Hassall would reduce the size of his book it could appear in the firm's shilling series of Contemporary Poets — as indeed it did, as *Poems of Two Years* (1935). The reply to Marsh's next letter was not preserved in the firm's archives.

27 February 1935

Many thanks for your letter of today. Before I show it to Hassall, I should like to make a suggestion which *may* be quite outrageous : if so, please consider it as *nul et non avenu*, as if I sin it is through ignorance of the conventions of the publishing business.

Your letter is not very enthusiastic, but I gather from it that your firm would, to put it at the lowest, not consider that the publication did them discredit. If therefore the difficulty is solely one of finance, would you consider the proposal that the difference between the actual cost of production of the whole book, and the amount which you are at present ready to risk on the abridgment, should be put up by myself and another friend of Hassall's who believes in him?

If this is out of the question, as it may well be, please turn it down at once, and I will put your present proposal before Hassall. If not, would you let me have the *roughest possible* estimate of what the racket would be, by return? The reason for my asking this is that the other friend is leaving England on Sunday for about three weeks, and I should like to communicate with him before he starts.

If the arrangement is feasible, we should both *prefer* to keep it a secret from Hassall, but this may not be possible.

CHARLES LANGBRIDGE MORGAN
1894–1958

Morgan had published two novels with other publishers before, in the summer of 1928, he offered Macmillans a manuscript entitled *The Edge of Life.** On its acceptance he wrote, 'It is a great pleasure and honour to me that my work should bear your imprint'. In the next thirty years eighteen of his books bore the same imprint.

Morgan had been encouraged from the start by the novelists George Moore (1852–1933), and Francis Brett Young (1884–1954).

8 More's Garden, Cheyne Walk, S.W.3, 1 August 1928
Dear Sirs,
  ... I confess that my own judgment of the title is confused by many changes of mind. At first I thought *First Love* a good title. It was my own earliest choice. It seemed then to have the merit of being a plain, dignified statement of the book's subject. Then it was suggested to me that the word 'love' has been so dishonoured by the films that it ought now to be avoided. Then Mr. George Moore, for very different reasons, condemned the title. But lately Mr. Brett Young has begged me to retain it, giving as his own all my own reasons for choosing it — that it has simplicity and beauty and is refreshingly unspectacular.

  But it is impossible to discuss this by letter. Perhaps you will allow me to call and talk it over with you? ...

  Yours faithfully,   CHARLES MORGAN

28 August 1928
Dear Captain Macmillan,
  Thank you for your letter about the title of my book. ...

* The book was announced under this title in Heinemanns' spring list, 1928, and as *First Love* by Knopf of New York.

It has been suggested to me that *Portrait of a Girl* would lead to a misunderstanding — namely, that the book was about a child. This hadn't struck me, but I think the objection is valid. The choice, I think, therefore lies between

PORTRAIT OF A YOUNG LADY

which avoids Henry James's title, but is perilously close to it, and

PORTRAIT IN A MIRROR

to which I am now inclined. If, meanwhile you would casually try these titles on one or two people and see which they like, I should be extremely grateful.

Yours sincerely,   CHARLES MORGAN

Portrait in a Mirror was published in January 1929 at 7s 6d. In order to assist its reception Morgan had persuaded Daniel Macmillan to let him contribute £125 towards the initial advertising campaign.

13 February 1929

Thank you for telling me that the book is doing so well. I have just come back from a week-end in Oxford. I dined one night in All Souls, and even they seemed to have read me. Almost as astonishing was the appearance of a woman undergraduate at my bedroom door before I was dressed — with a copy of the first impression and a request for a signature. She told me that it was worth £1 plain, and 'more signed'. I hope she knows. Anyhow the book is being talked about, which means much.

12 March 1929

I am always told that a good review in *Punch* sells more books than any other paper — if it comes in time. This week's *Punch* comes when it was most needed. Probably the little advertising fund to which I contributed by arrangement with your brother is already more than spent, for you have been very generous to my book; but if there is, in your judgment, justification for further outlay, I suggest that *Punch*, alone and prominent, might be of the greatest service.

It is a mirror unclouded. For Mr. MORGAN, essentially a poet, has the mastery of a prose which enables him to follow the lines of his thought with the delicate precision of a PROUST or a JAMES.

Please do not trouble to answer this. I write it only because the *Punch* review might otherwise escape your attention for a little while. You will know, as I cannot, what is practicable and what is best.

In May 1929 Morgan wrote to thank Macmillans for refunding the £125 which he had contributed towards advertising the *Portrait*. 'I had no sort of expectation that this money would be returned, nor any thought that I had claim upon it. I am therefore the more grateful for your generous courtesy.'

As a full-time dramatic critic on *The Times* Morgan had little leisure for novel-writing. Three years were to elapse before the appearance of his next novel, *The Fountain*. Meanwhile, in order to keep his name in the eye of the public, Macmillans suggested reprinting *My Name is Legion*, which Heinemanns had published in 1925.

12 June 1929

I am of course anxious that this book should be revived some day; there are parts of it that have more fire and movement than anything I have written; but it is a very uneven, confused book, and there are considerable sections of it (perhaps the best) which would shock many admirers of *Portrait in a Mirror* out of their lives. I think it is probably true that there might be a fair sale of *My Name is Legion* now, but the question in my mind is — is it worth it? I confess, though it is an immodest confession, that I am playing the long game with my writing. My aim is a steadily cumulative repute as an artist who makes no compromises and will publish nothing but the best that time and infinite care can produce. For this reason I have resisted every temptation, however profitable, to do signed journalism outside *The Times*, because I am old-fashioned enough to believe that, at any rate until he is established beyond all question, and probably even then, the constant appearance of a writer's name over work that he has not pondered and matured does him more harm than good. The public — I mean, the best of them — expect to go steadily forward from one work of art to another, and are, I think, irritated and confused by side-tracks.

My Name is Legion is by no means journalism, and some day, when there is no possibility of its being confused with later work, I should like to revise and re-issue it. But at the moment I feel that it might be a dangerous side-track or, to put it another way, that it might take the edge off the appetite which, I hope, *Portrait in a Mirror* has created. On the other hand, it is arguable that it would bridge an interval and that if all the announcements of it included the statement 'First published 1925. New and revised edition', no harm might be done.

I have stated the position as I see it. Now I am in your hands. Macmillans know better than I can what is the wisest policy. But before you go forward with *My Name is Legion*, may I come to see you and talk it over for ten minutes? The *Portrait* has given me a wonderful opportunity. If the next book, patiently written and considered, succeeds, I may be free from journalism, and I am very anxious not to take any possible risk with the future for the sake of some momentary advantage.

The plan outlined in the next letter came to nothing. Contracts were drawn up but not signed; and George Moore left his books with Heinemanns.

8 December 1931

Also — much more important than my own affairs — I shall come to you privately as an unofficial ambassador from George Moore and his solicitor. G. M. is extremely discontented with his present publishers and is inclined to move, bag and baggage, together with a new novel, *Madeleine de Lisle*, within three or four months of completion. I have found out from his solicitor that G. M. is, by his agreements, free to move all his works, except possibly *The Lake*. I am not at present authorized to make any formal proposition because his solicitor was afraid that, apart from any business considerations, Macmillans might not wish on moral grounds to become the publishers of some of G. M.'s writings — in which case it would be better to put the whole thing out of mind. I have therefore been asked to ascertain privately, before the project is any further considered, what your feeling would be on the moral question alone.

G. M. being what he is, I have waited several weeks to make sure that this is not simply a whim. Of course it may come to nothing, but it is at any rate seriously intended and persisted in, and his solicitor, not an impetuous man, has been through all the agreements, discussed them with me and asked me as a preliminary to solve the moral problem. He is aware that, if negotiations were begun, they might reasonably break down for business reasons ; Moore would understand that and, though he might be disappointed, would not be wounded ; but it would be better to persuade him to make the best of Heinemann than to run any risk of a moral objection at his time of life.

Possibly you may not care for the idea at all. In that case, he can be quickly turned from it. But the humour of my offering you a new author called George Moore appealed to me, and I thought it worth while to let you know at any rate how things stand.

A letter from Morgan to Lovat Dickson in 1945 gives some idea of the rewards of successful authorship in mid-century. The background is an investigation by a journalist into the tax liabilities of writers.

16, Campden Hill Square, W.8, 18 October 1945
Dear Rache,

I enclose Mr. —'s letter. It is very interesting, and I should think he has every prospect of success.

A point which may not have struck him is that a successful author differs from the managing director of a company in this : when the managing director retires, his income ceases ; when an author 'retires' he still has back-royalties from old books — if his publisher can keep them in print ! ! Therefore what an author needs is not so much a pension as a 'spread'. For example, I should like to have my whole earnings accumulated by Macmillans, and to be paid by them £*x* a year — the balance to be kept as a kind of Dividend Equalization Fund and the ultimate balance to be regarded as a tax-free capital sum to be paid to me in old age or to my heirs.

If Mr. — wants to use my figures, I am very willing, provided (*a*) that the questions don't come to me, for I am driven mad by income-tax ; (*b*) that any information provided by my accountant is provided *not* at my expense.

I am, I should think, a good specimen because I earn by my pen from so many different sources : Royalties (British, U.S., Foreign) ; Plays ; Serial Rights ; Films ; Journalistic salary. And my earnings greatly vary. For example, *excluding* journalistic salary, they have been in round gross figures as shown on the next page.

These figures (*a*) include [Mrs. Morgan's royalties] ;

(*b*) are what I receive after deduction of agency; (*c*) are for years ending 31 Dec. and so do not correspond with the tax-year.

£	£	£
1925— 128	1932— 6,393	1939— 4,464
1926— 43	1933—11,357	1940— 2,963
1927— 104	1934— 637	1941—11,764
1928— 43	1935— 880	1942— 385
1929—1,028	1936— 5,950	1943— 3,440
1930— 351	1937— 3,497	1944— 2,205
1931— 79	1938— 2,672	1945—10,000 (estimated)

This gives a total of £68,000, and an average over the last ten years of about £4,700 plus journalism.

Yours ever,   CHARLES

In 1945 Morgan joined the staff of the *Sunday Times* as fiction critic. Two years later, changes in editorial policy threatened him with the prospect of having to review more novels in briefer compass than he had bargained for, and he resigned his appointment.

Laugharne, Carmarthenshire, 12 August 1947

Dear Dan,

Your letter, and another from Harold, were the greatest possible encouragement to me. I had long doubts about leaving the *Sunday Times*, not because the salary was of much value if reckoned for taxation at the top range of last year's income, but because, I thought, it might *become* valuable if everything else shrank. For this reason I might have hesitated indefinitely. But the changes that the *Sunday Times* wanted to make seemed to me unacceptable, and I can only hope that the decision I made will prove to be right. That depends on my ability to write books and yours to publish them.

I am one of those people who are inclined to be over-anxious if they are not earning regularly month by month. For that reason I have stuck to journalism all these years so that I could write my books at leisure and in peace of mind. Peace of mind is the key to me — even to a fault — and your letters go further than anything else could do to give me the reassurance I need. It was kind and extraordinarily imaginative of you and Harold to write at that moment; it gives me the sense of continuity that is the greatest gift of a publisher to an author — anyhow to an author made as I am; and I shall always gratefully remember it.

Would you show this letter to Harold and let it express my thanks to him as well as to you? I don't want to burden his letter-bag at a time of political crisis, and anyhow it is to the firm that I am writing as well as to the two brothers who now represent it.

Yours ever,

CHARLES MORGAN

JAMES HILTON
1900–1954

Early in 1933, on the strong recommendation of J. C. Squire, Macmillans accepted a manuscript by the comparatively unsuccessful author of half a dozen novels published elsewhere.

42, Oak Hill Gardens, Woodford Green, Essex,
9 May 1933

Dear Mr. Macmillan,

I have for some time been feeling that *Blue Moon* is not a particularly good title for the new book, especially as so many people seem to think it has a musical comedy flavour. This morning my American publisher has cabled me to the same effect and says also that the title has been used already in the U.S.

I think, apart from getting a better title, it would be an advantage to have the same one on both sides, and I hope, if you agree, to have an alternate suggestion ready in a day or two.

Yours sincerely,   JAMES HILTON

11 May 1933

I am glad you are in agreement that *Blue Moon* could be improved upon, and I believe Mr. Squire thought so too. My own preference for an alternative is *Lost Horizon*, which seems to me both appropriate and attractive.

Though appropriate and attractive — and now famous — the new title proved not so new after all. Soon after publication Macmillans received a complaint from a writer whose novel *The Lost Horizon*, published a few years earlier and out of print, might at any time be reprinted 'to the manifest discomfort of librarians, booksellers, Mr. Hilton and (incidentally) myself'.

Hilton's *Lost Horizon* was an immediate success on both sides of the Atlantic, and in June 1934 he was awarded the Hawthornden prize. Daniel Macmillan attended the ceremony. *Goodbye, Mr. Chips*, first printed in the *British Weekly*, was published as a book by Little, Brown in Boston and by Hodder & Stoughton in London.

Ingoldsby, Woodford Road, Wanstead, E.12,
15 June 1934

After Tuesday's very pleasant affair I would like to express again my appreciation to you and your firm for your share in such success — which I am sure was in many ways considerable.

I think I mentioned to you when we lunched together recently that a long-short-story of mine, *Goodbye, Mr. Chips*, was attracting a good deal of attention in America. This story was originally commissioned by Messrs. Hodder & Stoughton for one of their publications, and as a close personal friend of mine, Mr. Cutts, who is on their staff, is really responsible for the commission having been given me in the first place, I feel that Hodders have a sentimental claim on the story if they wish to make extended use of it. They now suggest publishing it separately (as has been done in America) in book-form during the autumn (in time for Christmas sales), and I am inclined to consent to this, subject to their putting on the title-page some such phrase as 'By arrangement with Messrs. Macmillan & Company'. This, I know, is not strictly necessary (and of course it is subject to your approval), but I do feel strongly that I want to be regarded as a Macmillan author, and that such a clause would prevent reviewers and readers from imagining that I was contemplating any significant change of fiction-publisher.

I hope this arrangement, even if it is a little unusual, will seem to you reasonable. As regards a future full-length novel, I think I can say that I have no intention of considering any other publisher than yourself.

I feel that the publication of *Goodbye, Mr. Chips*, will help to keep my name before the public during the interim before the appearance of my next novel — a task on which I am eager to get to work, as soon as present commotions have subsided a little.

Perhaps you would let me know if you have any objection to the idea I have outlined.

For some years Hilton acted as a reader of novels for Macmillans. In 1946 Lovat Dickson went to America as a talent-scout. *Main Street*, by Sinclair Lewis (1885–1951), had been a best-seller of the nineteen-twenties. *The Grapes of Wrath*, by John Steinbeck (b. 1902), had won the Pulitzer prize in 1940. Macmillans did not succeed in 'grabbing' Steinbeck.

Hollywood, Calif., 18 March 1946

Dear Lovat Dickson,

Thanks for your letter of March 11th. I shall look forward to a talk with you by telephone, and this is just a note about Steinbeck. Beyond doubt he is one of the finest American writers and it certainly could be argued plausibly that *The Grapes of Wrath* was the best American novel since *Main Street*. I feel that one reason for its greatness was that Steinbeck found himself completely at home in writing it — i.e., the American background and his strong proletarian sympathies. Not since has he got his fine talents into such a favourable double-focus, if I might so put it. In *The Moon is Down* he wrote synthetically about an imagined background and since then he seems to have been groping for a return of what he must be aware of as a prime necessity for reproducing the earlier excellence. I think too that attacks on him by leftists, some of whom are jealous of his success and others of whom regard him as politically off the beam, have probably driven him into the somewhat magazine-story nostalgia of his last book *Cannery Row*. All this of course is just critical guesswork and if I were a publisher I would grab him if I could, equally for current performance and future possibilities. He is definitely 'a Macmillan author'.

I will try to think of a few others whom you might consider.

Best wishes. Yours sincerely,   JAMES HILTON

RICHARD HILLARY

1919–1943

Hillary was aged twenty-one when he was shot down in a Spitfire in flames in the Battle of Britain, seriously mutilated. He was twenty-three when, flying a night-fighter, he crashed and was killed. In the interval he wrote *The Last Enemy*. He submitted the first chapter of the book to Lovat Dickson at Macmillans in the spring of 1941, and completed it that summer in the United States. It was published six months before his death.

The following are extracts from a long letter written to provide Dickson with material for publicity for *The Last Enemy*. Viscount Halifax, later the Earl of Halifax (1881–1959), was British ambassador, and Sir Gerald Campbell (1879–1964) was British minister, at Washington; Duff Cooper, later Viscount Norwich (1890–1954), was minister of information; and Sir Walter Monckton, later Viscount Monckton of Brenchley (1891–1965), was director-general at the ministry of information. (Sir) Archibald McIndoe (1900–60) was the most distinguished plastic surgeon of the war years.

Autumn 1941

Dear Dickson,

Herewith nine pages of scrawl from which I hope you can obtain something useful.

How I came to go to America is as follows, but it's absolute dynamite so far as the various ministries are concerned, the M. of I. still being touchy as the devil on the subject, especially in Washington, so for heaven's sake be careful how you use it.

I had always wanted to write, and my long period of convalescence after my mastoid operation seemed an ideal time to start, especially as I felt I really had something I wanted to say at last, as opposed to just writing a day-to-day record of flying experiences. But I soon felt the need to do something more active — the book looked like taking months to finish as I find that when I dictate it bears no resemblance to anything that I would actually write. My right hand was still in something of a mess and writing was therefore a pretty laborious process. Then I had the idea of America. I couldn't do anything in this country, but having been put out of action I could, as an operational pilot, tell the American industrial workers something about the emotions of the men who flew the planes they were making — something of what their planes were doing — and try somehow to make something living out of the job of putting nuts and bolts into an airframe.

I therefore went to see Sir Walter Monckton at the M. of I., and after some discussion with him and Duff Cooper they decided to send me to the U.S.A., subject to Air Ministry approval. This was obtained and, so that it would not look as though I was on a propaganda mission, I went out officially attached to the Air Ministry at Washington. (This is very important, and I do not think the M. of I. should be mentioned.)

We went out by ship — the *Bismarck* came within thirty miles of us on her run for Brest — and arrived in New York on 1 June where I had a press interview with thirty reporters before going to Washington, where Sir Gerald Campbell, first minister and that day appointed head of the information services in America, took one look at my face and said that I must quietly disappear. My face was a lot worse than it is now, and the fear was that, should I go round the factories and talk, the isolationists would call it propaganda and the millions of the Middle West would say, 'We don't want our sons to die for Britain'. Finally, to cut a long story short, after an enormous storm in a teacup in Washington, he had his way (the President backing him, never having seen me, on the strength of a letter from Halifax). . . .

It was with some hesitation that I sat down to write the book, for I felt that when someone finally pointed out that the impact of this war was something more than a series of movie climaxes on the youth of the country, that it had some mental impact, the thing should be done well and be worthy of the subject. Whether I've succeeded I don't know. Finally I got so sick of the guff about 'our island fortress' and 'the knights of the air' that I determined to write it anyway in the hope that the last generation might realize that, while stupid, we were not that stupid, that we could remember only too well that all this had been said in the last war, but that, in spite of that and not because of it, we still thought this one worth fighting. . . .

It has been suggested that the great point of the book is that it does show the change over in character from hard-boiled conceit to something considerably more agreeable rather well. Can we make something of this perhaps ? . . . We might try and pretend that the generation fighting this war is considerably more intelligent than the generation which fought the last one in this country, whereas in Germany the opposite is true : therefore we have a hope of making a better peace and less of a balls of things afterwards. . . .

At the moment there is little more that I can think of except that I hope that if I have to take a staff job I may go back to Washington, and that, if not, Archie McIndoe can fix me up to fly again. I feel that I want to see some blood flow. I stopped, or was stopped, too soon. . . .

R. HILLARY

DAME EDITH SITWELL

1887–1964

129 Rue Saint Dominique, Paris VIIᵉ, 5 June 1935

Dear Sirs,

I have read today in the *London Mercury* that Mr. Yeats
will celebrate his seventieth birthday on the 13th of this month.
Most unfortunately and stupidly I have mislaid his address
in Ireland. I would be most deeply grateful if you would
have the kindness to send it to me, so that I may send him
some flowers.

It must be every poet's wish to do homage to Mr. Yeats;
but in addition to this feeling towards our greatest living
poet, there is, in my case, the memory of great personal
kindness.

I hope, therefore, that you will most courteously and
kindly waive what I know is the rule of all publishers, and
send me Mr. Yeats's address, for which I enclose an
addressed and stamped envelope, for I should be most
unhappy if his seventieth birthday should pass, and I should
not have the happiness and privilege of welcoming it.

I am, yours faithfully,   EDITH SITWELL

In 1938 Macmillans, who were Osbert Sitwell's regular publishers,
published a volume of lectures by Edith, Osbert and Sacheverell
Sitwell called *Trio*. The three authors were closely associated in the
public mind, and in 1940 they were libelled, as a trio, in *Reynolds
News*. In the resulting court action before Mr. Justice Cassels, which
they won, G. D. Roberts, K.C., appeared for the defendants, and
Daniel Macmillan gave evidence for the plaintiffs.

Renishaw Hall, Renishaw, near Sheffield,
13 February 1941

Dear Mr. Macmillan,

This letter would have been written days ago, but I've been so unwell, as the result of the strain we've been through. Osbert, Sacheverell and I can never, *never* be grateful enough to you for your great kindness in coming to witness for us. Your help was absolutely *invaluable* to us. And everyone there must have been most strongly impressed.

The papers with their usual low cunning and meanness have left out, in their reports, everything inconvenient to themselves. Nobody reading most of the reports would have any idea of the sternness of the judge's summing-up, for instance.

The buffalo, in his final speech, threw out a few hints, during about five minutes, about blackmail. Apparently, only the fact that we are not entirely destitute saves us from the charge of being blackmailers. So that, you see, only rich plaintiffs dare bring an action to protect themselves. Such a luxury is not for the poor !

They really are a revolting lot, the defendants. And during most of the time I was in the witness box they were making faces at me. As though their natural ones weren't bad enough ! !

It was *so good* of you to give up your time, in this odious case, and we are indeed so grateful that we can never express our gratitude. I do feel that we have all struck a blow for the arts.

Believe me, yours sincerely,   EDITH SITWELL

Edith Sitwell, already an established poet, became a Macmillan author with her *Street Songs* (1942), and remained with the firm for almost the rest of her life. Her *Green Song* (1944) was advertised in *The Times*, three days after publication, together with books by Eiluned

M

Lewis, John Buxton and 'D. Page' (D. P. Lambert), under the heading 'New Small Volumes of Verse'. She wrote to Lovat Dickson:

19 August 1944

My dear Rache,

I am much displeased by the advertisement of my *Green Song* which appeared in *The Times* yesterday. It is most disrespectful towards me, to bracket my poems with those of these young people whom nobody has ever heard of as *poets*, and whose name is yet to make, if it is ever made. (They may be quite good, I know nothing of them.)

It makes you look extremely silly, as everyone will think you do not know the difference between an established reputation and one that has not even begun; and it is calculated to harm me if my publishers convey the extraordinary impression that they are unaware of my position as a poet!

Also, please do *not* describe *Green Song* as 'a *small* book'. It is a short book, but it happens to be a book on a very large scale, as far as the poems are concerned.

I am extremely displeased. I will say no more. Yours ever,

EDITH

24 August 1944

Naturally you would not have published those three people unless you believed they have merit.

I believe Miss Eiluned Lewis wrote a charming prose book. But she is hardly yet of the same standing as Mr. Yeats, Mr. Eliot and myself. It has taken me thirty years' hard work to achieve my position, and I cannot afford to see it thrown away by my own publishers.

I realise the difficulties of doodle-bugs. But as long as a house of the reputation of Messrs. Macmillan continues to publish, they would not, I am sure, wish to belittle their own authors. And some expression of regret is really due to me. Would Charles Morgan allow himself to be classed with three unknown prose writers?

A well-known author who was staying here was so shocked that he brought the matter to my notice.

29 August 1944

Thank you very much for your letter. Believe me, this complaint I made has not altered, in the very slightest, the feeling of friendship I have for you. A 'business' complaint doesn't change, in the least, anything at all outside that complaint. Everything is exactly the same.

In the autumn of 1949 was published *The Canticle of the Rose*, 'selected poems by Edith Sitwell, hon. D.Litt. (Leeds), hon. D.Litt. (Durham)'. A proof of the dust-cover had carried an advertisement of books by herself and her brothers with the heading 'Sitwelliana': this was amended before publication.

14 July 1949

My dear Rache,

I am very grateful to you for having rescued me from that cover. It really would have been *disastrous*.

Osbert, Sachie and I are extremely displeased when we are treated as if our works are a *mass* production. We do not like to be treated as if we were an aggregate Indian god, with three sets of legs and arms, but otherwise indivisible. I should have been extremely annoyed if this 'Sitwellian' idea had appeared on the cover of my *magnum opus*. We have all three suffered very much from this. It vulgarizes and cheapens everything, and deprives all the work of its importance. People don't mean to be impertinent, but it *is very* impertinent to lump us all together indiscriminately. We are individual artists, and the fact that we are two brothers and a sister is the business of nobody else considering our work.

I shall be very grateful, too, if you will delete the part about Dr. Leavis from that particular place. I *should* like it to appear among the press cuttings. Dr. Leavis is certainly *not* of sufficient importance to place him in the blurb. But I *would* like the remark of his quoted among the press cuttings. Please may I have a look at the press cuttings before they are put on — just in case I could think of anything else.

Once again, really, Rache, I am so *very* grateful to you about this.

As you know, we are one of the most devoted families that has ever been, and are *extremely* proud of each other's work. But we don't like being treated as a hive, because it diminishes the importance of each individual.

I shall be in London for ages in September, and do look forward to seeing you.

In great haste, with love, yours ever, EDITH

In 1950 the Oxford University Opera Club approached Dr. Sitwell through her publisher with a request for permission to perform, with choir and orchestra, her poem-sequence *Façade* which had been published in 1922 with 'accompaniments, overture and interlude' by (Sir) William Turner Walton (b. 1902). She wrote to Lovat Dickson:

17 March 1950

Our letters crossed. Thank you so much for yours. These are obviously delightful young people, and I am touched that they should wish to perform *Façade*. Alas, it really is not possible for me to give permission for them to perform it *in the particular way they suggest*, but I will see if I cannot help them to perform it in a way for which I *can* give permission.

I am sorry that a *choir* is *absolutely out of the question*. If Walton had *wished* to set it for a choir, he would have done so. The sound of a choir would destroy the whole effect — it would slow and sentimentalize it. The orchestration is in the highest degree apt, hard and clear. I am sorry to disappoint the young people who were to sing in the choir. But it really *cannot* be. I don't know *what* Walton would say (or, indeed, what *I* should say).

Walton has arranged the *music* for piano duet, and although the effect would necessarily not be so hard and brilliant as it is with the small orchestra, at least it is *possible* — *would* be possible, I think, for it to be performed that way.

Then, I cannot let the poems be recited *without* music. They have to be done *with* music.

I think the best way would be for Mr. Brittain-Catlin, Mr. Shuldham, and Miss Mitchison to come and see me; for me to discuss the matter with the first, and for me to hear the two latter recite. I *must* hear them recite before I can give a final permission. I could then (if I can hire a gramophone) play over the records I have just made of *Façade* in America to them.

I will *try* and get a room and a gramophone for Thursday the 6th of April, and suggest that they should come to me at the Sesame Club at 3.30. . . . If they are wanting the words of 'Scotch Rhapsody' and 'Tarantella' I can let them have the former when I come to London. But I have not got the latter, and do not wish it to be performed anyhow.

Castle of Montegufoni, Montagnana, Val di Pesa,
Florence, 9 May 1950

Mr. Brittain-Catlin and the other young people came to recite to me. I liked them very much, and was touched by their enthusiasm. I may, however, tell you *in confidence* that they recite *appallingly*. I have easily never heard anything to touch it. *Façade* is extremely difficult to recite, it needs an extreme elegance in recitation, a virtuoso technique, and great experience. These dear young people recite it as if they were performing in an egg-and-spoon race.

I suppose I must allow my work to be ruined by them, because of their enthusiasm. And I have given permission for it to be performed, witholding from them my full opinion of the horrors of the performance.

What I did *not* expect was the enclosed grossly impertinent cutting,* written by a lout who accompanied them, and, uninvited by me, made his way into my presence and enjoyed my hospitality in order that he might write in this outrageous manner about me.

It is really shocking, and will have to be punished. I have not withdrawn my permission for the performance. But I have asked Mr. Catlin to send you this moron's name (I do not know it), together with the name of his college and of his tutor.

As it was at your request that I am allowing *Façade* to be performed (which will make it difficult for me in future to protect the work against requests of the same kind) and as you are my publisher, I shall be very glad if you will be good enough to write to this person's tutor and complain of his conduct, which is a breach of every law of behaviour.

I am too angry to write any more. I may add that Osbert is just as shocked as I am.

In 1950–1 Edith Sitwell visited the United States, where she gave recitals of her own poems and of speeches from Shakespeare's plays.

San Francisco, 19 January 1951

It was great fun in Hollywood. We had a very successful reading to which a great many film stars came — including Harpo Marx. As I was reading the sleep-walking scene from

* 'Biggest social event of the term will undoubtedly be the Opera Club's production of Edith Sitwell's and William Walton's segment of artless whimsy, *Façade*, which is scheduled for the fourth week. John Catlin is producing, and *all* the boys are taking part. . . . During the vacation John Catlin arranged an audience with Miss Sitwell, and all those readers domiciled in the metropolis wilted into the Sesame Club to meet the *doyenne* of drawing-room letters. Once inside, each reader read a poem from *Façade* to the authoress, and then heard the poems read back by Miss Sitwell. Later, tea was served, and . . . the *literati* sat at Edith Sitwell's feet: I saw the shade of Harold Acton run along the window curtains as the attenuated atmosphere of the 'Twenties pervaded the fragile afternoon'.—*Isis* (undergraduate magazine), April 1950.

Macbeth, I had just announced that 'Hell is murky' when a poor gentleman in the audience uttered several piercing shrieks and, after a struggle, was borne out, in a recumbent position and foaming at the mouth, by four men.

An onlooker said to me afterwards, 'Weren't you delighted? I've never seen anything so flattering in my life!'

The volume offered in the next letter, addressed to Daniel Macmillan, was not published by the firm.

Renishaw Hall, 23 October 1951

Dear Dan,

I do hope you will forgive me for sending you these poems in the hope that you will feel like publishing them.

I believe Sydney Goodsir Smith to be the greatest poet who has arisen since Dylan Thomas. The poems are not equal in merit, but at his best I think he is nothing short of *sublime*. Such fire, such concentration! — 'The Mandrake Hert' for instance (page 16) and the even finer 'Defeat o the Hert' (page 45). I don't know if you knew his work previously (his later work is *infinitely* better than the early, I think). I only read it for the first time this summer, and was enormously impressed.

This is, of course, *in confidence*, because it would not do if it got out. But I've just heard that he has been put up as a candidate for the rectorship of Edinburgh University. He seems to be one of the two leaders of the Scots poets. (Of course I don't know if he'll be elected.) I do hope you are very well, also Betty. Please give her my love.

Yours ever, EDITH SITWELL

SEAN O'CASEY

1880–1964

In *Winds of Change, 1914–1939* (1966) Harold Macmillan wrote
that O'Casey was among his greatest friends in 'the Irish school'.
'Although he claimed to be a Communist and, I think, an atheist, his
was a truly Christian nature; one of the kindest and most genuine men
I have known. He and Ronald Knox — in their different ways —
were saintly men.' O'Casey affected to believe that Mr. Macmillan and
his wife were 'Communists at heart'.

Macmillans published all O'Casey's plays from *Juno and the Paycock*
and *The Shadow of a Gunman* (1925) onwards, and six volumes of his
autobiography between 1939 and 1963. In 1936, under attack by the
Sunday Times dramatic critic James Agate (1877–1947), O'Casey
wrote a series of combative articles on the theatre, taking for epigraph a
sentence of Agate's: 'There is a nest of wasps that must be smoked out
because it is doing the theatre infinite harm.' George Jean Nathan
(1882–1958), had dedicated his *Passing Judgments* to O'Casey in
1935.

St. Martin's Street, W.C.2, 18 September 1936

Dear Sean O'Casey,

I am afraid that I have let you go far too long without
news of your collection of articles, *The Flying Wasp*, which
you sent on 5 August, but the holidays have caused the usual
delays. Now that the time has come it is rather difficult for
me to do anything but speak to you in two voices, first as
your friend, and secondly as your publisher.

If I may first counsel you as a friend, I think that you
would be well advised not to publish these papers in volume
form. One has, for one thing, to reckon with the time-lag of
the production of a book, which puts out of date what was

fresh and topical when the articles first appeared, and matters that seemed mighty enough for current journalism are apt not to appear so significant a few months later. I often find too that a good hearty piece of destructive criticism which is most stimulating and enjoyable in a weekly paper has somehow an effect of brawling in church when one encounters it later on between cloth-covers. It is not that I do not think that your 'apostolic blows and knocks' are well delivered or deserved, but I feel that the general reader with theatrical interests would tell himself that in these articles your gifts sometimes are employed on a theme scarcely worthy of them, and would wish for something less combative and more creative. . . .

As your publisher, however, I should be very sorry to see a book of yours published under any other imprint than our own, so I hope you will not mind if I make some suggestions of a more constructive kind in case you are really attached to the idea of this collection.

It would, I am sure, be a great improvement from every point of view if you were to re-edit the papers for that purpose, and give them a title which would suggest a unified theme, *Towards a Living Theatre*, or something of that kind, grouping and altering the essays with any additions you please, so as to support that theme. I should recommend leaving out articles in reply to criticisms of your own work such as 'In Defenso'. You would not, I imagine, find much difficulty in retaining all the destructive criticism directed at anything of permanent importance and working it in with your positive proposals.

These suggestions are offered with all due diffidence, and I should be interested to hear what you think of them. . . .

Yours sincerely,   HAROLD MACMILLAN

49 Overstrand Mansions, Prince of Wales Road, S.W.11,
                                        25 September 1936
Dear Mr. Macmillan,
    Thanks for your letter about the proposed publication of

The Flying Wasp. I wouldn't ask, nor do I expect, indeed I shouldn't care to allow you to publish anything of mine about which you had the slightest uncertainty. So, the question of publication by your firm set aside, I can freely say a word in reply to what you have said about the articles.

Most of the articles will be fresh enough — too damn fresh for a lot of people — when they are offered in book-form. Everything I have written, up to the present, has been 'combative', and the sword I have swung so long is now stuck to my hand, and I can't let go. These things that are said by me need to be said, and must be said, for England has no critic like George Jean Nathan of America, whose works are rarely read and never mentioned here. I shouldn't think of giving anything I said about the theatre such a title as *Towards a Living Theatre*, for such a title would be too academic and professorial for me to use. Besides *The Flying Wasp* is more lyrical, and much more to the point. Why should I leave out an article in reply to a criticism of my own work? My works are, at least, additions to the drama, and defending them, I defend the drama. Am I to leave it out because 'it is not done', or because it is not 'good form'? I hope I know something about good manners, but, on a question of principle, good form can go to the devil. Invariably I have done the things that are not done, and have left undone the things that are done, and I amn't much the worse for it. The theatre is more than good manners. As for 'brawling in church', well, Jesus Christ did it before me, and I occasionally follow in His steps. I believe these articles will give to young men coming into the theatre courage to say what they think,

> Let us our native character maintain ;
> 'Tis of our growth, to be sincerely plain.

It is so easy to be nice. I know these sayings will not make it easier for me, and I love ease ; but not enough to change what I believe to be the truth into politeness and nicety of speech and manner. All this is said in the friendliest manner and in fair and full appreciation of your effort to prevent me from making a fool of myself. But the fact is that there is here in England no criticism of things theatrical, and all truth is lost in cowardice, good feeling and polite deportment. I hope, and believe, that my articles will have some effect in bringing about a change....

With all good wishes, sincerely yours,   SEAN O'CASEY

Further discussion of *The Flying Wasp* took place in personal interviews, and Macmillans published the book in 1937.

In 1938 O'Casey was at work on the first of his autobiographical volumes, *I Knock at the Door*. (He depicts himself so working in the letter reproduced overleaf. In that letter he refers to the Maurice Macmillan of the fourth generation, who had lately left school and did not join the firm until after the second world war.)

Each of the volumes of autobiography was read in proof by Macmillans' solicitor as a precaution against libel, and by Thomas Mark, their chief literary editor, as a precaution against other dangers. The next letter, addressed to Daniel Macmillan, deals with *Rose and Crown* (1952).

Tingrith, Station Road, Totnes, Devon, 7 March 1951
Dear Mr. Daniel,

Thank you very much for your letter dated 6 March, and for your kind interest in the present work.

I don't think there is anything libellous in it. I certainly had no feeling of writing anything so derogatory while I was working at it. If I be inclined to libel anyone, I'm inclined to libel myself. But, as you wisely say, it is better to make as sure as assurance can be by getting a lawyer to look over it.

I am sure that no one can write anything worth a damn without annoying someone. Joyce did; Yeats did; Hardy did; and so did Tennyson. And Jesus annoyed a crowd of people. However, I haven't written anything just to annoy,

Your Ref:
MHM/DER.

April 28th 1938.

Forty-Nine.
Overstrand Mansions.
Prince of Wales Road. S.W.11.
Macaulay 2566.

Harold Macmillan, Ey.

Dear Mr Harold Macmillan:

Thank you for your letter asking me about "the book," but mercifully leaving out the bell and the candle.

I'm hard at work on it ⟶ and expect to be able to let you have a look at the first batch of sketches soon.

I hope you and your family are well, & that Mr Maurice has started in as a publisher.

Sincerely Yours.

Sean O'Casey

but simply wrote down what I felt I must write down. And that was done, not to annoy any person, but to free myself from annoying God. Of course some of my conceptions may be wrong — nay, all of them may be so — but they are all honest; though that isn't saying that they are true or proper. Let a man examine himself, says St. Paul, and I have done this often, and most often when I am writing, so as to try to prevent anything malicious creeping in to what I am setting down.

I should like, I think, to have the MS. back — as I mentioned in my first letter — for I have a few things to add or change in some of the chapters; and, with things as they are, I'm afraid I might get only page-proofs from the printers, which would be very embarrassing. Besides, I thought of giving an Inn Sign as title to each of the chapters, and would like to brood a little over the idea. I could let you have the MS. finally before a month has passed.

I will send on the agreement signed as requested later on, as soon as I get it witnessed. I presume you will deal with the Macmillan Company of America side of it.

All good wishes to you. Yours very sincerely,

SEAN O'CASEY

The first two volumes of O'Casey's *Collected Plays* had appeared in 1949; the next two volumes (1951) were the occasion for a review of his stature as a playwright on the middle page of the *Times Literary Supplement* on 21 September. The review was almost certainly by Anthony Victor Cookman (1894-1962), chief dramatic critic of *The Times*.

29 September 1951

Dear Harold,

Thank you very much for taking the trouble to send me the review from the *Times Literary Supplement*. I had not seen it, and so it was very welcome. I have no comments to make on it. The writer evidently knows a lot about my work, and about me too, and has, I think, set it down very cleverly; and very kindly, too. I am always grateful for sensible reviews. This writer (whoever he may be) loves the Theatre, and knows what he is writing about. I cannot expect, nor do I expect, that everyone should like, and agree with, my 'judgment'. I don't think 'judgment' to be the right word about what I state or seem to imply in play or biography. They are opinions only; honest ones, taken after thought and long and wide experience of men and things; but they are, for all that, far from being infallible. Only God or Time can vindicate or repudiate the judgment of man. To me one thing alone is certain — we are all one in the tremendous and glorious bond of humanity. Jew, Gentile, bond and free, Tory and Communist can never break away from this grand bond. We are born, we die, and we must do the best we can between the day of birth and the night of death. But this writer about the Theatre is one who deserves to be a writer about the Theatre, against so many who look upon this work as merely a job to be done and finished with so that they may be able to turn their thoughts to something else. Thank you again for sending it to me.

I have had a somewhat similar review written by Brooks Atkinson (a great friend of mine), drama critic for the *New York Times*, deploring the fact that my plays aren't being performed in New York. He gives, too, a fine send-off to the third and fourth volumes of *Collected Plays*. The odd thing about it is that no mention of the volumes has been made by any Irish journal; except a line in the *Irish Times* saying that they had been received. Actually, in *The Star Turns Red*, not only the words, but the judgment too, is that of the Bible. When G.B.S. read it, he saw it at once, and wrote to me saying, 'You have given them the Authorised Version.' We have grown afraid of the Bible. . . .

I hope you are keeping fit and well. My love to you and

Lady Dorothy, and to all that are yours. Very sincerely,

SEAN

In April 1954 Mark sent O'Casey proofs of *Sunset and Evening Star* with a long list of suggested modifications. In particular the solicitor had asked that certain living persons should be given fictitious names. O'Casey replied:

12 April 1954

Is it that once their names aren't given, it is all serene? I myself can't see how anything in it can be libellous. They argue on the right lines, and could hardly allege defamation. And, surely, a description of appearance can't be libellous. I myself have been called bony, gaunt, haggard, etc., and couldn't find fault with the description, because it is true. If one looks at the earlier pictures of Christ on the Cross, it will be seen that the figure is shown in the same way; though it isn't meant to be a caricature. . . .

Your remark, 'The person concerned on pages 297–298 is apparently no longer alive, but for that reason alone it would in our view be most undesirable to let the passage stand', leaves me cold. Look at what Byron said about Castlereagh a minute after his death; what the apostles said about Judas; what is said about Henry the Eighth; what is said about Luther. Besides, this idea is but a survival of the early idea that the dead were dangerous; that it was risky to offend the dead. It is the living who may be dangerous. If, on the other hand, you think the reference shows 'bad taste', then I sin in good company. Shelley showed bad taste, so did Shakespeare, so did Jesus Christ. I'm too much of a tough to care a damn about 'good taste' in morals. If convenient, I'd like another set of proofs, so that I could keep a copy of amendments made. . . .

By the way, the naughty words you have exorcized have

appeared in work before, and worse are in Shakespeare, and in the A. Version of the Bible too.

The next extract also was in reply to a letter written by Thomas Mark.

20 April 1954

I enclose the corrected page-proofs of the work, *Sunset and Evening Star*, done as well as abilities permit. A good many of the marked passages are to remain, as you will see. The passages selected by your solicitor have been amended so as to make them innocent, I think....

The 'expressions' that you don't like (and you've a perfect right to dislike them if you so wish), and of which you say 'certain expressions which we do not care to see in our own books even though they may have been used elsewhere' — I seem not to have made it clear that these 'expressions' have been used in your own books by me before, in the biographies and in plays. I wasn't just trying to shove them into your books and have a laugh when they appeared in print. And they rank into importance seeing they have been used by the Translators of the Bible and by Shakespeare, by Byron, by Chaucer — to mention a few only. I never use them merely for the sake of using them. To me they have on occasions an explosive power that no other word can have. They are not in any way against Christian morality, as any priest will tell you who knows a little about this subject. They are merely 'vulgar' words, and carry no necessity, for instance, of mention in the confessional, though others permitted do — the use of the name of God or of Jesus, for instance, in any light, flippant or semi-irreverent manner. Perhaps you would leave these controversial words to look out of the pages you may send to the American Company.

O'Casey accepted the changes for which the solicitor had asked. In the course of his reply Mark wrote: 'The objectionable expressions we mentioned are neither biblical nor Shakespearean, and you have kindly agreed to our taking them out.' He added that it would be best to send the American publisher the amended text.

St. Marychurch, Torquay, 28 March 1960

I have refused a number of requests for the use of my name in advertisements, and I don't agree that any play of mine, or any part of any play, should be used for such a purpose.

I therefore decline to give the permission asked for to use a part of the play *Red Roses for Me* in an advertisement on behalf of Messrs. Guinness & Company. This refusal has no moral connection with any dislike or objection to the lowering of a glass of their beer.

INDEX

'A.E.' (George William Russell), recommends Stephens, 15, 296–7, 302, 303; confused with his namesake, 297–8; editor of *Irish Statesman*, 299–300; recommends O'Connor, 300–1; royalty payments, 306–7; *The Candle of Vision*, 298–9

Abbey Theatre, Dublin, 293

Abbott, Edwin Abbott, fears on publishing *Philochristus*, 145–7; and advertising, 147

Academy, 136

Acton, Lord, and *John Inglesant*, 196–7; *Letters to Mary Gladstone*, 196

Agate, James, and O'Casey, 360

Archer, William, and *The Cup*, 115, 116; and *Cashel Byron's Profession*, 192; *English Dramatists of Today*, 116

Aristotelian Society, 265

Arnim, Countess von (*née* Beauchamp), marriages, 268, 269; her anonymity, 268–9; and reviews of *Vera*, 270; *Elizabeth and her German Garden*, 268; *The Enchanted April*, 270; *The Solitary Summer*, 268

Arnold, Sir Edwin, confused with Matthew Arnold, 103–4; *Poems*, 104; *The Poets of Greece*, 104

Arnold, Matthew, 162; and advertisement, 13, 103, 105–6; confused with Edwin Arnold, 103–4, 105; on his title-pages, 104; terms of publication, 105; on Jeens's vignette of Wordsworth, 106; *Essays in Criticism*, 102; *Guide to Greek Poetry* (projected), 107; *Isaiah xl–lxvi*, 104–5; *New Poems*, 102, 104; 'Obermann Once More', 102; *Poems*, 103, 104, 107; *Poems of Wordsworth* (editor), 106

(vignette facing p. 57); *Schools and Universities on the Continent*, 103

Athenaeum, 105; and Countess von Arnim, 268

Atkinson, Brooks, and O'Casey's *Collected Plays*, 366

Atlantic Monthly, 200; Henry James and, 170

Austen, Jane, *Pride and Prejudice* (illustrated by C. E. Brock), 232

Austin, Alfred, 186; and advertisement, 13, 188; and authors' politics, 186–8; poet laureate, 188, 189; reply to review in *Literature*, 188–9; *Lamia's Winter Quarters*, 188–9; *Savonarola*, 13, 186, 188

Australian Town and Country Journal, 210

Authors, Society of, foundation, 190, 193; Shaw and, 194

Authors' terms: colonial rights, 198–9; commission publishing, 72, 146–7, 242, 243; copyright, 32–3, 61, 64–5, 84–5, 86, 94, 179, 212, 225; down payment, 171, 225, 256, 275; foreign (American) rights, 72–3, 199, 256, 304, 305; half-profit system, 217–18, 315; royalties, 247, 261, 262, 302, 303, 305, 306–7, 342; serial rights, 170, 247; shared profit, 256

Balzac, Honoré de, 202

Barnes, William, his use of repetitive words, 109; *Poems of Rural Life in Common English*, 109–10; *Poems of Rural Life in the Dorset Dialect*, 109

Barrie, Sir James, and Hardy's funeral, 332

Barry, Alfred, 196, 197

Edith Sitwell

D. G. Rossetti

Robert Louis Stevenson

Henry James

Sean O'Casey

Edmund Gosse

Maurice Hewlett

A. E. Housman

Samuel

Hugh Thomson

Walter H. Pater

James G. Frazer

Charles L. Dodgson